# THE TURNING SEASON

T0307428

MICHAEL WAGG

# THE TURNING SEASON

## DDR-OBERLIGA REVISITED

pitch

First published by Pitch Publishing, 2020

Pitch Publishing
A2 Yeoman Gate
Yeoman Way
Worthing
Sussex
BN13 3QZ
www.pitchpublishing.co.uk
info@pitchpublishing.co.uk



A CIP catalogue record is available for this book
from the British Library.

ISBN 978-1 78531 728 6

Typesetting and origination by Pitch Publishing

Printed and bound in India by Replika Press Pvt. Ltd.

# Contents

Acknowledgements . . . . . . . . . . . . . . . . . . . . 11
Vorwort . . . . . . . . . . . . . . . . . . . . . . . . . . . 12
A brief history of the Oberliga. . . . . . . . . . . . . . 26
The magic of Mr Schmidt. . . . . . . . . . . . . . . . 36
Jena Rules . . . . . . . . . . . . . . . . . . . . . . . . . 44
Leaning . . . . . . . . . . . . . . . . . . . . . . . . . . 58
Halle: a tragedy . . . . . . . . . . . . . . . . . . . . . 68
1966, and all that . . . . . . . . . . . . . . . . . . . . 76
Block F, Row 9 . . . . . . . . . . . . . . . . . . . . . . 93
The violet revolution . . . . . . . . . . . . . . . . . .104
A spy in Sonnenberg . . . . . . . . . . . . . . . . . .116
Sparwasser shoots . . . . . . . . . . . . . . . . . . . .130
Hinterland: a fiction. . . . . . . . . . . . . . . . . . .148
Lauzi: singular. . . . . . . . . . . . . . . . . . . . . . .171
The myth of Bischofswerda . . . . . . . . . . . . . .183
The loss of Jörg Stübner . . . . . . . . . . . . . . . .197
Blue Monday . . . . . . . . . . . . . . . . . . . . . . . .219
Crossing the line . . . . . . . . . . . . . . . . . . . . .235
Appendices . . . . . . . . . . . . . . . . . . . . . . . . .244
Select bibliography . . . . . . . . . . . . . . . . . . .254
Notes . . . . . . . . . . . . . . . . . . . . . . . . . . . .255
Picture credits . . . . . . . . . . . . . . . . . . . . . .256

# Acknowledgements

MASSIVE THANKS to: Haydn, Fouldsy, Duncan P. and Duncan H. who joined me on the road; Phil Earle; Nick, Andreas, Janusz, Chris and Beke in Berlin; Denis Roters; Bernd in Erfurt; Jens in Jena; Martin Fischer and Barbara Happe at Haus Auerbach; Matthias in Leipzig; Sebastian Bona; Heiko, Burkhard and Nils in Aue; Mike in Chemnitz; Uwe Karte, Andre and Bastian in Dresden; Martin in Magdeburg; Jens in Cottbus; Alex in Eisenhüttenstadt; Paul Scraton; Alan McDougall; and Massimo Furlan.

All at Pitch Publishing and Duncan Olner for the cover.

And to the former Oberliga players who kindly gave up their time to speak to me: Karl Drößler, Ulf Kirsten, Hans-Jürgen Kreische, Joachim Streich, Axel Tyll, Frank Siersleben, Dirk Stahmann, Niels Mackel, Harry Rath and Axel Schulz.

To my friends in south London and at Dulwich Hamlet FC, and to the actors and road managers I've toured Germany with: Prost!

Most of all thank you to:

Jan Stöver, a real travelling companion who I couldn't have done it without: who drew the maps and graphs, was a brilliant first reader and so much more.

Susan and Malcolm Wagg for all their love and support.

My brother David for sharing the football with me.

And to Sarah, for everything.

# Vorwort

THERE'S A postcard on my wall that I picked up in a town called Hof. I took it from one of those stands you find near a pub doorway with a selection of cards advertising something or other. But this postcard isn't selling anything. It's fascinated me since I found it 17 years ago, niggling away at me like a missed sitter.

I can't remember much about Hof but I'm sure it's a lovely town and looking at a map now I see it's in the north-eastern corner of Bavaria where the old West meets Thuringia and Saxony in the old East. It's just seven miles from where the Inner German border once ran its course. In the top left-hand corner of the card is part of a pennant, the type exchanged before a match for sporting friendship, with a series of bold characters printed on it like a clue to a Cold War thriller:

**WM74 DFV 22.6.1974 HAMBURG DDR–BRD**

Then three images: in black and white a close-up of a footballer just about to strike the ball with some force, two other bodies sliding over each other to stop it happening. There's a colour picture of a section of football fans behind a high, metal fence with flags draped over it in black, red and gold. The third is another image in black and white, two players standing shoulder to shoulder talking. It's after the match, the sweat picked out in dark patches on their shirts. One shirt is white with a black round-necked trim and a crest with an eagle on it. The other shirt is darker with a large V-neck and three thick letters above its crest: DDR. Then cutting straight through the middle of the card the words,

*'Sparwasser schießt … … Kaiser kotzt'.*

I imagine the commentator's voice rising in volume and pitch as the far-reaching blow is struck. I imagine hushed, urgent conversations and the scribbling of notes. I imagine a ball kicked high over a wall that's never really come down.

The original, real commentary was simpler I think, something more like *'Sparwasser? … und Tor!'* A tone of disbelief barely hidden. But I've stared at the words on the postcard for 17 years, fascinated by what this other, tabloid version might mean. I'm staring at them now on the S-Bahn from Leipzig-Halle airport at the start of my journey. I tucked the card into my notebook before I left London. There's alliteration in the German, the 'Kaiser Kotzt' kicking home the line; but the English translation is no less bold and in rhyme, *'Sparwasser shoots … Kaiser pukes'.*

* * *

The Olympic Stadium, April 2018. The opening ceremony of PAM, Munich's three-month festival of free public art. The festival has the overall title 'Game Changers' and presents artists' responses to significant shifts in the city over the past 100 years. Starting at the declaration of the short-lived Bavarian Soviet Republic in 1919, the art works move through 'paradigmatic shifts' in the city's history, stopping to consider, among other turns of events, the inauguration of the Olympic

Park and Stadium in 1972 and the welcoming of refugees at its central station in 2015, 'Visible game-changers in how societies reinvent themselves.'

Here at the festival opening the event chosen to kick things off is a piece of performance art called Re-enactment, or *Foot*. Its protagonist, its game-changer, is absent and will be played by an actor. The event being recreated tonight is a football match that took place in Hamburg in 1974, and the man at the centre of that match has said that on his gravestone just this word and date would be enough to explain who is buried beneath.

He is a man from a city 500km [311 miles] north of here which just 30 years ago was in another country, a country behind a wall that changed the game too. One game in Hamburg will be relived here in Munich, in that *other* other country, Germany, which now includes Halberstadt and Magdeburg and Aue and Zeitz among its towns again. Swiss-born artist Massimo Furlan, who has created the work, will

*To Sarah*

*Jedermann sein eigner Fussball*

Berlin Dada

play the part of a goalkeeper and will change his jersey from black to green at half-time, just like Sepp Maier did.

In Hamburg in June '74, the game changed late on. It was the first and only time that West Germany met East Germany in a football match. At least in a proper football match with spectators and all. The national teams had competed against each other a couple of times before in behind-closed-doors games – known in Germany as *Geisterspiele* or 'ghost matches' – to determine which of the Germanys would send a team to the Olympic Games.

They had in fact played two more of these qualifiers in front of crowds; as well as facing each other in the 1972 Olympics itself (in the very Munich Olympiastadion where Furlan's performance is happening); the DDR won that one 3-2, but let's not let that get in the way of a good story. This was the real thing: a competitive, televised, tournament match in the group stage of the World Cup finals – in West Germany. It didn't matter that both teams were already through to the second round, nor that the losing team would turn out to have arguably the easier passage to the final (*West* Germany, who went on to win the cup). This was a battle of ideologies: communism v capitalism, East v West, a politically-charged *Bruderduell.* Well it wasn't, it was a football match, but the ball is round, and against all the odds *East* Germany won. DDR 1 – BRD 0. The goal in the 77th minute was scored by a man called Jürgen Sparwasser, the man absent in Munich tonight. He'll be played by the actor Franz Beil. And soon Beil will disappear too.

> *'As a child, Massimo Furlan used to play in his room for hours with a foam ball while listening to the running commentaries of the football games of the Italian championship on the radio. He would mime*

> *all the players' actions, and when the commentary was interrupted because of the poor quality of the transmission he would resume the thread and include his own name. Thus, he became a world champion, again and again, scoring countless goals.'*

I was starting to really like Massimo Furlan.

Furlan the artist has moved from the bedroom to the stadium and has gone on to perform his *Foot* re-enactments all over Europe. He's played the role of Michel Platini in Paris, Zbigniew Boniek in Warsaw, and also given a Sparwasser himself in a previous version of this event ten years ago in Halle. His idea is to re-enact a football match from the past in its entirety with just one player on the pitch. The other 21 players are imagined, as are the referee and assistants, the coaches and subs, and the ball. There is a crowd there to cheer him on, or rather people assuming the role of a crowd to relive a match that has long since finished – listening on radios to the original commentary to the game – but apart from the one fully kitted-out player all else is invisible in green space.

For the version here in Munich, Furlan has decided to up the ante and use two performer-players, Sparwasser and the goalkeeper he scored past, Sepp Maier. Furlan and Beil have studied the movements and gestures of the two players through the full 90 minutes and play the game as it happened, with every twist and turn, jog, dash and curse. Two players and 20 ghosts; a dance in stadium space; football theatre.

* * *

I have another obsession beyond the Hof postcard which dates back to around the same time and my first visits to Germany. I fell in love with the country then and with one town in particular. I'm sure it's possible to fall for a place and not know why, with all the stubbornness that comes from the resulting puzzled looks. The love digs in. *We'll always have Neustrelitz.*

Seventeen years ago I was on a European theatre tour and one leg of it was through the state of Mecklenburg-Vorpommern. Our show was an adaptation of George Orwell's *1984* and I spent much of the second half hanging upside-down with my head in a tin box where some rusty nails made the sound of scratching rats. I was Winston Smith in Room 101. That was the downside. The upside was that we played in some beautiful places.

On this particular leg we played Greifswald, Stralsund, Rostock, Schwerin and Schwedt, as I remember. Schwedt caused much amusement for the word sounding a bit like *sweat* in English and the fact that it sits on the banks of the Oder.

We also played Neustrelitz. I loved it there; an unremarkable town on the shore of the Zierker See, drawn to its small pockets of faded grandeur, to its lake and ruined schloss and to its beautiful theatre. I now know that it wasn't really Neustrelitz I was drawn to, despite the fact that I told anyone who'd listen that one day I would live there, but to a wider territory and Neustrelitz became the emblem, a type of club crest, of a growing pull towards many of the towns of the former DDR.

On that first tour I also became beguiled by the words I saw, particularly in the football pages. There's a Dadaist delight in club names like Waggonbau Dessau, Motor Mitte Magdeburg, and Guts Muts Dresden. Imagine playing for Aktivist Schwarze Pumpe! It may be that the nightly hanging upside-down and imagined rats were playing with my mind, but I can distinctly remember repeating the phrase *Europapokal-der-Pokalsieger-Sieger* as I drifted off to sleep. I've since spent more time in many of those towns, usually working in theatres, but lately the draw has taken a different turn.

I'm a lower-league football fan too, in awe of the unbearable beauty of the empty terrace, and I wanted to travel where these two worlds meet: the strange, shabby romance of the cities of a country disappeared, and a world where football and football clubs, however seemingly insignificant, kick and scream, and change. I also fancied touring eastern Germany without having my head in a tin box every night. It wasn't until towards the end of what became a series of journeys that I realised another reason I'd picked that particular time to look back to. I was 16 years old in 1989, and football-crazy.

I think football clubs can tell us something of the communities they're part of and at their best they sit at the heart of the places they play for. But I'm an outsider here too, an away day fan cheering for both sides. There's a German word referring to away trips, adopted in English but that's little used now in either language: *Bummel.* Jermone K. Jerome used it for the sequel to his *Three Men on a Boat*, the three men now on land and bummeling on bicycles to the Black Forest, while German football supporters of the past would travel to away matches as *Schlachtenbummler*. Theirs was a *battle* bummel while my odyssey, I hoped, would be an altogether more peaceful venture.

I started to describe my own journey as a bummel. But it was to be a bummel through a country that no longer exists, via its football league, a wander-plan of away days. I was heading for the 14 cities which had a football club in the DDR-Oberliga – the East German first division – in autumn 1989. Sadly a return to Neustrelitz wasn't on the list as its club was a third-division Bezirksliga outfit at the time, denying me a chance to visit the previously and fantastically named club BSG Mechanical Arithmetic Neustrelitz. The 1989/90 season wasn't the last round of competition in East Germany: the 1990/91 season started pre-German reunification and ran its course, while it could be said that the last authentic season started in 1988. But I chose 1989 as my starting whistle, my *Anpfiff!* That was the year of the *Wende,* the turning point, and that was *the turning season.*

When the 1989 season kicked off the Berlin Wall was standing firm as it had done for nearly 30 years. By the end of the season it was gone. The people had pushed it over. Thirty years on, it has now been gone for longer than it stood and divided and I wanted to go back and trace some of its lines, through the lines on a football pitch, however faded. I don't know why I felt I had to, but as historian Alan McDougall has pointed out in his study of the game's relationship to state and society, 'Football's lack of importance, one might say, made it important.' (McDougall, 182)

Two years after the *Mauerfall* (the fall of the Wall), in the newly reunified Germany, the East German Oberliga was merged into the West German Bundesliga. To get a sense of that integration you need only glance at former East German representation in the German top league in the 29 seasons since. At the end of the 1990/91 season two eastern clubs were given a place in the Bundesliga, six in the second division, while the rest would play in the then-regional third tier. In terms of population or geography East Germany was roughly a quarter of the size of West Germany so the decision to place only two of its teams into a top league of 20 was disproportionate. The effects of that decision, based on an assessment that it would take the clubs of the DDR time to establish the economic foundations to survive in the new system, are still felt today. I saw them on my journey round every terrace curve.

In the years since German reunification there has never been more than two former DDR clubs playing in the top league at any one time, for much of the time only one, and for a long period none at all. At the time my journey started in early 2019, of the 14 clubs that competed in the 1989 season, three were playing in the second division, four in the third, five at the semi-professional and regional fourth level, one at the sixth and one at the seventh level, both amateur leagues. Thirty years ago all of these clubs played in the top flight. Like much of East German life the Oberliga was swallowed into an existing structure it had little chance of coping with.

Until Union Berlin were promoted to the Bundesliga in 2019, there had been no team from the east in the top division for ten years. To me the Leipzig-based club run by an Austrian energy drinks company doesn't count, and it won't be mentioned again. All of the clubs of 1989 are now playing at a lower level than they did then, most of them significantly so and many of them struggling to survive. But they play on in one form or another. *We'll always have Neustrelitz.* And give me the lower league over fizzy drinks football any day. I was looking for small stories not just big ones, a portrait of each club in miniature. The club was the starting point, and the year, 1989, the game changer.

Forty years earlier, in July 1949 when East Germany was yet to exist as a country, there was a football match between two neighbouring local teams. Sonneberg was in the state of Thuringia in the post-war Soviet administration zone, while Neustadt bei Coburg, just three miles away, was in the American zone in Bavaria. The border between these occupying zones, between what was to become just three months later East and West, was marked by the halfway line of the pitch. As Alan McDougall has described, the two towns had been connected for centuries by cultural and family ties (284); they were practically the same place, but now the people of each town had to watch from their own side of the line, while the players had been granted inter-zonal passes for the day to allow them to enter the opposing team's half during the match. Otherwise it would have been a fairly dull affair and certainly a long-ball game.

After the match, which Sonneberg from the 'east' won 2-0, the authorities opened the border for the day. As the two teams walked towards each other (as McDougall notes referring to a photograph that marked the occasion) one held a banner reading 'We want the unification of Germany'. The other team's banner said 'and so do we'. But the border games were just beginning and it would take 40 years for the final whistle to blow, if it has at all.

Back in Munich, when the 77th minute comes and Sparwasser shoots the stadium floodlights will be cut and a single spotlight will pick out the Magdeburg man as he wheels away, one arm in the air, before tumbling into a tentative forward roll. That's what's in the script. East beats West. Game-changer.

But there's another ghostly turn here. In the middle of the first half Beil as Sparwasser tumbles to the ground holding his ankle. He waves an arm towards the ghosts on the bench while the crowd continue to cheer, now deep in their own roles at the strange spectacle. Some of the older fans might have checked back through their collective memory for an injury on that night 44 years ago, scrabbling to recall whether it really happened like that in Hamburg or if the artist has added some theatrical embellishment.

But there's no such artistry at play here. Beil's injury is real, adding another surreal layer to the phantom action, where fact already met fiction. And after the intervention of a streaker, who hugs Furlan before leaping into the long-jump pit, Beil is stretchered off and Furlan as goalkeeper continues on his own: a lone black, then green figure dancing round the empty penalty box on a Bavarian spring evening. The crowd cheer him on and their volume rises as one as the fateful moment nears. The stadium lights are cut on cue and the spotlight picks out the goalkeeper first, sitting despondent in his goalmouth before cursing the absent defenders all around him. Then it refocuses to briefly scan the pitch, flitting nervously across empty grass like a searchlight, until it finds him. The light follows the invisible form of Jürgen Sparwasser and, in his impossible shadow, a country disappeared.

* * *

## A note on the text:

Chasing Sparwasser's shadow, this book is a response to my own journey. I wanted to respond as quickly as possible to each of the places I visited. I'm not attempting a full history, nor writing about politics or politicians, and neither do I seek to analyse, condemn nor condone the social and political structures of the former DDR; that's for bigger brains than mine. I've attempted something simpler – to look around, watch a match and meet people – and my response is, I guess, as political as any concerned with people and the places they live.

By omission I'm not ignoring that there are other serious issues associated with football and society in this context – I say very little, for example, about the history of hooliganism or the contemporary presence of the far-right, associated with some of these clubs, and many others across Europe at the time. But that's not the book I've chosen to write. Similarly, for example, much has been written about BFC Dynamo, then and now, but my response was to make a fiction inspired by what I imagined as I walked the streets of Berlin.

I make no apology for the romanticised nature of this. I wanted to be selective and creative, linking my wandering with a football league that finished long ago. The result is impressionistic and personal; a patchwork. In his book *Tor! The story of German Football*, Ulrich Hesse-Lichtenberger suggested that the four-decade history of East German football 'may very well be one of the game's most fascinating tales still waiting to be told properly'. (Hesse-Lichtenberger, 278). I make no claims to have done that, but I hope I have made a start.

I set off in February 2019 and finished the journey in March 2020, and wanted to respond within the 2019/20 football season, 30 years on from 1989/90. I soon realised how complicated it all is, and that I could easily spend the next 30 years trying to shape this book. One day maybe I'll go back and do it properly! But the timeframe felt important. Coincidentally I was in mainland Europe, watching football and meeting people, during much of my own country's process of trying to remove itself from the EU. I am European and remain so, and am glad I could be in Germany to say so.

I refer throughout the book to the *Wende*. Die Wende, which translates as the 'turning point' or 'turnaround', was the period of sociopolitical change in Germany around 1989–90. The word has been used variously: to refer to the time of the fall of the Berlin Wall; or to the events of autumn 1989 which led to the fall of the Wall; or to a broader period of political and social change which includes the subsequent reunification of Germany and encompasses all of this. For the most part I use it to mean this broader period of change and which I've connected to East German football's *turning season* of 1989/90.

A few other items: I have changed some of the names of the people I met, to respect their privacy. Occasionally I've merged aspects of one personal story into another. I have left many other things out – facts and stories that would be part of a more conventional history of a football league. I'm writing here about the men's game, and don't cover women's football. There is so much that should be written about the women's game in this context, once a national league was finally established far too late in 1987, and elsewhere in other contexts, but that's for other books. I hope I might write one of them.

In relation to language, for the most part I use the German acronym DDR (*Deutsche Demokratische Republik*) when referring to the country from 1949 to 1990 rather than the English GDR (*German Democratic Republic*). I also use East Germany for the country in that period, and east or eastern Germany for the area of Germany today. I've also tried, wherever possible, to use simplified versions of the names of football clubs. These club names, name changes and additional acronyms are complicated, albeit full of wonder, and warrant a book of their own at least as niche as this one.

But I've tried to keep it simple. As examples, I mostly refer to Dynamo Berlin, rather than Berliner FC Dynamo; to Lokomotive Leipzig, rather than 1. FC Lokomotive Leipzig; or to Stahl Brandenburg, rather than BSG Stahl Brandenburg; etc. And further into a story I'm likely to use just 'Stahl' or 'Brandenburg' or 'Dynamo' or 'Leipzig', if I think you'll know which club I'm talking about. Apologies if you don't. Sometimes I've veered from this plan, and that is either my choice or my fault.

To add to the name game, there are numerous FCs, SCs, FVs, SGs, BSGs and more, used in the East German game. For the most part I've ignored them, though have occasionally explored them along the way. It's not that I don't think they're important, I've just tried to keep things moving and occasionally lost the will to live!

I set off on this journey knowing very little – as well as speaking nowhere near good enough German. I've made lots of mistakes along the way and some of them, I'm sure, are here for you to read. All faults are my own, but then that's all part of the journey. So before we set off, and to help us on our way, here's a brief history – of the brief, strange history – of the *DDR-Oberliga*:

# A brief history of the Oberliga

EAST GERMANY existed for 41 years; its football league for a touch longer than that. The first championship kicked off one month before the foundation of the country in October 1949, and its last season was completed seven months after German reunification in October 1990.

Following the end of World War II Germany was initially divided into four Allied Occupation Zones. The Soviet-occupied zone in the north-east would become East Germany, under the ruling SED (*Sozialistische Einheitspartei Deutschlands,* or Socialist Unity Party of Germany). Berlin was split in the same way, with roughly the eastern area of the city, East Berlin, becoming East Germany's capital. West Berlin would become part of West Germany while geographically surrounded by East Germany. In the aftermath of the war many associations in Germany, including sports and football clubs, were disbanded, but new clubs were soon established or variants of their pre-war incarnations.

By 1957 the umbrella organisation for all sports in East Germany was the DTSB (*Deutscher Turn und Sportbund,* or German Gymnastics and Sports Federation). The DFV (*Deutscher Fußball-Verband der DDR*, the East German FA) was established in 1958 and was the largest of the sports associations under the DTSB. Fourteen years after East Germany, West Germany established a national football league championship of its own with the birth of the Bundesliga in 1963.

The new football championship had kicked off in September 1949. Initially called the *Zonenliga*, before the end of its first season it had become the *DS-Oberliga* (DS for German Sports Association), and then in 1958, with the establishment of the DFV became the *DDR-Oberliga*. It was renamed the *NOFV-Oberliga* (Northeastern German Football Association) for its final season in 1990 with reunification approaching and numerous clubs changing their names.

The first champions were Horch Zwickau. The last were Hansa Rostock. But of course these clubs didn't just play to win titles and trophies. There was much more at stake, according to the state ideal at least. Professor Mike Dennis, in his essay *Behind the Wall: East German football between state and society*, explains, 'Football was expected to strengthen the identification of East Germans with their political and social system, to help break the diplomatic isolation of the GDR ("ambassadors in muddy boots"), to demonstrate the superiority of state socialism over the capitalist "class enemy" and, in general terms, to boost the reputation and prestige of the GDR.'

The Oberliga comprised 14 teams each season, ran roughly from August to May, and offered two points for a win throughout. There were a few exceptions to this such as the seasons starting 1950–53 when the number of teams was increased; a brief experiment with seasons running through the summer, as in the Soviet system; and the seasons starting and following that experiment, when teams played each other only once (1955) or three times (1961/62 as the system was returned to 'normal').

All sports men and women in the DDR were officially amateur, although in the football world at least this was not commonly the case in practice. Clubs were mostly associated with a particular industry or occupation and it was through this employment that the players were, officially, paid. Despite a number of modifications, and plenty of tangled threads in other areas, the structure of the league, and those below it, remained fairly straightforward: at the top level was the Oberliga (upper league). The second level was the Liga, which between 1971 and 1984 was split into five regional divisions (the wonderful word *Staffeln* in German), and before and after that into two Staffels (North/South and later A/B), roughly compromising clubs from Berlin, the central states and the north in one division; clubs from the south in the other. The more localised levels below this were the *Bezirk* (country) and the *Kreis* (district) leagues. In addition to the leagues was the annual national cup competition, the FDGB-Pokal or Free German Trade Union Federation Cup. Waggonbau Dessau won the first cup; Hansa Rostock the last.

These are the basics and though the world of DDR football turned often and strangely, I think they're enough to follow the journey ahead. But if you're up for a swift detour for more detail before we begin, I'll pass the baton to Ulrich Hesse-Lichtenberger.

'Strangeness crept in early,' he says in his book *Tor!* 'The old clubs – denounced as "bourgeois" – were disbanded after the war, replaced by "sporting groups" (SGs) which would soon evolve into communal, multi-sport clubs that were linked with certain lines of industrial production. No more Borussias: now it was Chemie (chemical industry), Aufbau (construction industry), Stahl (steel workers), Lokomotive (state railways) or Wismut (ore mining). Less obviously heroic occupations received exhortations as their new names such as Empor (upwards!) for public servants and Vorwärts (forwards!) for the army. The tricky area of the media was represented by clubs called Rotation (from the German for "rotary press") and, of course, Dynamo became the name associated with both official and secret police.' (Hesse-Lichtenberger, 281–2)

These words were added to the city or town name to make up the football club name, and for our own purposes we should add: Fortschritt (the textile industry and agricultural machinery); Energie (energy providers); Carl Zeiss (optical instruments); Hansa (the Hanseatic history of the region); and Rot-Weiß (who play in red and white!). Some of these SGs, by the way, were also known as BSGs *Betriebssportgemeinschaft* – enterprise, or company sports group. Meanwhile, Professor Dennis takes up the baton, 'In 1954/55, 21 Sports Clubs [SCs] were removed from the BSG [or SG] system and were established as centres of excellence for the promotion of elite sport.'

And haring forward ten years or so Dennis hands back over to Hesse-Lichtenberger:

'As of 1 January 1966, 11 selected clubs were made independent of their multi-sport parent organisations and were turned into clubs solely for football. Thus Dynamo Berlin now became FC Dynamo Berlin, Empor Rostock became FC Hansa Rostock and Aufbau Magdeburg became 1. FC Magdeburg. These clubs were known as "focus clubs" … They were supposed to be supplying the national team with talent and to that end every promising player was ordered to play for one of these teams.' (Hesse-Lichtenberger, 284)

Professor Dennis picks it up again, 'The reorganisation of sport had assumed great urgency as the GDR would be fielding, for the second successive time, a separate national team at the 1972 summer Olympics in West Germany.'

While the DDR record in the major international football tournaments is less impressive, in Olympic football East Germany would add to their bronze medal from the 1964

Games (playing as the play-off-winning representative of an all-German Olympic team) a further bronze, a silver and a gold medal, in Montreal in 1976 – a result of that year's further focusing of the previous 'focus clubs' down to a further six specialist centres of excellence!

Meanwhile the Oberliga kept going strong, in its own peculiar style; and to bastardise Gary Lineker's quip about German football in general, 'Football is a simple game. Twenty-two men chase a ball for 90 minutes, and at the end *Dynamo Berlin* win!'

That's not altogether true of course, though Dynamo Berlin did win the league title for ten consecutive years between 1979 and 1988, and are probably the first team that springs to mind, not often in a particularly positive light, when the subject of Oberliga success rears its head. Dynamo Dresden didn't finish far behind them with eight titles, while Carl Zeiss Jena won the most Oberliga points overall and remain top of the Eternal Table.

Another aspect of DDR football that fans from elsewhere will have memories of is its appearances in European club football. Despite some big wins along the way, against the likes of Juventus, Barcelona, Benfica and Newport County, the overall record is modest: out of the 15 teams which played in one of the three UEFA competitions only one lifted a trophy; two others reached a final and the two big Dynamos, Berlin and Dresden, never got beyond a semi-final. Notable peculiarities among the European stories include PSV Schwerin's appearance in the European Cup Winners' Cup, despite having finished 14th in the East German second division the previous season (they lost in the first round to Austria Vienna). There are other things likely to be recalled in the general context of East German football too, and they appear as outrageous and daft as they probably were in reality.

Professor Dennis explains it well:

'The basic features comprising this allegedly "abnormal" world of football behind the Berlin Wall include: the high level of political interference in the game; the indoctrination of players in socialist ideology and the inculcation of a socialist friend–capitalist foe image; the frequent and bewildering renaming and relocation of clubs; the delegation of players to other teams, often against their wishes; illicit payments to footballers at all levels of the game since the early 1950s; and a running battle for control over football between the sports central authorities and club sponsors. The list can be extended to include the defection of top players to the West, the cooperation of several referees, officials and players with the Stasi, and the intermittent doping of players of the national team since 1965 and those of BFC Dynamo and SG Dynamo Dresden since 1977.'

That was all part of the journey and as the Oberliga came towards its staggering end, in the *Wende*-time of 1989/90, there were other things on people's minds besides the shenanigans on and off the pitch, and in its final season Oberliga attendances fell sharply. The population of East Germany was around 16 million. Throughout its history average Oberliga attendance had been consistently 9,000–12,000, with a slight boom in the mid-1950s and another in the mid-to-late-70s.

There were some notable single whoppers though. A crowd of 100,000 watched Rotation Leipzig against Lokomotive Leipzig in the Zentralstadion in 1956, still the record attendance for a domestic match in Germany (while I'm loath to overcomplicate things here, I should explain, crudely, that Rotation Leipzig later became FC Lokomotive Leipzig, the 'Lokomotive' we'll come to later, while the 'Lokomotive' above were *SC* Lokomotive Leipzig who later became Chemie Leipzig. Leipzig football is complex, but basically it was a big crowd!). Then in 1987 for FC Lokomotive Leipzig's Cup Winners' Cup semi-final against Bordeaux in the same stadium the number was said to be way beyond that – nobody really knows by how much – and may never be surpassed (Appendix D).

However, from the end of the 1970s crowds were starting to drop off in many leagues across Europe and while the DDR didn't really follow suit, its average attendance had fallen to 8,300 in the turning season of 89/90. And for its final Oberliga season the crowd average was just 4,800, the lowest in its history and less than half of what it had been for most of its 40-year life.

Since 1990 the structure of the unified German leagues has shifted often and continues to be modified but currently the top level is the Bundesliga: followed by the 2. Bundesliga; the 3. Liga, established in 2008; five fourth-level Regionalligas, but that appears changeable; and numerous localised fifth-level Oberligas. Crudely, moving down the pyramid structure from the top flight, the German system becomes regional and operates as semi-professional sooner than the English system. During the course of my journey I'd come to see the Regionalliga Nordost as the closest I could get to the DDR-Oberliga. Geographically it covers a very similar area and in terms of performance, again very crudely, seems currently to be a natural level for many of the clubs of the turning season. This was particularly true at its inception in 1994, when it gave an even clearer reflection of DDR-time, with two-thirds of the league sharing an Oberliga history, the other third being teams from west Berlin. As I set out in February 2019 five of my clubs were playing in the Regionalliga Nordost and, loving the lower leagues, I've become very fond of it.

Before we head off a couple of necessary commendations: Union Berlin barely gets a mention in what follows, despite the fact that they are currently (from 2019/20) the only real team from eastern Germany in the Bundesliga; and the only one to have made it to the top flight for ten years. Union Berlin was very much part of the Oberliga story but in 1989/90 it was a second division club. To date there are only five former Oberliga teams to have played in the Bundesliga in the 30 years since reunification: Union Berlin, Hansa Rostock, Dynamo Dresden, Energie Cottbus and, for one season only, Lokomotive Leipzig.

And what of the most successful football club of them all from the former DDR? Turbine Potsdam, who had previously won six national titles, have gone on to win a further six Bundesliga trophies, three domestic cups and two Champions League finals. Turbine Potsdam is a women's team. Formed in 1971, today they share the Karl-Liebknecht-Stadion with men's Regionalliga side SV Babelsberg in a leafy area of Potsdam near Berlin. Mike Dennis explains, 'Not until 1979 were women able to take part in a supra-regional competition, albeit without the official support, status and privileges associated with the men's game. Turbine Potsdam was by far the most successful team.'

Official support for the women's game coming too late, the DDR national team played only one fixture, losing 3-0 to Czechoslovakia in May 1990 in Turbine's Potsdam stadium. It is telling that Turbine Potsdam were one of the very few clubs in East Germany where the women's section had access to the same facilities and treatment as the men's section. Today, it is the women's team that can rightly claim to be 'Champions of the entire East' in the modern game. They are currently fifth in the Bundesliga and the journey goes on.

Throughout my own journey I have been very grateful for the research carried out by numerous writers and historians, including some of those quoted above. But the largest debt I owe is to Alan McDougall's brilliant and exhaustive study *The People's Game: Football, State and Society in East Germany*. The third section of his book deals with football, the people's game, not only as something to watch and discuss and shout about, but as a game to play. It's not all about the Oberliga. And while recreational sport (*Massensport*) was sadly not part of my own journey – despite hopes of a five-a-side in Bischofswerda – it was a huge part of life in the DDR. McDougall explains that by 1990 there were 5,534 registered football clubs in the country, comprising 30,200 teams, with 424,587 members. And that roughly one in every 40 DDR citizens was, officially, a footballer. (McDougall, 245)

Quoting the journalist and Carl Zeiss Jena fan Christoph Dieckmann, he suggests that in the people's game there were three kinds of football in the DDR, three ways to get your kicks if you couldn't get to the match itself: tuning in to live radio commentary of the seven Oberliga matches on a Saturday afternoon was the first; the 'illicit dreams' of Western television on a Saturday night, where you might be able to catch highlights of a Bundesliga match, the second (unless you lived near either Rügen or Dresden, which couldn't receive Western signals and each became known as a 'Valley of the Clueless'). The third way, less glamorous, took place on a Sunday, just as it did in my own childhood and maybe yours, on sloping park pitches made of mud. Here you might dream of *making the difference* in the match between 'Traktor Dingelstadt with "Boxer" Konnecke in goal and Stahl Elbingerode'. I know I did. The names are different, but the dream's the same.

Vorwärts!

Rostock
BERLIN
Brandenburg
Eisenhüttenstadt
Magdeburg
Cottbus
Halle
Leipzig
Bischofswerda
Erfurt
Dresden
Jena
Chemnitz
Aue

# The magic of Mr Schmidt

DANIEL SCHIMPF wheels away in celebration to face the cheers of the 150 or so Brandenburg fans, at which point I turn away too, my back to the pitch. Not because I'm attempting a one-man *Poznan* celebration, nor because I don't like Daniel Schimpf – far from it – but because I don't want to miss the main action: the scoreboard updating to signal *Heim* (home) '1' – Gäste (away) '0'. I watch as Mr Schmidt – his orange hi-vis brighter than the light of the scoreboard bulbs – bolts up the steps at the back of the board, and I wait.

I think Schimpf's goal on 56 minutes was a close-range finish after a fairly scrappy move. But I can't be sure as my attention was only half on the pitch, the other half taken by Mr Schmidt and his friend reminiscing about 1986 and the big matches here, the good old games against Gothenburg and Coleraine. Moments earlier the half-dozen vocal Brandenburg supporters were singing those two names to the tune of Auld Lang Syne, '*From Gö-te-borg to Col-er-aine*'. Old acquaintance is not forgot here, at the Stadion am Quenz. Especially when your club once held the Swedish giants to a score draw in the second round of the UEFA Cup, but now plays local football at the seventh level. IFK Gothenburg went on to lift the UEFA Cup that year, while only four years later German football reunification signalled the start of Stahl Brandenburg's steady climb down the football ladder. Many of the clubs of the east, including from the Oberliga, were left behind after 1990 and are still catching up today, and none more so than the steel workers' team from the Frequency Stadium.

It takes about 30 seconds for the '0' to become '1'. Quite a long time, but then the scoreboard is a pretty old piece of kit. The bulbs making up each letter and number date it somewhere in the 1970s, those electronic scoreboards made of dots of light redolent of World Cups throughout that decade and into the next. The flicking to '1' in this case has a hesitant, stuttered quality, with the '0' disappearing slowly then a pause of a second or two before the '1' fades in. Wiring on the blink, maybe? Mr Schmidt is probably having a look at it now with torch and pliers in hand. But then maybe something else is happening inside that rusting, two-legged box? Something altogether more miraculous.

Stephen had spotted us earlier, just as we'd arrived at the stadium gates and were taking pictures of a blue and white painted mural with a panorama of the town, the steel works and the stadium floodlights. The real floodlights are long gone now, taken down in the mid-90s as the club's decline and its wrangles with the council began. Stephen points out that after the match we should have a look at some more murals, including a long one bearing a version of the club's full, and very long, name – *BETRIEBSSPORTGEMEINSCHAFT STAHL BRANDENBURG (seit 1950)* – which we'll find along the street at the far side of the ground.

Stephen painted them himself and is clearly proud to point us in their direction. His daughter is less bothered. We ask him why we'd seen no evidence of this sort of club street art in the town itself. He explains that there's no point painting in town as it would quickly get covered over by fans from the other Brandenburg club, Brandenburger South, who rather confusingly play their matches in *North* Brandenburg.

Brandenburg an der Havel, 50 miles west of Berlin, is a town of 70,000 souls, and two clubs. The population has fallen from closer to 100,000 in the 30 years since 1989 as the decline of local industry encouraged many, particularly young people, to head further west. Stephen is still here though. As is his dad.

Moments after our chat at the gate Stephen appears again, this time spotting us taking an interest in the retro scoreboard and trying to find a good position to get a photograph. He waves us towards it, shouting that we're fine to go through the pitch gate, round the running track and have a closer look. By the time we get to the cracked terracing just below, Stephen has popped up again and after a brief chat with his dad is showing us up the metal steps behind the scoreboard that lead to a door which will take us right inside the magic box. Mr Schmidt follows us. Stephen, we learn, is Pierre Schmidt's son.

The first impression is of a hideaway – a cosy box room, like the rows of shed-houses on each of the allotments or *Kleingärten* on the edges of the city – a place to be alone and protect a bit of your private self, your *Privatsphäre*, and maybe as far from the state's prying eyes as it's possible to be. It's also a dusty place, a space to make a mess and get some work done, in this case maintaining the electrics. Plug sockets everywhere, trailing cable and bulb boxes. A well-worn desk with a jar of screwdrivers and a pot of paint. A kettle and a mug.

Pierre Schmidt tells us that he usually watches the match from outside, below the board on the terrace steps, but that when it's too cold during the winter months he watches from up here. He gets hold of a jug of glühwein, climbs up and settles down. But how can he see through the scoreboard, I ask, is there a window? And there is, sort of. In fact there are lots of them. Mr Schmidt takes hold of a thin steel pin poking through one of the metal joists and pulls it out.

Of the 14 teams that competed in the 1989/90 Oberliga, Stahl Brandenburg are now playing at the lowest level, the seventh-tier Landesliga Brandenburg-Nord, where they're currently sitting mid-table. The fall down the leagues from the very top division in DDR days, and those two heady rounds of the UEFA Cup, to this seventh level has been a not so slow and a very steady one. In the first season of reunified German football they finished bottom of the 2. Bundesliga (Nord). Three seasons at the third level and one at the fourth were followed by a solid ten years at level five, before slipping to the sixth tier in 2006 before another step down just last year. These relegations were not always the result of poor performance, as re-organisations of the league structure then and still now have meant some movement between levels. But the steps down the ladder have been steady. And the visit of IFK Gothenburg remains the highest rung.

The 1989 season saw Stahl Brandenburg finish in a very tidy tenth place. That time round the fans had a lot to enjoy: a 4-0 home win against Carl Zeiss Jena, and a 2-2 draw in the return fixture on the last day of the season; they also put four past eventual champions Dynamo Dresden. Either side of the Berlin Wall falling they lost away to Energie Cottbus and drew at home with Halle. The season also brought an away win against Lokomotive Leipzig, a big name in more ways than one.

It's in Stahl Brandenburg's name and nature to show a steely, make-do-and-mend attitude, despite all that football reunification and the swallowing of East German industry has thrown at the club and the area, and they show no sign of giving up now. Clubs like this one really need their fans, on a very practical level, and the hard-core are here to stay. Stahl's Quenz Stadium is surrounded by the old steel works buildings and rows and rows of workers' housing. It is deeply rooted in its community and forges on. It also helps when one of your fans is a genius.

And there, in a flash, all is revealed. Mr Schmidt has removed the steel pin. Everything here is steel. He grips one panel, the one with 'Heim' written in biro on the back, and prizes it out. This is a moment of magic, better by a mile than Schimpf's scrappy goal. He's holding a white Styrofoam board, about the size and shape of a swimming float. In fact it might *be* a swimming float. It's painted black on one side, with the addition of perfectly painted white dots, each about the size of a tennis ball, arranged to form an almost angular '0' for the home team's score. The '0' is a brilliant replication of the pixelated version from those scoreboards of the 1970s and '80s. I glance to my left and right and there stacked up are neat piles of identical foam boards, each one painted with perfect dots like this, one for each letter of the alphabet, and more for the numbers 0–9. The system is a perfectly formed, fully working *manual* scoreboard. I gasp and I think Jan, my travelling companion, does too. As Pierre Schmidt is not merely a genius, he's a magician. And if an artist need not only conjure the idea but also to execute it in form, Pierre Schmidt is also an artist. A bright idea, brilliantly done.

Mr Schmidt says he has three sets of alphabets to spell out the team names, and presumably more than one set of numbers too, as otherwise a score draw would be impossible. I can't calculate quickly enough if this would have covered the clash with FC Eisenhüttenstadt, when they were in the same league last season before Stahl were relegated once more, but I'll take Pierre's word for it – even with the addition of the umlaut! And I'm sure he would even have had it covered (had he needed to) back on 9 September 1989, despite the fact that three Os, three Is, and two Es are required to display 1. FC Lokomotive Leipzig, plus the additional *E* needed for Stahl

Brandenburg – not to mention the fact that there's a '1' in the visitors' name and the match finished 1-1. Mr Schmidt's a magician after all. I'm only glad that he doesn't spell out the scorers' names on his board too. On that day, Bernd Hobsch for Lokomotive and Jens Pfahl for Stahl.

From outside, even as close up as the rows of mossy terrace behind the home goal just underneath us, you would swear, or rather wouldn't question, that this thing, while a bit dated, was a fully functioning electronic machine. It was indeed electronic until the mid-90s, hence the trailing cables and sockets. But then it packed up as these things do and the local council which owns the ground didn't get round to repairing it. It fell into a bad state by the new millennium, rusting and becoming unstable. So the council decided to knock it down. After all, there was a place to display the match score on plastic boards propped up at the window of the stadium speakers' box just round the terrace curve.

But Pierre wasn't having that and so stepped in with his ingenious fix. First he set about dealing with the rust on the scoreboard hut, sanding and cleaning the outside and repainting in Stahl blue and white. Then he cut up his foam panels, painted one side black and started the task of adding the dots, in tune with the style of his beloved club's glory days. *From Gö-te-borg to Col-er-aine.* After a match Pierre or his colleague swap back the panels they've used that day with plain black ones, as if turning the scoreboard off. And in the early days, on the odd occasion he forgot to do this and left the score on display, he had phone calls from workmates who lived in view of the stadium bemoaning the waste of electricity. Mr Schmidt, who doesn't overdo such things, can't help but smile.

The council was still talking about tearing the box down, as well as other parts of the stadium which were also becoming run down. But they too were starting to be looked after by other fans, including Stephen, who set about repainting as much of the stadium as they could in their spare time. Pierre told the council that if they ever tore down the scoreboard he'd 'kill them!' And he meant it. We could see that today when Stephen told us the story. In his understated, no nonsense way Pierre is very proud of his makeshift scoreboard. And he should be. It's a trick of the eye. A surreal, steely solution to score-keeping in the modern world. But most of all, his heart is in it.

That's not always the case though. Pierre is a fan and he's only human. So when Chemie Premnitz equalise in the 93rd minute, after 20 minutes of looking like they were always going to, he's really in no rush to update the score. He gives it a couple of minutes, finishes his cigarette and ambles over to the metal steps. The opposition can wait. A stark contrast to the spring in his step when Schimpf scored earlier, and we watched him rush to climb up to his box of tricks, his granddaughter not far behind him. Pierre's granddaughter seemed as excited as we were to watch the scoreboard update, maybe even to get the chance to operate it herself. And the thought that this little girl will one day take on the task, when her *Opa* hasn't the legs for it anymore, of keeping the score at the Steelworkers' Stadium week-in, week-out, is a magical one.

*Postscript: Three days after our visit to Brandenburg, in a second division match in Guatemala, Deportivo Carchá's Luis Acuña slotted home a winning penalty, then celebrated the goal by climbing the ladder up to the scoreboard and changing the '0' to '1' himself. He was booked by the referee.*

# Jena Rules

I CAN report that Pitch Five is flat. It is well lit, regularly proportioned, has a circle in the centre and rectangular boxes to mark the goalkeepers' areas. Furthermore it has no obstacles. No stones, shrubs, nor students lolling about in midfield. This may be as expected, but it could have been so different, had the troublemakers not been removed, and not just the students. I wonder what it would be like if there was a rhododendron bush in the centre circle, or a cherry tree on the wing? I pick up a stick and throw it for the dog.

It took me a long time to find Pitch Five. Trudging through the mass of sports facilities that surround the Ernst Abbe Sportfeld, I could have done with a Carl Zeiss Jenoptik telescope to help me find it. Yoga, aerobics, basketball, swimming, football training with shooting practice and five-a-sides, and finally a young man wearing nothing but a tiny towel outside the back door of a sports hall. I presume he'd had a hot dip and was now taking a balancing cold jolt, but he did give me rather a jolt as I turned the corner. I shouldn't have been surprised though, despite the near freezing temperature, as I'm in the middle of sporting paradise here. Paradise Station is one of the two main train stations in Jena. Though there's certainly nothing paradisiacal about the smell from the overground water pipes as you walk from Jena Paradies, through the Oberaue Park, to the home of FC Carl Zeiss.

As I'm beginning to realise is a theme on this wander-plan of mine, nobody else seems to be heading for Pitch Five tonight. The prospect of a 'friendship' match between the Carl Zeiss Jena reserve team and FC An der Fahner Höhe, from the sixth level, not enough to entice them away from keep-fit. I'm getting plenty of exercise though, having been on my feet, bummeling briskly through Jena, for the past ten hours. From the statue of Carl Zeiss to the memorial to Ernst Abbe; a whizz around the Optics Museum and a great deal of jogging behind the extraordinarily helpful, and swift, librarians at the Friedrich Schiller University Library.

Fahner Höhe, a more relaxing prospect, is a collection of villages just the other side of Erfurt: Jena's arch-rivals in footballing terms, and where I arrived from yesterday. As I head down another dirt track, having got stuck a second time behind a wire fence, I begin to hear the low level murmur of a competitive match, as if there might even be more than a handful of people enjoying the friendship. This is Paradise after all.

I refuse to be disappointed, so I quicken my step, pass another large sports hall which is the main training centre for FC Carl Zeiss, past two more grass practice pitches, and I'm there. Watching football at a low enough level to hear the voices of the players at a spoken and not just shouted level, and to hear the bounce of the ball as well as the familiar lovely thud of ball on boot, is a great comfort. It helps us understand what the players are actually doing, rather than what the television or the big stadium scene suggests they ought to be; it helps us actually watch the game. And maybe even to understand it. Though in my case I doubt that very much.

It helps too when the pace of the match is that bit slower, but that can't be said for this one. The pace here is frantic and feels to me at least as quick as those fleet-footed librarians, and probably twice that of the first team match we saw last Saturday just over there in the Ernst Abbe stadium. I'm very pleased to report that I helped maintain the pace on three occasions, when the ball ran out of play and straight towards my weary feet. I cushioned a pass back to the Fahner Höhe number six the first time, but then must admit to taking a touch too many the second. This is an artificial pitch with just a single metal leaning bar surrounding it and nothing to stop the ball rolling off. The third time the ball comes near me I'm not able to get anything on it and have to chase after it, like a dog for a stick.

* * *

I don't know the dog's name but let's call him Hermann. He races towards it and instead of bringing the stick back, bounds up the steps to the house and in through the light blue metal surround of the Winter House door. Hermann knows that the lawn must be kept clear at all times. It's in the rules. And so I'm left alone for a few moments in the middle of the lawn – I look back up at the house. It could be 1924, in Weimar Germany.

I'd been standing in the middle of Schaefferstraße in front of Haus Auerbach taking a photo, when Hermann and his master arrived back from their morning walk on the Windknollen hills a short jog away. They stopped to find out what I was up to, he a cultured-looking man with short grey hair, a black polo neck and tracksuit bottoms; he a brown and black short-haired terrier. Then to my surprise and delight this kindly man and his dog invited me to have a quick look inside the house, clearly used to people gawping at it from the street, but explaining that we would have to be quiet. I thanked him and followed Hermann inside.

Doctor Fischer is a professor of zoology and evolutionary biology at the University of Jena and his wife, Doctor Happe, a lecturer in folklore and cultural history, and they live in a bona fide, original Bauhaus building. I explain that my bummeling type of research is not architectural but connected to football in eastern Germany, and that this visit to have a quick look (at just the outside, I thought) of a famous early example of a Bauhaus home is a detour before I start the day's real wander-plan. I would later realise that I was very much on the trail of Bauhaus throughout my bummel, as centenary exhibitions popped up in every town I visited.

Today though, I explain, I'd planned to explore the legacy of Carl Zeiss and Ernst Abbe, Jena's most well-known sons. I'd already discovered these two are impossible to avoid here. I'd planned to look at optics and lenses and binoculars, and the history of the Carl Zeiss factory which since 1903 (with the odd detour itself including a brief period named after Abbe rather than Zeiss) has been in the name of the town's most successful football club. I didn't expect to find any football here at the Bauhaus house, maybe just Hermann chasing his stick. But Jena is a football town, and just as it's impossible to avoid Carl and his factory, Ernst and his optics, so the image of the game refracts in the most unexpected of shapes. The Doctors Fischer and Happe listen sympathetically, and are kind enough not to let on that for me to have arrived in their living room unannounced and start gabbling on about football is frankly weird. Their house, though, is beautiful.

It's made up of large white rectangles, a 'cubic ensemble', each about the size of a goalkeeper's area, designed to form the whole by Walter Gropius in 1924, who rather underplayed it as a 'big box of bricks'. One of the Bauhaus founder's earliest commissions, it was the first house he designed with a flat roof, and was built for Felix Auerbach, a Jewish professor of theoretical physics also at the University of Jena and his wife Anna Auerbach, a prominent campaigner for women's rights and suffrage (I was starting to think everyone in Jena is an academic – I'd met a Hungarian biologist in the pub the previous night enjoying Manchester United v PSG). Felix and Anna were movers and shakers in this city of science and light. Felix took over the professorship originally established by Ernst Abbe, while it was Anna who was the driving force behind commissioning this thoroughly modern house. It is a stunning example of an early Bauhaus building, perfectly restored in every detail both outside and in, including the 37 different pastel colours originally designed by Alfred Arndt and painstakingly reinstated by its current owners after they bought it in a much neglected state in 1994. The DDR authorities it seems didn't much care for this Bauhaus house. Today it appears to float.

Both Felix and Anna Auerbach (known as *Fea* in tandem) were significant people of Jena, heavily involved in not just the academic but the cultural, sporting and political life of the city from their arrival here from Breslau in 1889 to their deaths in 1933. They were forward thinking, encouraging to artists and musicians, and engaged in all aspects of Jena life. This new box of rectangles, just like their previous house, was a hub for scientists and musicians, artists and thinkers. Gropius himself spent time here. Edvard Munch painted Felix Auerbach's portrait here, and it hung in the busy music room upstairs. Meetings were held to discuss the issues of the day. Wassily Kandinsky and Paul Klee popped round to discuss line and colour and, no doubt, the starting 11. As did, I imagine, a PE teacher called Hermann Peter and a man from Sheffield called Joseph 'Joe' Findlay.

I'm guessing at this last pair, and can find no evidence of what is almost certainly impossible, but this chance meeting with one professor and his dog on a quiet street in Jena has opened an improbable and unexpected football door, like peering through a Carl Zeiss lens. I look through the high windows into the back garden. It is no surprise that there is no clutter on the lawn, nor that the walls of each of Gropius's floating boxes are as straight as the lines on Pitch Five, and its roof as flat.

At half-time at the friendship match the team from the villages is leading 1-0, and there's nothing to do but wait. Half-time is usually a busy time for fans: queue up for a drink or snack, the same for the toilet, check the scores of the other matches, try to warm up. But at a match at this level there's nothing to do in the interval but wait and, if you're lucky, get that quick nip to the loo, which in this case is in the changing rooms of fifth division club SV Schott Jena. Otto Schott, a chemist and glass manufacturer, whose factory workers formed the club in 1896 was, unsurprisingly, also a regular visitor to Haus Auerbach. Anyone who was anyone in this town was a friend of *Fea*.

I take a picture of a cage full of footballs and wait while the substitutes have a run around. The Jena subs have 'Carl Zeiss' emblazoned across their tracksuit tops in a 1960s style, calling up the memory of past glories as, statistically, the DDR Oberliga's most successful team. Despite all Dynamo Dresden's success and then their Berlin namesake's string of ten titles from 1979 to 1988, it is Jena who won the most points overall in Oberliga history. They are officially top of the Eternal League: 1,097 points, to Dynamo Berlin's 1,092. That was hard to imagine at the first team's lacklustre showing against Karlsruhe on Saturday in a 3. Liga fixture, when the sights around the Ernst Abbe Sportfeld held more pull than the action on the field. This is often the case at a ground with history, especially for a first time foreigner, but there was a lot to take in there off the pitch: the elegant wooden building that holds the famous clock tower; the classic 60s scoreboard; the noise and smoke from the ultras in the Südkurve; the Newport County flag hanging under the main stand.

Random bonds between clubs are a common theme when for both parties a trans-Europe trip is a relatively uncommon occurrence. The bond here between Carl Zeiss Jena and Newport County springs from Jena's miraculous run to the 1981 European Cup Winners' Cup Final. That season saw the Thuringians knock out no less than Roma, Valencia and Benfica to reach the final against Dinamo Tbilisi, across the border at the Rheinstadion, Düsseldorf. They were leading until the 67th minute but went on to lose 2-1 after a late, excellent individual effort by Vitaly Daraselia, and failed finally to join Magdeburg as a European cup competition winner.

But Jena still stand alongside Magdeburg and Lokomotive Leipzig as the only other DDR team to reach a European final. In the quarter-final they played Newport County, drawing at home and then grabbing the win with captain Lothar Kurbjuweit's free kick in front of 18,000 people at Somerton Park. It's unlikely that many real Jena fans were able to travel to south Wales that night but the link formed from distance lives on. A week after my visit to Jena, Newport County were due to face Manchester City in the fifth round of the English FA Cup, and Jens was desperately trying to work out if he could get there. I meet him underneath the main stand at the Ernst Abbe Sportfeld and his opening gambit is, 'How far is Newport from where you live?'

Jens from Jena is a busy man. So I was very grateful for the chunk of matchday time he gave up to welcome me to the club, to chat about its history and hand over a pile of papers about the 1989/90 season, including pages of stats annotated with his own smiley face (arrow up)-sad face (arrow down) system to indicate his team's league performance. He also presented me with original copies of *FUWO* (*Fußball Woche*, the East

German weekly football newspaper) from the summer before the final Oberliga season, which I was happy to pose with for a photo for the next matchday programme.

Jens has been the editor of Jena's prize-winning programme for three years. Called *Anpfiff* (Kick-off) it's been voted the best match programme in the 3. Liga by the German Programme Collectors' Association for the past two seasons. He edits it in his spare time and is one of that special breed of fans who devote endless hours as a volunteer for the club that, sometimes, puts a smile on his face. 'It's a labour of love,' he says, tapping his heart.

I look at the biggest of his highlighted smiley faces and see that it describes the period from late February to early May 1989 when FC Carl Zeiss went on an unbeaten run, including seven wins, to land them firmly in a very smiley fifth place for the season. But at the end of that run of results, and with just two matches left in the season, comes a big sad face, arrow down. Not only a result of that first defeat for months, but because of who it was to: Rot-Weiß Erfurt – local rivals, certainly as far as Jens is concerned (and who incidentally held the title for best 3. Liga match programme when Jens took over *Anpfiff*!). Their 4-1 win against Jena in mid-May meant securing the two points that kept Erfurt from relegation, and to add insult to this injury it also propelled Jena's rivals into the following season and the big scrap for post-reunification Bundesliga places. By this point Erfurt were flying, finished third in the final Oberliga and qualified for the 2. Bundesliga as well as for the UEFA Cup. The boys from the Optics factory finished sixth and also qualified for the second division but the sudden switch in fortunes still rankles in Carl Zeiss country.

FC Carl Zeiss Jena or its predecessors can look back at its Oberliga history and count three league titles, nine runners-up spots and four cup wins among the achievements, the first of each of the league and cup wins playing as SC Motor Jena. That last cup win in 1980 led to the trip to Newport and on to the final. Their golden years were from the mid-1960s through the '70s, coinciding with two of their most significant players' best years. Eberhard Vogel moved from FC Karl-Marx-Stadt to play for Jena throughout the '70s, finishing his career with the record highest number of Oberliga appearances and the second highest number of Oberliga goals (after Joachim Streich). The colourful Peter Ducke, a pop star alongside Dresden's Jörg Stübner, was a Jena player for his whole senior career and finished third in the all-time goalscoring list behind Streich and Vogel. Vogel was also the man who scored the decisive late goal in that Olympics match between East and West Germany in Munich in 1972. Plenty to shout about back then at least, while the years since reunification have seen Jena bounce between the second and fourth divisions and survive as best they can.

'Nothing much has changed since the *Wende*,' Jens explains, referring to the turning point for all aspects of East German life, including its football. 'It's still really difficult for our clubs, in relation to teams from the west.' The older fans in the seats of the main stand above us still talk of the 'good old days' in reference to the Oberliga era, and Jens adds, 'Now our world is a smaller place and it's difficult to build a union of supporters across the club.'

He smiles as he remembers European Intertoto Cup matches, a competition seen as fairly insignificant in much of western Europe, but for those clubs in the East it was at least a chance of competing on a bigger stage. He says, 'You could smell victory there, in those games; victory beyond the DDR.' He then skips forward to the 2008 German Cup semi-final where 80,000 people saw Jena take on Borussia Dortmund. They lost 3-0, but for fans like Jens it's possible, and important, to skip back and forward in time like this, between highlights either side of the *Wende*, like stepping over the Wall as if it were a white line on a park pitch, the memories unending and as clear as glass.

At the Optics Museum on Carl Zeiss Platz there are rows and rows of glass cabinets, demonstrating the seemingly endless possibilities of a lens. Microscopes, telescopes, binoculars, spectacles, optical illusions, laser technology and planetaria. There's also Ernst Abbe's hat and gloves and a stuffed bird with a camera strapped to it for a bird's eye view of the action. Abbe deserves the tributes here as someone who was not only a Nobel Prize-winning physicist but a workers' rights reformer who, among other things, introduced the eight-hour work day to the Carl Zeiss factory. Marvelling at the ground-breaking optical formulae he discovered, I wondered if FC Carl Zeiss should have put them to use in the latter stages of their Cup Winners' Cup Final against Dinamo Tbilisi. But the thing that stopped me in my tracks was labelled *Unendlichkeit.* Infinity. *Put your head in the mirror box and look around. Discover infinite space and complex perspectives.* Okay.

I stand spellbound gazing down into a box about a metre square, in which the placing of a few round mirrors creates a view that goes on forever.

> *The opposing surfaces of the cube are parallel to each other, so that the light can run back and forth almost infinitely between them.*

Terrifying as the image of my own repeated ugly mug under a cap with a Carl Zeiss Jena badge pinned to it is, the way the view continues down and down into an infinite hole opens up … something … and my mind wanders; how flat Pitch Five was, but how we refer to the attacking end of a pitch as up (*up field*, *up top*) and so the area for defending, the opposite, must be *down*, as if the pitch is always on a slope, like a magic mountain, and not flat at all; how we talk of hitting the *back of the net*, as if the striker had walked off the pitch, round behind the goal to the spectator's position and whacked the ball at the back of it, thus never scoring a goal.

*It becomes a huge room full of confusing perspectives,*
*in which you can also see yourself from all sides.*

Then if the goal is just a line reaching up from the paint, how impossible it is to hit it anyway, only cross it, and if the goal, as in modern design, is a rectangular space with the net pulled back to four corners, then how it's only possible to hit the back of the *goal*, which is in fact the *front* of the net; help! I guess it's best not to think about these things too much and just enjoy the game.

I refocus and look deeper down into the box, and there right at the far, impossible end of my vision, I can just about make out the silhouettes of four people deep in conversation.

There they are: Hermann Peter, Joe Findlay and *Fea* (Felix and Anna Auerbach), their dog barking back up at me. I remove my face quickly from the box for fear of letting out a yelp in the quiet of the museum and I look up. It is 1895 and I'm standing at a table in the Winter House of Haus Auerbach. Hermann, Joe, Felix and Anna are putting the finishing touches to a document that will pass through the football ages, not so much break down borders as flatten bushes.

On 1 January 1896 the Jena Football Club published a set of rules of the game. The *Jenaer Regeln* are the first formal German rules and among the oldest football rules in the world. The most famous of them is, 'The playing field should be free of trees and stones, as flat as possible and covered with low grass.'

A good start, and not surprising that this was considered an important step as the Jena club at that time played on the fields of the Oberaue, or upper meadow, between the town centre and Pitch Five (which is flat), and on which the Ernst Abbe Sportfeld stands today. The Oberaue was, and still is, covered in trees, with the River Saale running at its western edge. This is as it should be, as a footnote in the Jena Rules states that proximity to water is welcome. I don't think they state how close the water should be to the playing field though, so I imagine a moat in front of the Jena goal.

The same footnote suggests a 'draught-free location' is also welcome, though that could be 'train-free' as the word used (*Zug*) can refer to either. But in any case it seems like a sensible idea to keep draughts or trains off the pitch. The rules also stated that the goalkeeper's area should be rectangular, rather than the previous semi-circular shape and I'm sure this is evidence enough of the couple from the floating boxes, *Fea*'s input. Their Bauhaus house wasn't built at the time of the meeting to establish the Jena Rules, so we know this meeting can't have happened here, but it did happen somewhere; and Doctor Fischer did mention a vague recollection that he'd seen Felix Auerbach's name in reference to the Jena Football Club so, in any case, let's not let details like facts spoil our flight of fancy. The box of mirrors proves that time is, well, flexible. So I look through its lenses and join Hermann Peter, Joe Findlay, Felix, Anna and the dog in the Winter House pawing over plans to transform future football.

* * *

Felix and Anna Auerbach were forward-looking and open-minded; an avant-garde couple in this city of light and science.

But the original thinking of such minds sees the dark as well as the light, and the perspective shifts suddenly soon after their house was built. In early 1933, just as the Nazi Party took power in Germany, the Auerbachs made the decision to end their own lives, together, in their bedroom upstairs at Haus Auerbach. We can only think they saw the horrors to come, their futures made unbearable. Doctor Fischer told me this outside in the street before he invited me inside and is why, I think, quietness was encouraged. Such sadness here at Haus Auerbach. After such possibility. And as I stand here now, among the light and the colour and the modernity, Hermann the dog chasing round the garden on a bright February morning, I think of them. *Fea*. Their house appears to float.

The poet Richard Dehmel wrote a poem about Anna and Felix Auerbach which I read later in the University Library. I feel very lucky to have spent a few precious moments at the home that's been made inside the extraordinary Auerbachs' house.

*Where far away the world has roamed*
*tandem shooting stars ignite,*
*and attempt with all their might,*
*fusion in each other's light,*
*that is where we feel at home.*

I look up just as the Carl Zeiss reserves score a late winner against FC An der Fahner Höhe. This, after hitting the post and the crossbar twice. The pace hasn't let up. The pitch is flat, with nothing in the way of the action. No trees, no stones. Thanks to *Fea.* Jena Rules. There are 17 of us watching this match now. I am not alone. In fact I feel at home, too. The ball strikes the underside of the crossbar, bounces down and off the goal line at an impossible angle.

# Leaning

I DON'T know my Pythagoras from my Pommerenke. I'm no scientist. I did GCSE physics, but that was a long time ago, and my understanding of geometry (or is it trigonometry?) is spectacularly rudimentary. But nevertheless, armed with a schoolchild's protractor I've just picked up in the One-Euro Shop, I'm marching off to the Steigerwald Stadium on a scientific mission.

It felt like a good idea last night about midnight when I was sitting in a leather swivel chair staring at Erfurt Cathedral. I was drinking a Schluntz Pils brewed here in the city. There's a picture of a medieval *Bürger* on the bottle. Back then the *Bier Rufer*, or beer caller, would walk the streets of old Erfurt, through Anger, over the Krämerbrücke with its half-timbered houses spanning the length of the bridge, and past the fish market, ringing his bell to let people know where the freshly brewed beer was on offer; after having tasted it for quality control of course. Probably the best job in the world. But sitting there in the leather swivel chair is pretty good too. I don't have to tell you that it is stunning. The view of the cathedral that is, not just the Schluntz.

The *Dom* is a magnificent sight. Its main bell, I've read, is the largest medieval bell in the world still in use. It's known for its pure tone. A far cry, I think, from the Rage Against The Machine song that rang out to welcome the Rot-Weiß Erfurt players into the Steigerwald Stadium yesterday. But there's more than one tone out there and more than one church. It's true that the football stadium is for some a type of church. Though for me it's not stadiums necessarily that move me, certainly not of the generic shape springing up these days, but rather a particular type of football place that is the football *ground*: secular, sacred and usually falling down. And in this case it's not the whole ground I'm thinking of but part of it, or rather four parts. I'd come to think that the floodlight masts at the Steigerwald Stadium might just be as arresting, as glorious even, as the towers of this cathedral. I'm sure I'm wrong. But to hell with it.

The hail is lashing down, but I'm on a mission. I've moved from Holy to haily, marching past the fish market, over the Krämerbrücke and through Anger on a pilgrimage of my own. I'm going to measure the angle at which the floodlight masts – the *Flutlichtmasten* – at the Steigerwald stadium *lean*. I've long thought that their lean is the beautiful thing. It's not the angle that attracts me, but the result of it. How great is the lean?

No one at the match yesterday could, or would tell me the exact angle of the lean. They probably assumed I was joking, but no I'm deadly serious, or at least deadly. I was sure someone at some point had written it down, or would be able to check the original plans for the masts, erected in 2003 in place of the previous ones which had a lot less curious a lean. But no, so I have to find out for myself. With my one-Euro protractor. Scientifically.

Which is why I'm battling down Arnstädter Straße in a hail storm. I've just passed a building with a large mural from DDR days chiselled and painted into its side, with images representing tools of the workers – a hammer, a chisel, brooms and hods – and a motto among the symbols suggesting, roughly, that 'behind all good societies are good workers, and behind all good workers, good societies'.

A good worker needs their tools, so I've got my protractor in my top pocket.

Half an hour ago as the hail started I was walking round the Juri-Gagarin-Ring, the busy ring-road circling Erfurt old town. Huge *Plattenbau* concrete buildings, one of them with the cosmonaut's name on it, loomed large, and it struck me that *Gagarin's Ring* would be an excellent title for a sci-fi story. This persistent hail, as if from space or the future, makes me think that maybe I should be writing that book instead of this one; rather than attempting to measure the precise angle of the floodlights at a German fourth division football ground. Still, *Vorwärts*.

An hour later and I'm at the home of Rot-Weiß Erfurt, having spent the last 45 minutes protractor in hand as the perfect personification of extreme amateurism. Football in the DDR, as noted, was officially amateur at all levels so this is perfectly apt. But I am also utterly hopeless. The hail has turned to heavy drizzle, the cold biting at my fingertips as I fumble about trying to get both an accurate measurement of the angle of the lean and at the same time a phone photo of the protractor with one of the masts in the background, to prove that I've been here and done it. I only have two hands and I discover that you need at least three to do this, possibly more in this weather. In the end I settle for two pictures, one of a magnificent mast and another of my protractor at rest. I then faff about for far too long than is sensible, only pausing when people pass by so they don't offer to have someone come and take me back to the *Krankenhaus*.

In the spirit of amateurism and with my trusty scientific instrument I commit to getting my best guess. For a good 20 minutes I am convinced that my measurement of 17 degrees is spot on. Then I lose confidence in this, after a passing pensioner gives me a startled look, and start to think it's probably more like 10. This is disappointing as that's hardly a special lean. And, I've realised, results often depend on the way you look at them. Literally in this case as depending on the angle of my own head, and the position of my protractor in relation to it, the reading changes significantly.

I've tried to even things up by getting as close to the ground as possible, as a guideline. Surely the earth is flat, I think. But still varying results. Then I try to rest the instrument high on a fence so it appears from my eyeline to be the equal height of the masts. Everything's blurred though, particularly with my glasses covered in drizzle; which makes me wonder whether if I squint hard enough with both eyes almost shut and think of a number between 1 and 90, that might be the answer. Equally, depending on which way round I hold the protractor a reading of 20 degrees starts to look more like 160. But I don't think that can be right.

My reading I decide has to reflect the fact that the floodlights lean inwards and light up the football pitch rather than passing pigeons. This is a breakthrough. I'm learning something and don't need to ask an expert after all. So with renewed rigour I have a final go, with the protractor perching on a low wall and half a brick to keep it steady. From a crouching position I take my final reading. It has to be, I can't feel my fingers anymore. I can report that the angle at which the floodlight masts at the Steigerwald Stadium lean is 25 degrees! Give or take.

The floodlights masts are beautiful. There are four of them – of this I can be absolutely certain. That's where my engineering understanding ends, but I'll offer my technical description of one mast regardless: At the front there are two thick legs leaning out to stabilise, and at the back two more thinner metal wires which are pointing inwards towards the main base, so that there is effectively a cage of four stands which is the floodlight mast and which is the thing that is leaning at 25 degrees (or thereabouts), then as they meet the ground those four stands come to a point at the main base, at the back of which are two thinner wires going outwards from the base and up to two thick prongs which are on the back side, which is then replicated on the front side, so whereas the two thick prongs on the back side lean outwards and meet the two thinner wires which then continue right to the top, on the front side the two large stabiliser legs point outwards, so that there are essentially two legs at the front, two legs either side and two thinner wires from the back meeting the legged point higher up on the back side, as those thinner wires continue right to the top where the point at which the two legs meet is approximately a fifth of the way up the whole mast and in the middle of it all is a ladder to climb up. To change a bulb.

I hope that's clear. Any questions, please look at a photo.

You'll see there's an elegance to the lean of these things and a hint of menace too. There's a curiosity, a questioning, but also something hopeful. As an attack forms on the pitch below the crowd moves forward instinctively, hopefully, holding their collective breath. As the ball's about to hit the back of the net I wonder, does the crowd lean in line with those masts behind them? At 25 degrees? I hope so, with every angle of me.

It's a shame we didn't get a chance to test this theory at the match yesterday. But Rot-Weiß Erfurt looked scientifically incapable of troubling the Germania Halberstadt defence, in a second home defeat in a row following the winter break. It was the 20 or so travelling fans from Halberstadt who did the leaning-in, for Philipp Blume's first goal and Dennis

Rothenstein's calmly dinked clincher; while the rest of the Steigerwald congregation, including us in the Südtribune, remained resolutely upright.

This is a long way from the days when the Georgi Dimitrov Stadium stood here on the edge of the Steigerwald. Rot-Weiß Erfurt was a solid, if undecorated, DDR-Oberliga club, spending all but two seasons since 1966, and their reformation as one of the football focus clubs, in the top flight. In 1980 they reached a cup final, losing out to rivals Carl Zeiss Jena 3-1 after extra time. Equally, since reunification they have fared reasonably well, spending most of their time at the third or fourth level, with two brave forays into the 2. Bundesliga. But it is their team from the 1950s which is the one that would truly make the fans lean in. Playing then as Turbine Erfurt they won consecutive Oberliga titles in 1954 and 1955. And still at the time Erfurt joined a new Germany in 1990, in the first post-reunification season, there was cause for one last lean forward. Uwe Schulz's neatly-timed 65th-minute strike saw the Red-Whites take the lead in a second round UEFA Cup match against Ajax, perfect for a 25-degree lean-in. It's just a shame that Jonk, Bergkamp, Pettersson, Blind and Van Loen all scored for Ajax across the two legs, to stand the Thuringians back upright.

Today though we did finally get the chance to lean towards some modern day goal action when, after the main match, a tip-off from fanzine seller Bernd led us to the vast Thüringenhalle where a youth tournament was in full swing. On offer here was all the excitement we'd missed back at the Steigerwald Stadium. Spectacular finishes, over-exuberant (i.e. sweary) parents, great passing football from young players, male and female in various age groups, and fizzy pop and homemade cakes to boot. Plus the modern footballer-styled temper tantrum of the star striker of the host team Motor

Erfurt Gispersleben, all of nine years old, in protest at a disallowed goal.

The Thüringenhalle is an impressive hall for football and much else and has seen its fair share of protest over the years. In the town library I bumped into Bernd again (he's not to be confused with the other famous Erfurt Bernd – *Bernd das Brot*, a children's TV character in the form of a grumpy loaf of bread). Bernd is significantly more jolly, works in the library, and pointed me towards some books on the history of Rot-Weiß and the area around the Steigerwald. I think back to the angry protest of the young Gispersleben striker, storming off to the changing rooms behind the large podium stage. And I find a photo of that same hall, a packed Thüringenhalle in late October 1989, hundreds of people sitting, more standing at the back, many more outside, for a public meeting amid growing calls for social reform here in Thuringia and across the country. On the podium stage is a very long table which looks precariously perched.

The demonstrations were to reach their peaceful climax less than two weeks later; but I think back further to the Erfurt artist Christoph Jahn whose *Pianola* gallery and bar I passed earlier today, near Anger, on the way to measure the lean. Jahn was imprisoned after his friend fled to the West in the mid-1980s. Looking through the gallery window at what I could see of his muted, playful abstracts, I wondered if he was locked up in the narrow cells of the Andreasstraße prison which, along with the Erfurt Dom, I can also see from the swivel chair where I started. I was standing in those cells earlier today, the doors a foot thick, decorated now by a memorial exhibition with images of protest in Thuringia throughout October and November 1989. I could feel the pulse of it all rising, amid much else, the Anger. I leave the chair and rush down the road. It's kicking off.

A football match. In a pub just over the road from the old Andreasstraße prison, I watch Hamburger SV take on Dynamo Dresden. There's a young 20-something wearing a Rot-Weiß scarf. I'd seen very little evidence of the club outside the area around the Steigerwald Stadium, almost nothing in the town itself, so was pleased to spot the scarf, to find a fan.

'Erfurt's not really a football city,' he says. 'In Magdeburg if they're in the second division they have 20,000 fans – if they're in the fourth division, still 20,000. The same in Dresden. In Erfurt if we're in the second division we'd get 20,000, but in the fourth, maybe 5,000 at the most.' Football is fickle and often paradoxical. Loyalty leans in to discontent in the hard times. German football culture in particular, very much still today, has a fine tradition of protest.

'Yes we have a big stadium,' the young fan goes on. 'But we have no money. Like Chemnitz. The stadium's not the problem. It's the people making the decisions. When we were in the 3. Liga they tried to save money by buying fourth division players. But we need better players to survive in the professional game.'

Will he keep the faith, I ask. 'In general it's okay, yes. I think the good times will come back.' I ask if young fans like him think of those days in the top flight, in the DDR-Oberliga, as the good times. 'Well the past is part of our history. Yes we talk about that, but about the future too.' And what of the future? He leans in, hopefully. 'The good times will come back,' he says again.

Hope. I'm in the courtyard of the Cafe Arche on a street called Grosse Arche, staring at a tree. It was planted when the building was restored after years of neglect and the pub was opened. On a small sign nailed to the tree it archly states, '1989. An Oak Tree'. As lacking in arboreal knowledge as physics know-how, I am easily fooled. The sign is surely intended for gullible hunters of the spirit of '89, like me; delighted by the mighty oak planted with the peaceful revolutionary hope of November 1989. I check with the chef when he pops out for a fag. It's a joke. This is a cherry tree, planted in 1990. I am reeled in.

Still even this satirical cherry tree is a stark reminder of that time and of how much has passed, like water under the Krämerbrücke, since. Its trunk is about a foot wide, reaching from roots which push up the cobble slabs beneath. Despite the joke, the cherry tree looks old. It is standing firm and – as they say down the road at rivals Carl Zeiss Jena's home – 'steely and not for sale'. It was born at the end of one Germany and the start of another. A new beginning or a buying up, I don't know.

I take a final sip of Schluntz Pils and look back up at the cathedral. The last time I looked it was gloriously lit by its own floodlights, pointing up from the ground at a certain angle, bathing the bold buildings in Erfurt reds and whites. But now when I glance up again the lights have all gone out. Someone's pulled the plug, perhaps telling me it's time to go to bed. Not floodlight failure I'm sure, but the angels and the angles at rest. And before I turn out the light I think of Christoph Jahn and others like him in their prison cells, like those just over the road, the doors as thick as the trunk of a cherry tree.

After all this angle angst in Erfurt, I am certain now that the *Flutlichtmasten* are as filled with hope as that tree 30 years on. They are at least as beautiful as these magnificent cathedral towers, now disappeared in the dark. Of that I'm certain. And then I get it – my Eureka moment, I doubt very much – but never mind the science, those floodlight masts, they're urgent. That's the difference. They light up the match. They shine a light on the effort, the huffing and the puffing and the protest. But more than that, they're solid *and* precarious. That's why I love them. *An Oak Tree. 1989.* They lean so far they could fall.

*Postscript: Midway through the following season, 2019/20, Rot-Weiß Erfurt were withdrawn from the league due to insolvency, all points won against them deducted. They hope to start again at the fifth level, the familiar-sounding Oberliga.*

*Meanwhile, as I continued on my own journey I visited a number of stadiums where I found myself thinking, 'Damn it. I think those floodlights have a bigger lean than at Erfurt.' This was particularly true at the Ostseestadion in Rostock. But I still love the Erfurt lean most of all.*

# Halle: a tragedy

EARLY IN the second half I look down to the terrace step just in front of me. A man in his late 50s, a woman in her early 20s and a younger man, perhaps 30, still haven't stood back up from their half-time rest. The people in front of them are all standing now so their view of the match is completely blocked. I wonder if I should tell them the action has restarted. Then I look closer, and see that the older man is crying. He looks like he's been crying for some time. The woman has a hand on his shoulder. Then I look to the younger man and see that he has been crying too and is now trying hard not to start again. Clearly something has happened for this small group, something very sad, so I try not to stare and look back up to what is a poor match, but bathed in bright sunshine. I don't mention it to my companions, Duncan and Lutz, but I can't help but glance back occasionally to the man crying and the other man trying not to.

Halle, on the banks of the River Saale, is a town of tragedy. It was from the roof of a farmhouse just outside town that Katrin, the young, mute daughter of *Mother Courage*, banged her drum to warn the people of Halle that soldiers were about to sack the city. In Bertolt Brecht's play, set in the Thirty Years' War, Katrin bangs her drum furiously, intently (not unlike the ultras drummers to our right this sunny afternoon), until a bang too far and she is shot dead. She's finally found her voice and paid a tragic price. Her mother, *Courage*, holds her dead body and sings to it, then packs up her cart and drags it off to another town, dragging the tragedy with her. Maybe she moves on to Wittenburg just down the road, we don't know, the play ends there.

There was a young prince from Denmark who went to university in that town down the road, and in 1871 Wittenburg University was merged with Halle to create the Martin Luther University of Halle-Wittenburg. I've just walked past some of its grand buildings and the theatre which has *Sein oder Nichtsein, das ist die Frage* painted on its walls. 'To be, or not to be?' I imagine Hamlet and his mates – Horatio, Rosencrantz and Guildenstern – hanging out outside the Mensa building having a vape, with the other bright young things on this street called *Harz*.

Hamlet is in my heart, so I have to pause here. Not because of the play particularly, but because the word is in the name of my club, Dulwich Hamlet of 1893. Hamlet's young age adds enduring fascination to his tragedy. But there's something deep, maybe deeper, about the tears of older age. And while crying isn't necessarily a sign of tragedy of course, and these are both plays, there is something about the man on the terrace step this afternoon. I see him carrying the tragedies of Halle on his shoulders, and the loss.

Turbine Halle is not entirely lost, nor forgotten, but almost. I've moved to another ground. There's a great view down across the Volkspark and the west of the city from up here at the Sportanlage Felsen. Here at the *Felsen* (the Rock) the birds are chattering away as if to amplify the quiet, nothing-happening-here-ness of a Thursday morning in February at a very, very lower league football ground. The only other people I can see are two kids kicking into a net on the artificial practice pitch, listening to hip hop at a very sociable volume;

and two men, maybe a father and son, loading the back of a car with decorating stuff. The younger man is doing the carrying.

I stand looking at the main pitch, the turf in good condition. The only resemblance it has to a stadium is from the grass bank on the far side, with a dozen or so concrete benches dotted around for standing or sitting on, or for a mid-match nap. They look like stone coffins. This is a far cry from the 1920s plan, never realised, to build a modern cultural centre on Lehmann's Rock beside the River Saale just a few hundred yards south of here. Still on the trail of Bauhaus that started in Jena, I discover that one of the 24 entrants to the architectural competition in 1927 was Bauhaus founder Walter Gropius, whose visionary design called 'Hanging Gardens' included a sports forum. Imagine how Halle football might have been revolutionised by its teams playing a Bauhaus-inspired passing game beneath the 'hanging boxes' of Gropius' Grandstand.

Turbine Halle currently play at the eighth level of German football, the Landesklasse Saxony-Anhalt, in front of crowds of, I guess, a handful. But in 1949 as *Union* Halle, and again in 1952 as *Turbine*, they were DDR-Oberliga champions, the top of the pile in the recently established East German football league. Back then a Bayern or Dortmund equivalent from over the hills, far from where they rest today.

The club still exists and it's clearly cared for by the few, but there's another strain of misfortune here too. After the 1953 workers' uprisings Turbine lost a number of players after they defected to the West. The club was struggling to form a team and at that point a new club was founded across town in the south called Chemie-Leuna Halle. Chemie (linked with the chemical industry) took many of the remaining Turbine players and was also given its place in the top league. I don't think Turbine were relegated through the normal poor results, but rather it was decided the new club would take their place. Chemie-Leuna went on to become Hallescher FC Chemie (also known as Chemie Halle) and is the Halle club of 1989 and later Oberliga history. While Turbine were essentially subsumed into Chemie, a foreshadowing of the swallowing up of east German football into the west post-1989. This is the tragedy of Turbine. But Chemie Halle, and its successor Hallescher FC, have had more than their share of real tragedy too.

Chemie Halle had their best Oberliga season in 1970/71, finishing third behind Dynamo Dresden and Carl Zeiss Jena, to book themselves a European adventure the following year for only the second time in their history. They were drawn against PSV Eindhoven in the first round of the UEFA Cup and managed to hold the Dutch side to a goalless draw in the first leg at home. The second leg, though, never happened.

In the early hours of 28 September 1971, a fire broke out in the ground floor restaurant of the Hotel 't Silveren Seepaerd. It spread quickly up through the hotel, which had no fire exits, no fire proofing or alarms and few extinguishers. Many of those trapped in the upper second and third floors had to jump down on to the flat roof of the kitchen where people held out bed sheets tied together to catch them. Most of the 86 guests escaped this way, but tragically 11 people died that night and 19 were injured. The playing and coaching staff of Chemie Halle were staying at the hotel that night, the night before the second leg.

Nine of those who lost their lives did so in their hotel rooms, while two people died attempting to jump to safety. Twenty-year-old player Erhard Mosert broke his leg this way while international defender Klaus Urbanczyk suffered career-ending injuries attempting his escape, after bravely helping people from inside the building along with reserve goalkeeper

Volkhard Jany. Part of Urbanczyk's leg was amputated days later. Most tragically for the football club, 21-year-old midfielder Wolfgang Hoffmann missed the target of his jump to safety and crashed through a skylight. He died in the fall.

Chemie Halle immediately withdrew from the competition after a dark night for the club, which has never been forgotten. One of the PSV Eindhoven players at that time was Guus Hiddink, who in 2006 on the 35th anniversary of the tragedy was by then the PSV manager and helped to organise a remembrance match in Halle between his Eindhoven team and Hallescher FC. The East German version of the club never again qualified for a European match, while Hallescher FC did play in the 1991 UEFA Cup, losing out in the first round to Torpedo Moscow. Bill Shankly was wrong. Football is not more important than life and death.

* * *

Chemie Halle were a solid DDR-Oberliga club, playing in the top league for all but four seasons from 1966 to 1991. They started the post-reunification era in the 2. Bundesliga but by the Millennium were down to the fifth tier. They've since spent the last 18 years at the fourth or third levels and have a modern new stadium built within some of the stone walls of their old Kurt-Wabbel-Stadion. A metal plaque has been placed on one of the walls with the date *September 26, 1997.* This is not a slightly misdated anniversary of the fire in Eindhoven but another tragedy altogether, which struck 26 years later. I glance back down at the stone steps. The man is still crying.

On 26 September 1997 it was an evening match. An excited crowd gathered inside the Kurt-Wabbel-Stadion for the Regionalliga clash. It was a special one. This was the first local city derby for many years, between Hallescher FC and

Vfl Halle 96. The Halle football landscape is a knotty one, with numerous splits, merging, folds and re-formings, and requires a graphic map to navigate it, but essentially all the Halle clubs share some sort of history.

To mark this special occasion it was decided that a parachute team of ten would enter the stadium minutes before the start. The last of the parachutists would deliver the match ball ready for kick-off, but that never happened.

Something had gone badly wrong. Matthias Becker was in the first group of five who jumped, carrying flags of the two teams. Becker's parachute failed to open and with the ropes knotted he hurtled towards the ground. Travelling at high speed he veered from the pitch and towards the ticket office near the *Badkurve* – where we're standing today. Becker struck a queue of people as he landed and he and one other died on impact. Two other people died later as a result of their injuries.

Matthias Becker was a 37-year-old father of three. The others who lost their lives were 28, 21 and 18 years old. The youngest was a youth team goalkeeper for Hallescher FC. The match was of course cancelled immediately. Future swimming champion Paul Biedermann was there that evening, an 11-year-old boy from Halle. He would never go back inside the stadium after what he saw.

* * *

But many do still come here, dragging their cart down Kantstraße, and Halle football is well supported. Twenty-two years later under an unusually bright February sky the match today is an uneventful one. Halle came in to it in third place in the 3. Liga, pushing for one of the two automatic promotion spots to the second division, which would be their highest level since that first reunified season in 1991/92.

But the team doesn't seem to have much spirit for it today, and despite controlling much of the ball are content to keep Sportfreunde Lotte, today's lowly visitors, from troubling Kai Eisele's goal. Maybe they have other things on their minds, sharing the weight of two acts of tragedy. The closest thing to a goal comes when Eisele is able to tip a long-range shot over the bar early in the second half, just about getting his fingers to it. And that's more than can be said for one of his predecessors.

Chemie Halle finished the 1989/90 season in mid-table with few notable results, barring perhaps the 3-0 win against Rot-Weiß Erfurt the night before the Berlin Wall fell, and a 5-0 defeat to Magdeburg two weeks into the uncertainty of two Germanys. They scored 38 goals that season, and rather neatly also conceded 38 – all of them past goalkeeper Jens Adler. That means that we can be pretty sure that Adler touched the ball at least 38 times, picking it out of the back of his net. But ten months later, with reunification only weeks away, thankfully the third act of Halle-related history turns tragicomic.

Adler, who still works at the club as a goalkeeping coach, was 26 when he was selected for the squad for the DDR national team's last ever football match, a friendly against Belgium in Brussels in September 1990. With East Germany leading 2-0, Adler was brought on as a late substitute for first-choice goalkeeper Jens Schmidt – presumably a sporting gesture by coach Eduard Geyer to allow him to pick up his cap.

Adler became the last ever man to win a cap for the DDR, and while German players don't actually get a cap, nor refer to them, if they did I'm sure Adler would have been very proud to get his hands on his. The only trouble is he didn't get his hands, or his feet or even an eyebrow on the ball. In his minutes between the posts he failed to touch the ball even once. This third act – the tragedy of Jens Adler – might just bring a smile to Halle fans' faces.

I hope so, as the final whistle approaches here in the match against Sportfreunde Lotte, and the unexpected sun continues to beat down to the sound of the drums. I glance down again and sense the very faint beginnings of a smile on the terrace steps below us. The group of three is still sitting down, still not able to take in the action. But beer has been fetched. And it has been drunk. I can't see whether that smile is really possible, but these are Halle people and something tells me they're going to get through it. I hope they do. They've been through so much already. I see the young holding their older friend, singing to him and carrying him home.

# 1966, and all that

A GERMAN side lines up in the tunnel about to step out into an iconic stadium to play one of the biggest matches of its lives. It is 1966. Among the opposition standing beside them is the goal threat who wears number ten. He has high hopes pinned to him and a famous hat-trick's not out of the question. He's wearing a plain red shirt today, with white shorts and red socks; while the German team is naturally sporting its iconic strip – in yellow and blue? Hold on.

Shouldn't that be white and black? Black shorts, white shirts with black trim and a badge with an eagle on it. Isn't their captain the *Kaiser*, and the opposition number ten Geoff Hurst? Surely the people will think it's all over.

It isn't. It's a freezing Wednesday night in December. Snow shovelled to the edges of the pitch for a third round clash in the Inter-Cities Fairs Cup. This is not the World Cup Final or Wembley Stadium in June, nor is it the team of West Germany led by Franz Beckenbauer. At the Zentralstadion in Leipzig the yellow and blue strip, albeit with a rare red trim, belongs to the railway workers' team from Saxony. This *is* 1966 and all that, but it is the year of Lokomotive Leipzig.

If the archive footage is anything to go by the stadium is full with nearing 80,000 fans. But the floodlighting appears dim and it's hard to see them. The players appear shadowy figures, skating in the reflection of the Saxon snow. The stadium lights are just about bright enough to pick out the opposition number ten though, confirming it's definitely not Geoff Hurst. The opponents in red tonight are Benfica from Lisbon, one of the great sides of the day led by one of its greatest players. While the captain of Lokomotive Leipzig, just a few steps ahead of him in the tunnel is a slight, short, balding man with a comb over, called Karl Drößler.

'As we were waiting in the tunnel leading out to the pitch at the Zentralstadion we came together,' Drößler tells me. 'As I can recall it I said to the boys as the team captain, "Today it's our weather."'

1966 is not a year etched exclusively into the memories and second-hand imagery of English football fans. Other things happened too, beyond the Hurst hat-trick, The Beatles' *Revolver* and the miniskirt. And while 1966 is an *annus mirabilis* for England international football, it is also a pivotal year for the East German game, key to the history of many clubs from the DDR and particularly to that of 1. FC Lokomotive Leipzig. Their road is winding, as long as any other club in the country and longer than most. In 1966 not only was the club re-formed anew, adding the current *Lokomotive* to their *Leipzig* amid the greater football restructuring that established the 11 focus clubs, but on a Wednesday night in December the railway workers' team in yellow and blue lined up against Eusébio.

I meet Karl Drößler before a match on a crisply cold but bright day over 50 years later. It's February 2019 and today Lokomotive Leipzig are lining up against Union Fürstenwalde in the Regionalliga Nordost, at the German fourth tier. Drößler, now in his 80s, is as busy as ever on a matchday so I'm delighted to grab a chat with him on the steps into the glorious wooden grandstand at Leipzig's Bruno Plache Stadium, before he's whisked away to meet a Spanish TV crew.

He's a kind, dignified man in corduroy, a black workers' cap over a now bald head. He was losing his hair even then but the memory of that night in December 1966 is still as bright as today's February sun; the weather then, as Drößler says, on the home side's side: 'I said to the boys, this is Petrus's [the weather God's] contribution. He wants us to win, so let's do him a favour!'

The match in 1966 was in the third round of the *Messestädte-Pokal.* The Inter-Cities Fairs Cup – which later morphed into the UEFA Cup – was designed to promote international trade fairs and originally only open to cities that hosted such a fair; which is perhaps why Birmingham City made it to the final two years running. It's also why Lok Leipzig were often involved. The city has a notable trade fair tradition and is known locally as *Messe-stadt.*

That night *in Fair City* there were 75,000 people in the Central Stadium. If the live view was clearer than the faded footage shows, they saw an own goal by Benfica's Jacinto after 25 minutes and an Augusto equaliser just before the break. Then early in the second half two excellent strikes from forward Henning Frenzel finished the first leg. The ghostly film shows snow piled up on the sidelines and frozen mud in patches across the surface, challenging even *The King* to be able to make things tick.

At the time Eusébio was one of the best two players on the planet: he'd shone more brightly at the World Cup in the summer than even his friendly rival Pelé, and left England with the Golden Boot. But the footage from Leipzig shows only flashes of skill mixed with a good deal of struggle. A tough tackle to regain possession sees him get a shot away, here; a swift one-two despite the hardened pitch, there; then he narrowly wins a header on the edge of the Leipzig box, nicking it off the balding head of captain Drößler. By the end of this frozen first leg the Saxons led Eusébio's Portuguese giants 3-1 and Drößler led the team back in.

'After the game I did regret not speaking any Portuguese. I'd have loved to hear the thoughts of Eusébio and the other players. He was obviously disappointed, unhappy and grumpy. But before he left he gave me a signed picture and said in English, "Thank you for your fairness."'

Karl is clearly very proud of that moment, and leading his team out against Eusébio into a full Central Stadium cheering his beloved Leipzig on was surely the happiest point of his playing days. 'Not quite,' he says. 'The circumstances were very special. We played a league game in Rostock – it was 1962. The final score was 2-2. I called and they said "nothing has happened yet". The next morning we got the early train back to Leipzig. Back in those days there were no mobile phones so we rushed to the post office and called again. "It's about to happen," they said. So me and my team-mates waited at the Hotel Astoria next door to the Hauptbahnhof and eventually the message got through: a healthy little baby girl has arrived, my daughter Heike.'

Karl Drößler is a remarkable man with quite some breadth of experience. After a distinguished playing career with various incarnations of the Leipzig club he turned to science, studying biology at the city's university and gaining his doctorate there and later a professorship. He studied and worked in London for a year in the 1980s, a rare thing for a DDR citizen, and by 1991 was Chair of Animal Physiology and Immunobiology at the University of Leipzig, while at the same time guiding the football club through the *Wende* period of change, as its chairman. But he's never forgotten where it all started.

'When I was ten years old I fell in love with football. Of course I was dreaming of packed stadiums applauding me. But here I was in Hohengandern, a tiny village near Eichsfeld in

Thuringia, with no sports field or sports hall. But the dream came true: in March 1959 we played in Zeitz, the stadium was sold out and we won 2-1. The papers judged that "I showed a firm display and have the potential to see through some tougher matches as well." It was the day I realised what a great feeling it is when dreams come true.'

Drößler and his team-mates did indeed move on to tougher matches and were no strangers to the dream of European glory either; nor were they strangers to the Fairs Cup or the wintry conditions that seemed to follow them around. He recalls the adventures the club had in the same competition the previous year when they faced a Leeds United team who would go on to win the cup three times.

'We played Leeds United in late 1965. We lost the first leg at home 1-2. But we still had a chance. Elland Road was covered in snow and ice. The ground workers did everything they could to clear the pitch. But we couldn't train there. So we went to the local greyhound track. One of the journalists had the idea that it would be good to take a photo of me and a dog jumping over a fence. So we did.'

Matthias is my host in Leipzig today. He has an encyclopaedic knowledge of all things Lokomotive Leipzig pre- and post-1966, and has co-written two encyclopaedia-sized histories of the club, one covering the modern era (from 1966 onwards) and a second, award-winning book covering the full history of the Leipzig club from its founding in 1893. He sends me a newspaper clipping and sure enough there's a large photo of a young Drößler leaping over a fence, holding on to the lead of the hound leaping beside him. This unorthodox training session must have taken it out of the captain as he didn't start the match at Elland Road the following day, which finished goalless. On a weather-ravaged surface, conditions once again favoured the Saxons up to a point, as the colourful match report in the *Doncaster Evening Post* suggests:

'Where light-weight Leeds struggled in perplexity to conquer the pitch, the Germans stroked the ball around with fluency and purpose … As a lesson in snow-soccer, it was enthralling. A 32,111 crowd cheered them off at the end, thrilled by their classic style.'

But despite the Leeds players continuing to show the 'desperation of drowning men clambering aboard a life-raft', they clung on to their 2-1 lead from the first leg, with the visitors ultimately misfiring. The report concluded, 'But, as Leeds had found to their advantage in the first leg, Leipzig's finishing was atrocious. A blind grannie with a pop-gun on a golf course could have done more damage.'

The following year they did do a bit more damage. In the 1966/67 competition they knocked out Djurgårdens in the first round after a 3-1 win in the Olympic Stadium in Stockholm, then saw off Liège in the second round to tee up the clash with Benfica in the last 16. The 3-1 win in the first leg gave them a real possibility of reaching a first European quarter-final.

But they'd have to wait a while for the return leg which didn't happen until March 1967, in the bright lights of Lisbon's Estádio da Luz. On home turf and in significantly more clement conditions Eusébio started to take control. After a goalless first half his shot from the edge of the box struck a Leipzig player on the arm and he stepped up himself to convert the penalty. Two minutes from the end his remarkably powerful header from outside the box doubled Benfica's tally. On the away goals rule this would have been enough to see Benfica through and to end Leipzig's run. But in between these two Eusébio strikes, up stepped the Lokomotives' own number ten, Henning Frenzel.

Frenzel is also here for today's match against Union Fürstenwalde. Sitting in the wooden grandstand near the simple desk which serves as a press box, he is never far away from his old friend Manfred Geisler. Geisler was also in the side against Benfica in 1966 and was as ever looking out for his mate. Known as Frenzel's bodyguard, Geisler patrolled the midfield ready to dive into tackles to keep the pressure off and allow the striker to do his thing. 'Geisler's still Frenzel's bodyguard today,' Matthias jokes, pointing to him in the stand. 'If you bother him now, Manfred will step in.'

Frenzel did his thing after 81 minutes, forcing the ball over the line from close range after a scrappy move from a corner, and this was enough to hold Benfica at bay.

Weigang
Giessner
Franke Faber
Geisler
Engelhardt Drößler Zerbe
Naumann Frenzel Löwe

Leipzig won the tie 4-3 on aggregate. But the Inter-Cities Fairs Cup dream would end a month later, in Kilmarnock of all places. Leipzig won the first leg of the quarter-final by a single goal but lost the return leg 2-0. Kilmarnock then lost out to Leeds United in the semi-final, who in turn lost the final to Dinamo Zagreb.

The railway workers' team would have to wait a while for another real chance at European glory. The team of 1966 was from a golden generation – that of Drößler, Löwe, Frenzel and his bodyguard Geisler – but there were two other Lok Leipzig European adventures to come before the turning season.

Neatly spaced out, the first of them came in the 1970s before the final fling in the late '80s.

In the 1973/74 UEFA Cup the Lokomotives rolled past Torino in the first round, then Wolverhampton Wanderers in the second: the 4-4 draw on aggregate seeing Leipzig through on away goals. In the third round they knocked out Fortuna Düsseldorf, then drew 1-1 with Ipswich Town in the quarter-final, but progressed on penalties to set up a third encounter with an English club in what was their first semi-final.

The home leg against Tottenham Hotspur at the Zentralstadion saw a crowd of 74,000 and a narrow 2-1 defeat for Leipzig, so Lok travelled to White Hart Lane for the away leg with the tie still alive. They failed to make the final leap as Spurs won 2-0. But they had got one step closer to a first European final. That would come, eventually, after a further 13-year wait, and would be against another of the giants of European football. Karl Drößler wouldn't have it any other way.

Lokomotive Leipzig beat Union Berlin 5-1 in the FDGB-Pokal (the East German cup) of 1986, to set up their foray into the European Cup Winners' Cup for the following season. It would prove to be the closest they'd get to European silverware. They saw off Glentoran of Belfast in the first round; Rapid Vienna in the next, after extra time. Swiss club Sion were beaten in the quarter-final, which set up a tight and momentous semi-final clash with Bordeaux. A 1-0 away win for Leipzig in France was followed by the reverse for Bordeaux in Leipzig (after Uwe Zötzsche had a penalty saved in normal time), taking the tie to a penalty shoot-out. Zötzsche made amends scoring his, and it was 5-5 after six penalties each when Bordeaux missed their next kick.

As momentum in the competition had grown all home legs since the second round had been played at the vast

Zentralstadion, rather than the Bruno-Plache-Stadion, and the official attendance for this semi-final was 73,000. 'But it was more like 110,000, at least,' says Matthias. No one really knows how many were holding their breath as Leipzig goalkeeper René Müller stepped up to take the seventh penalty and blast the Lokomotives into their first, and only, European final. Never a team to do things by halves, they would face Ajax of Amsterdam in the final in the Olympic Stadium, Athens.

Müller
Kreer Lindner Baum Zötzsche
Scholz Bredow Edmond Liebers
Richter Marschall

A photo of that 1987 *Europapokal-der-Pokalsieger* team hangs on the wall of the boardroom bar today. I look up at it as I sip an instant coffee and eye up the cheese sandwiches. In fact I can't miss it. It's massive. Blown up to about the size of a six-a-side goal, the yellow and blue Adidas strip screams of former glory. This bunch faced an Ajax side with Arnold Mühren, Frank Rijkaard, Marco van Basten, and a young Dennis Bergkamp on the bench. It was Ajax captain van Basten's single goal that won it on the night and finally ended Lok's dream at the last greyhound hurdle.

Journalist and author Uwe Karte was a young fan in Leipzig at the time. Appropriately born in 1966, he has fond memories of those European nights leading up to this one, 'In 1982 Lok played against Barcelona, in '85 against Milan, then in '87 it was Bordeaux. I was there. It was wonderful. I think it was one of the biggest moments in East German football history: to win such an important match *in* the DDR.'

Looking back he suggests a final (*Endspiel* in German) may not feel as significant as other occasions, as finals tend to happen elsewhere, on neutral ground. Magdeburg's in 1974 was in Rotterdam, Jena's in 1981 in Düsseldorf, and Lok Leipzig's was in Athens. Even the DDR Olympic gold medal was won in Montreal. So it's the semi-final, and particularly the home leg of it, that often carries more potential romance, particularly if it's also the second leg and means celebrating with your own fans – this is especially the case for East German clubs where foreign travel for real fans was almost impossible.

In 1974 Magdeburg won their semi-final home leg against Sporting Lisbon at their own Ernst-Grube-Stadion, and Leipzig did it in style at the biggest of them all on home turf. 'The Central Stadium was the biggest stadium in *Germany*, not just in East Germany,' says Uwe. 'It was a dream. I don't think they'll ever be more fans watching a football match in Germany than at that match against Bordeaux in 1987.' (Appendix D)

The old Zentralstadion was indeed massive and the new version of it, completed in 2004 and still pretty sizeable, sits inside the walls of the old one.

If you're going to face anyone on the big Europe nights then why not face Van Basten in 1987, Martin Peters in '74, Eusébio in '66? And despite the size of the blown-up team photo in the boardroom bar, it was the 1966 team who ultimately feel like the golden boys. Those boys are still here in the wooden grandstand today: Drößler, Frenzel and his bodyguard Geisler, now golden in years, looking over the modern game as icons of a different time, in a former country. And if their club wasn't born in 1966 then it was – not for the last time – re-born.

1966 is not only central to Leipzig's history but to East German football in general. In the months preceding it football got serious in the DDR as 11 dedicated FCs were formed out of the existing Sports Club structure: Dynamo Dresden (who retained their 'SG' tag), Union Berlin, Carl Zeiss Jena, Karl-Marx-Stadt, Vorwärts Berlin, Berliner FC Dynamo, Hansa Rostock, Hallescher FC Chemie, Magdeburg, Rot-Weiß Erfurt and Lokomotive Leipzig. The new system was born out of an inferiority complex in the national game. The national team was struggling to compete, failing to reach major international tournaments, and the focus on a smaller number of specialist clubs working to produce a higher standard of player was seen as the answer to this as well as to domestic success in European club competition. Eight years later the DDR did qualify for a major tournament and in the same year Magdeburg lifted a European trophy, so something worked. 1966 was where this process started, but for the club from Leipzig, like many of those reborn in '66, the history goes back a lot further than that. In Leipzig's case right to the very beginning.

Earlier in the day Matthias picked me up at the side entrance to Leipzig's magnificent main station and whisked me just round the corner to a building on Büttnerstraße. Some scaffolding and a skip or two remained after recent renovation, and there was little to see besides a small plaque on the wall and the front part of what remains of the original building. It was here, or rather in the restaurant *Zum Mariengarten* at the rear, that the German Football Association (the *DFB*) was founded in 1900. Matthias isn't personally responsible for this but I shake hands with him anyway in front of the plaque, to thank him.

I've long been fascinated with German football and it feels right to start my Leipzig tour here. Our handshake seems apt too, not only as a nod to German–English football encounters and a wink to 1966, but to seal mine and Matthias' reflected odd obsessions. Matthias is an Anglophile who has lived in Manchester and talks fondly of the great matches he's seen at the likes of Saltash United and AFC Blackpool. But he's got a lot to be proud of here at home too. Not only as his Leipzig club was one of the founding members of the German FA and host of the meeting to establish it, but because they would soon become its first champions.

Originally formed as *Sportbrüder* Leipzig in 1893, then merged with *VfB* Leipzig to form *VfB Sportbrüder* in 1898, the club was renamed VfB Leipzig in 1900. Three years after the founding of the FA, VfB Leipzig won that first German championship, beating DFC Prag 7-2 in the final at the Exerzierplatz Altona near Hamburg (home of Altona 93, also born in 1893). Heinrich Riso scored a hat-trick that day and the Leipzig legend was born.

In his book *My Century*, published in 1999, Günter Grass makes it the key event of his 1903 chapter, playing on the myth that surrounds the first German final:

> *'But to get back to Altona: it was a decent match, if nothing spectacular. Still, even in those days, when Leipzig was the undisputed champion of Germany, reporters liked to spice up their stories with the stuff of legend. In any case, word got round that the reason Prague had been so slow on the uptake, especially during the second half, was that the night before, they'd had a grand old time with the ladies of the Reeperbahn. Well, I have it from Herr Behr, the referee, in his own hand: "The best team won!"'*

If that was the birth of the club, in the earliest days of the German football story, then its rebirth in 1966 was followed by a *re*-rebirth in 1990, after the *Wende* season. Karl Drößler became the chairman with the thorny task of guiding his beloved yellow and blues into an uncertain world.

'At the time of the *Wende* all the big sports clubs were more or less state-owned enterprises. The management structure was organised like this: on top the *Clubleiter* (chairman), then the deputies, chief of the youth academy etc. It was mandatory for a secretary of the SED to be part of the management team too. All clubs were financed by the state and their organisations. Overnight all that funding was gone. But shortly before the reunification Konrad Mecke, a club board member and director of DDR railways in Halle and Leipzig, organised a "farewell present" of two million D-Marks. Otherwise the club would have gone bust.'

Karl goes on, 'At that time, like in many other areas of what used to be the DDR, a workgroup was formed at the club to check the Stasi papers they could get hold of. One guy told me I was lucky that they hadn't found any evidence in my file of any activity as an IM [*Inoffizieller Mitarbeiter* or unofficial collaborator]. I became chairman of the club in autumn 1990 because I was "politically clear".'

If the *Wende* period wasn't precarious enough then the next *re*-rebirth of Leipzig football was to take place in 2004, amid a further period of peculiarities that mark this club out. The graph representing Lok Leipzig's fortunes is a dramatic one: it rises from winning the domestic cup final in 1986, to taking on Ajax in the Cup Winners' Cup Final the following year, and further still to competing in the Bundesliga after reunification, now renamed VfB Leipzig once again. But still in the relatively early years of a reunified German league this steep upturn was followed by an even steeper downward slide, this time right to the very bottom.

That single Bundesliga season was 1993/94 – European Cup winner and England international Tony Woodcock was briefly the manager the following season. Then after four seasons playing in the 2. Bundesliga and two years at the third level, financial problems during four further seasons at the fourth tier Oberliga Nordost meant that, just ten years after playing in the top flight of German football, its first champions were declared bankrupt and dissolved.

They picked themselves up and started again, as 1. FC Lokomotive Leipzig, at the lowest possible rung, the 11th tier (Kreisklasse 3), and from there slowly began the climb back up. The fans stuck by the team and even while playing at this most modest of levels had a famous return to the Zentralstadion where they'd entertained the likes of Eusébio, Diego Maradona, Jean Tigana – and Ray Wilkins – on those noisy European nights. Not quite as noisy but surely as noteworthy, in 2004 over 12,000 fans gathered to watch an 11th division match between Leipzig and Eintracht Grossdeuben, from a tiny Saxon town of about 2,000 people – in fact against the tiny town's reserve team! During that season the 44-year-old Lothar Matthäus, a World Cup winner in 1990, turned out for the Lokomotives. While to further the absurdity, earlier in the season a 62-year-old Henning Frenzel had made a 30-minute appearance in a game against Paunsdorf Devils. The club obviously felt experience was the way forward and upward and that's *some* experience. Frenzel proceeded to nip past the young defender tasked with minding him and head home the 16th goal in a 20-0 win.

Frenzel lost his minder that day, but his bodyguard is here today, a smiling Manfred Geisler in the wooden grandstand above me. As is Karl Drößler of course. A grin forms under Karl's moustache too as he glances across to the ultras gathering to sing at the Fan Curve behind the goal – their section named *Fankurve 1966* is also, rather absurdly, at least 40 metres away from the action.

Drößler remembers the singing back then, in the strange old days, 'I'm sure we played the most games against teams from the west in the late '50s and early '60s. In December 1959 we went to Hamburg to play a friendly with HSV. On our way back we stopped in Hannover. West Germany were playing Yugoslavia that day and the HSV people were nice enough to organise tickets for us. The chief of our DDR delegation agreed to it. There were some rules obviously: during the German anthem we were allowed to stand but not to sing. The problem was my brother-in-law lived in West Germany and he'd become part of our delegation. So there we were before the game and everyone was quiet, except for my brother-in-law. He was a passionate singer in a choir and gave it everything he'd got. After that the delegation leader was not allowed to travel to the west for two years.'

Back in the here and now, come kick-off I'm on the *Gegengerade* (the stand opposite the main stand), and today's crowd of 3,241 is in good voice too. It's turned into a surprisingly beautiful day, and things are going surprisingly well on the pitch too. Lok Leipzig are two up after only 15 minutes. Then soon after the linesman turns his ankle in a divot just down below us. He waves to the referee and struggles on for a few minutes more, but can't continue. The lino hobbles off. There's a call over the tannoy for someone in the crowd to take over. I half expect Professor Drößler to put his hand up, swap his corduroy and cap for a 1960s tracksuit and come trotting out to run the line. But someone else offers sadly, a Lok fan who happens to be a qualified referee. The Fürstenwalde officials agree to this potentially partisan man calling offsides and after a 30-minute sun and beer break we're off again. It's 4-0 by half-time.

By the second half I've moved back to the grandstand and I'm sitting beside Matthias in the press box a row back from Henning Frenzel's bodyguard. The Bruno-Plache-Stadion (*das Bruno*) – named after a Leipzig athlete, electrician and pre-war Communist Party politician – was built in 1922 with a capacity of around 40,000. Today the stadium holds around 10,000 (with volunteers currently helping with the work to increase that), with seating here in its wooden grandstand, one of the few of its kind still in use and a beautiful example. It was extended in 1932, almost doubling in length and today it's impossible to see the join in its story-filled beams. The wooden stand at *das Bruno* has seen it all: national finals, international matches (Germany against Switzerland, Bulgaria and Finland), 2. Bundesliga fixtures and a Bruce Springsteen concert.

And just as Karl Drößler cycles here for the match these days, the stadium was an end-of-stage venue for the 1955 Peace Race – an international amateur cycle race known as the 'Tour de France of the East' running between East Germany, Czechoslovakia and Poland. The *Friedensfahrt* riders entered the stadium on Connewitzer Straße with 5km [3.1 miles] to go and raced round the track to finish under the gaze of the wooden *Haupttribune*.

The fans were treated to two sports that day, the race entering *das Bruno* shortly after the final whistle of a 1-1 draw between Rotation Leipzig (an earlier version of Lok) and Bayern Munich.

Even before that the wooden grandstand had seen its fair share of drama. The structure was badly damaged in a storm in 1935 when a full section of the roof was blown off, while in its very first season it watched over the ill-fated 1922 national final replay between Nuremberg and Hamburger SV. The first match in Berlin couldn't be settled despite going on for over three hours. The replay at *das Bruno* saw 60,000 squeezed into a ground that held 40,000, to see Nuremberg's Willi Böss sent off in the first half for kicking an HSV player in the stomach, before a succession of injuries and another sending off left Nuremberg with only seven players on the pitch. The referee

Peco Bauwens called it off in extra time, it was never replayed and there was no winner. Match abandoned.

Thankfully today's match isn't abandoned, despite the injured official. But it's a one-sided affair. The Leipzig goalkeeper Benjamin Kirsten – son of DDR legend Ulf Kirsten, whose career straddled the *Wende* – might as well join the six travelling Fürstenwalde fans for a beer behind his goal. It's still an eventful match though: five goals, a penalty, a sending off and a supporter running the line. But it seems that Karl Drößler has abandoned it himself, at some point in the second half. I don't blame him. He's had a busy day answering questions, memory lines back and forth from a cold night in 1966 to a bright February day 30 years after the turning season. He turned 82 yesterday and still cycles to every match here at *das Bruno*, whatever the weather. His own personal Peace Race. 'He's a star,' I say to Matthias as we leave. 'And Frenzel too. And Geisler, the bodyguard … 1966 *and all that*.' 'There were no stars in the DDR,' says Matthias, with a wink.

# Block F, Row 9

ALEX IS 18. Harry Rath is his hero. Harry has hung up his boots now but just a couple of years ago, in a different country, he was still barking orders out on the field as captain. Alex remembers swinging his black and white scarf in the air as his team came out for its first match back in the first division two years ago, on 12 August 1989.

The club from the town once called Stalinstadt had been in the Oberliga just once before, for one season only, exactly 20 years earlier. But they finished bottom of the league and were quickly relegated.

So 12 August 1989 was a big day and the scoreless draw against Wismut Aue was not a bad start. Alex was there as ever with his mates on the home curve behind the goal. That was the best place to get some noise behind the team and under the skin of the opposition.

But today is an even bigger day. It is 18 September 1991. At the game against Aue few knew what was just around the corner but now a new Germany has been forged, 11 months ago, and soon Harry Rath will lead the team once again, as manager. Alex decides to take his family seat in the *Gegengerade* opposite the main stand. He can take it all in much better from here, savour the spectacle of a new Europe spreading out in front of them. He will always be able to point to the spot: Block F, Row 9.

The crowd has been swelling since late afternoon when the day-shifters clocked off. They'd been watching the clock all day, ready to race home, grab hats, scarves and foam cushions, and get to Forest Street to enjoy the build-up. It's not difficult to keep an eye on the time here: there are clocks everywhere in this town but no one knows why.

By kick-off the crowd packed into the stadium at Waldstraße has reached a near-full 7,000. The black plastic seats here in the *Gegengerade* were installed in 1989 for that first season back in the top flight and they've been in good use ever since. These past three seasons have seen good times for the iron workers' team. They finished 12th in 1989/90 – one place above Wismut Aue – surviving by a slim goal difference to earn another season at the top. Then, remarkably, they reached the cup final the following year and, despite losing 1-0 to Hansa Rostock in Berlin, had the good fortune that Rostock also won the league, allowing Harry Rath's boys to take their place here tonight – in the European Cup Winners' Cup. They're not fazed, even at these dizzying heights. On 18 September 1991, Eisenhüttenstadter FC Stahl, on the far eastern edge of an *East* Germany that's still fading away, are facing Galatasaray of Istanbul.

Despite being part of a society that was closed off in many respects, East German football was very much part of wider European football culture and even in 1991 the stadium clock was still ticking.

As it reaches the 42nd minute, Frank Bartz decides to clock off from defensive midfield duties and take a first foray forward. Hirsch and Podsiadlo will cover him he's sure, as he wins a tackle and slides a pass out to Wenzel on the left. Bartz should go back now but decides to keep going. His pass hasn't quite reached Wenzel who has to dart infield and fight to try and keep possession, backed up by Bitzka biting at Turkish heels. This creates a pocket of space on the inside-left channel and Bartz ghosts into it, edging ever further forward. When Ralf Sack finally picks up the loose ball and takes control, Bartz makes his move. Sack sees him heading for the space at the left-hand corner of the box and slides a pass into his path. Bartz doesn't pause for breath and runs on to it, his left leg already swinging back and forward without breaking stride to smash a low, hard shot towards the bottom corner of the Galatasaray goal. In the next moment the clocks will stop. Eisenhüttenstadt is the New Town where time stood still.

* * *

Alex looks up. There's a voice coming through the loudspeakers around the ground, originating in the rickety box at the back of the main stand. He looks around him and across at the black plastic seats in Block F, but they are empty. All of them. Dotted around, a dozen or more are cracked or broken at the base and collapsed. Blocks D and E are not quite empty but almost. There are about 25 people there, including one young family and a man with a plastic horn. The fans of both teams playing today are mixed in without the segregation of an Oberliga or a European game. Times have changed strikingly. Alex rubs his eyes. He tunes back in to the voice on the loudspeakers. It's his own.

Alex is 46 years old now. He's been the FC Eisenhüttenstadt youth team coach for 15 years, as well as the regular matchday stadium announcer. He tells the crowd, of about 100 souls for today's sixth division fixture with Petershagen-Eggersdorf, not to forget that the €5 entry fee also includes a free glühwein from the kiosk, then runs through today's line-ups. When he's done that he turns to me, puzzled, and asks what I'm hoping to discover in Eisenhüttenstadt; a question which really means, 'What on earth are you doing *here*?' I tell him I think football clubs can tell us something of their communities and that really I'm looking for small, positive stories connected to each of the places I'm visiting. He smiles, rubs his eyes again. 'The positive story here is that we still exist,' he says.

I have to confess that my description of Frank Bartz's goal in 1991 is purely fictional. He did score that night, that's a fact, and played in midfield rather than his usual left-back spot. Eisenhüttenstadt did take the lead in their only ever European match – before conceding an equaliser minutes later, going behind in the second half and then shipping three more in the return leg. But I've found no footage to be able to relive it and pass it on. I could ask Alex to describe it from memory of course, but he's busy with the present-day job of laying cable for the live video feed of today's match – technology in stark contrast to the scoreboard clock he drags the cable past, which is not just broken but frankly knackered. The pine trees form elongated shadows across the pitch below us, ghostly imprints of a long shot.

I've seen plenty of ghosts around Eisenhüttenstadt today. Ghosts of workers clocking in and out of the biggest steel works in East Germany; ghosts of town planners creating wide, ambitious streets and rows of concrete *Plattenbau* blocks to house happy families; ghosts of a football club which briefly punched above its weight in those liminal years either side of two Germanys; and the ghosts of those who sat on the dozens of foam cushions stacked high in Alex's announcer's box. Joseph Stalin's ghost is here too, his name used for the town in the 1950s when everything was new and shining and sang of a Socialist dream in concrete and steel. I didn't see the ghost of Tom Hanks, but it'll be here somewhere, chugging down Lindenallee in a Trabi.

Eisenhüttenstadt, literally Ironworks City, is in the state of Brandenburg 70 miles east of Berlin. It lies just a few miles to the west of the River Oder which forms a border between Germany and Poland. Before 1950 the town didn't exist. I ask Alex what the area was like before the town was built and he points to the clump of pine trees behind the away end and the broken scoreboard. All forest. These days the standard here is closer to park football than the top flight so those trees, the roots of the place, and the leafy feel of a stadium on the edge of a once ambitious town seems somehow as it should be.

There is an original old town to the east called Fürstenberg, even closer to the Oder and Poland, and Eisenhüttenstadt was constructed right next to it. Or rather the iron works was. 'First was the steel, then came the city,' says the website of ArcelorMittal which now runs the industry here. The steel works factory was called *Eisenhüttenkombinat Ost* and was, and is, mammoth. Then came the residential areas and infrastructure for the workers and their families and *Hütte*, as the locals call it, was born. Both were part of a grand Soviet plan to build a new town and industry in the Soviet style as the first proper socialist city in the DDR: a model city. A symbol of 'high hopes and hardships', as Alan McDougall puts it, 'it was an exemplar of the new socialist community, a place with affordable housing, no church towers, good schools and hospitals, and a wide range of cultural amenities.' (McDougall, 251)

A 'collective spirit' drove the town's construction during the first decade of East German history, when it was initially named Stalinstadt and then renamed Eisenhüttenstadt in 1961 during the de-Stalinisation period. From pine tree beginnings, by the 1980s there were 50,000 people living here beside one of the world's largest steel producing plants, employing around 12,000 workers. And if you're building a new world for a new community you need a football team.

The football ground was just one part of the modelling of this new world for the workers and was placed at Sportanlagen

Waldstraße, but soon became known as the Stadion der Hüttenwerker (the ironworkers' stadium) and if you followed the team you followed the *Hütte*. The club itself was initially called BSG Stahl Fürstenberg Ost, with a nod to the older roots that did exist nearby, but that didn't sound nearly new world enough so it was soon renamed BSG Stahl Stalinstadt and then BSG Stahl Eisenhüttenstadt. Stahl equals steel. With a sizeable and growing population there was a good chance of fostering a winning football team, especially taking the example of somewhere like Aue, another club built directly on local industry with under half the population yet a regular top-flight team. But success for the new town team was hard to come by.

Until 1989 the *Hütte* spent most of the DDR era playing in the second division, with just that one previous promotion to the Oberliga in 1969. That was followed by relegation the following season, not just back to the second but to the third level as a further penalty for 'non-socialism'. In the model socialist city of all places, wrists were slapped for 'damaging the principles of socialist society', when against the sporting spirit of the state they were found to be paying their players.

Few high points followed throughout the 1970s and much of the 80s, until they won the second division (Staffel A) title in 1989 to usher in those notable three years either side of the *Wende* – years in which they not only survived at the top table (Alex proudly and somewhat ironically reminds me that his team was still, somehow, in the top division when the DDR disappeared) but also opened their stadium gates to Europe and the Cup Winners' Cup. If they hadn't achieved this unexpected, late run of success it's pretty certain the club wouldn't have been remembered long enough to have ever been forgotten.

Incidentally they also hold the record for the most draws in one standard Oberliga season – out of the 26 matches in 89/90 they won two and drew 14 of them. But Eisenhüttenstadt were very much part of the turning season and they do have the good old days to remember *before the ghost town*. As the stadium gates were opening to Europe, so the factory gates were opened up too, with the changes of the *Wende* ushering in big business. In 1990 the *Eisenhüttenkombinat Ost* was privatised.

* * *

I found it hard to locate the town, let alone the factory or the stadium. Arriving on the train from Frankfurt an der Oder I marched off confidently in the direction of signs for 'Zentrum' only to realise 45 minutes later, in the middle of a gathering of senior citizens in a café behind the town hall that I was in fact in Fürstenberg, not Eisenhüttenstadt. I retraced my steps and started again at the station – another long walk, this time heading down the wide Straße der Republik into the new centre. But the new centre is now old. Time, I realised, stood still when Frank Bartz hit the back of the net.

Huge swathes of *Plattenbauten* in salmon pink and yellow fade into the grey sky. The line between unloved and derelict is a thin one and it's hard to see which is which along here. Once I reach the corner of Karl-Marx-Straße I can finally see Eisenhüttenstadt centre up ahead. Restored, clean and elegant low-rise buildings line both sides of the street sweeping impressively up to the town hall and the shops at Lindenallee. But behind the bus stop is another story: a six-storey grey-brown block of a building, graffiti-covered, with its lower windows boarded up and above them every other window smashed. In faded letters, each the size of a window itself, stuck to one side of the building and reading vertically it says 'Guest House'.

I like bleak Soviet concrete, but this is something else. I've rarely seen quite such a sad place. And I've toured to Billingham! The front of the City Hotel Lunik is weary and scarred. The library opposite looks a bit more cared for (so maybe the *Hütte* are bookish types) and the town hall is smart and grand. But there are no flowers in the beds outside it, only bare soil. Fürstenberg was almost deserted, save for the small party of senior citizens, and Eisenhüttenstadt on a Saturday afternoon is much the same. I pass an elderly man at the crossing to Lindenallee. I want to ask him if he worked at the steel works and went to Oberliga matches at Waldstraße. But he doesn't look up. His shoulders are hunched and he looks tired. He looks like the City Hotel Lunik.

Things must have been so different in 1950. A brand new town made of great shining building blocks and colourful flowers in the neat beds outside the town hall. To the people here there must have felt so much potential. Then in the 1960s and '70s heyday, with so many jobs for so many of them, money in their pockets and a healthy working life, things were surely good. They may still have been in 1989 with the steel works going great guns and the football team reaching the very top too: young families streaming down the Straße der Republik, flooding the stadium and factory gates.

Then came the *Mauerfall,* and I wonder what the people here thought. We were doing all right but – did they have any sense then of what this change would mean? And how much did they realise in those late months of 1989 what turning meant turning into? There is spirit here, but it's hard to find. The city is of course still alive, but the sense I get on these streets now is that it has been sinking for these 30 years into a slow, difficult emptiness. Like a ghost as big as a city, it is translucent.

The wide streets built for ambition are empty too. This one feels somehow like an American street and as I reach the corner of Beeskower Straße where I turn off for the Hüttenwerker's stadium, there's a Burger King opposite. I stop on the other side and look up, as I've realised this place encourages you to do. I'm standing in front of a ten-storey apartment block, brightly painted in white, blue and orange, with balcony canopies that speak of holidays long gone. The smart-looking Art Nouveau-style café on the ground floor is closed, I'm not sure if permanently, it's hard to tell. The café's called C'est La Vie.

In 1989 the population of Eisenhüttenstadt was 52,000. It's now about half that and is ageing. The *Eisenhüttenkombinat Ost* workforce has reduced from 12,000 to about 2,000. Since privatisation the plant was initially owned by Belgian company Cockerill-Sambre and then since 2006 by the Indian steel magnate Lakshmi Mittal, chair and CEO of ArcelorMittal. Mittal also owns a decent percentage of Queens Park Rangers FC, but doesn't seem to have been tempted to put any of his considerable fortune into helping the struggling football club in Ironworks City.

In 2005 while the club was playing at the fourth level Oberliga Nordost they were withdrawn from competition and folded. A campaign was launched by fans to raise much needed funds but it couldn't save the club from insolvency. A new club was formed the following year and they struggled on at the fifth, then sixth level before a local merger in 2015 created FC Eisenhüttenstadt. The steel has gone from the name but not from the spirit and they fight on. Alex explains that in the good old days attendance of 6,000 to 8,000 was the norm at the Hüttenwerker Stadium but that these days it's less than 100 most of the time. Or if a cold wind's blowing across the Oder as low as 30. Times are hard. In 2005 Lakshmi Mittal was third in the *Forbes* list of the world's billionaires and the following year was first in the *Sunday Times* Rich List, with an estimated wealth of nearly £15bn. Meanwhile, FC Eisenhüttenstadt gives out free glühwein. They get my vote.

Desperate for a win today, Alex is hoping my visit will bring the team some luck, and after hitting the bar with a great strike from distance the *Hütte* bag a penalty after 30 minutes and then see out the second half for a well-earned three points. Some 95 people will wander home happy down the wide Straße der Republik, but not before the players slip through the perimeter fence to chat with their families and friends and sip a celebratory glühwein themselves. Meanwhile, the beaten Petershagen-Eggersdorf players settle for a post-match cigarette on the changing room steps.

Harry Rath is delighted. Eisenhüttenstadt is his club. I meet him briefly upstairs in the clubhouse and he takes me back to 1989. 'It was a very special season for me,' he says. 'I was the captain and had led the team up from the second division. But then I had a knee injury so missed a lot of matches. At that time, though, football had a huge meaning for the town.' I ask him how that compares to today, to a clash with the likes of Petershagen-Eggersdorf. 'Well, now football is just one piece of the city,' he says. 'One normal, small piece. But the meaning of football was huge back then. At that time Vorwärts Frankfurt/Oder was the big club in the area. They had the money and the state support, and the players here were very motivated to get better than the players from the bigger club. We were the outsiders.' They still are I think. 'Like Asterix and Obelix,' Alex adds.

Ever the underdogs, Harry's proudest moment as an Eisenhüttenstadt player was winning promotion to the top flight in 1989. As the manager he adds the German cup matches against Hertha Berlin and Werder Bremen in the late '90s and early 2000s as his highlights, uncommon times. Harry's son Marcel Rath is here today too. Marcel started out at Eisenhüttenstadt as a young player but went on to a career at Hertha Berlin, Energie Cottbus and St Pauli among others, as well as to play for the Germany under-21 team and score for them in a world championship.

Harry is clearly very proud of Marcel and has enjoyed following his career westwards. But I sense that he's most proud that his son started out here, at the club that has been part of his life for so long. Harry has played, coached, managed, or advised at the *Hütte* for almost 40 years and he's still going strong. He's seen a way of life change immeasurably in Eisenhüttenstadt, seen a city come and go, faces fade to grey. I ask him what he hopes for this year, 30 years on. 'To survive,' he says.

And what of Frank Bartz? Today Frank works in a car showroom just down the road, about 200m from the stadium and from the very spot where the ball hit the back of the Galatasaray net after leaving his left foot all those years ago. It's still travelling, I'm sure. Frank still comes to matches whenever he can, but he's working today so can't make it. Maybe he's hoping Tom Hanks will pop in to buy a car from him. The Hollywood star has been here twice, apparently fascinated by the new town and its hopeful planning. On his second visit he bought a Trabant, a classic DDR car. I hope he went to a match too, to cheer on the *Hütte*. Meanwhile, Frank clocks in and clocks out. His ghost hovers at the edge of the box.

# The violet revolution

HEIKO LACES up his boots and wraps a violet scarf around his neck. It's mid-October and it will be cold tonight, even in the brightness. He finished his shift early to be ready in plenty of time. Everyone did. The buzz has been building all day, at the factory gates and on the allotment plots that slope above town. He fumbles in the dark to button up his jacket, just about ready to go out into the light, and puts two hands firmly on the wooden handles of the doors. Heiko holds his breath. *Glück Auf.*

Aue is a small town in Saxony, in the far south of what was East Germany. Today about 17,000 people live here, a population about the size of Oswestry or Ramsbottom. Twenty miles north of the Czech border, it nestles in the Ore Mountains (the Erzgebirge) where the Schwarzwasser empties into the Zwickauer Mulde. An *aue* is a meadow or floodplain. In 1989 the town was home to 26,000 people, the Soviet-led Wismut mining company and a football team that had punched above its weight for 40 years, the lifetime of the DDR. Today on the outskirts of town along the historic Silberstraße is the Zoo of Minis with its collection of over 400 diminutive animals, 'Pygmy marmoset, dwarf otter, dwarf ghost cat … While everyone is fascinated by the size of a whale, or stands in awe in front of a giraffe, hardly anyone has seen horses that are only 70cm tall, or monkeys that are smaller than a hamster.' Aue is a unique place, a small town with a big heart.

I stand with Heiko in the snow high up the hill looking down over the allotments to the Erzgebirgsstadion. Dotted on the hillside below us among the bare pines are a couple of rickety wooden boxes, open on one side and with a bench carved out inside. From here you can sit sheltered looking directly into the stadium from the quiet of the hillside watching the action unfold down below. These must be the best seats *out of* the house.

Heiko starts to tell me about that night in October 1989. Those that can remember it among the regulars at the *Fan Projekt* on Bahnhofstraße where Heiko has an office, remember it in bright colour and sharp focus. The *Flutlicht-Premiere* they call it. I wonder if Heiko is superstitious. He's from *Bergbauland* (mining country) after all and maybe you have to be. I notice that 13 October 1989 was a Friday. Six days before, at the DDR's 40th birthday party in Berlin, Mikhail Gorbachev had spoken of reform while tens of thousands of demonstrators took to the streets. Other parts of the country might have still been in the dark about this, but they were already heading towards the brink. In Aue, the meadow in the mountains, on Friday the 13th, Heiko and his Wismut Aue team are on the brink too. From the dark into the light.

There's only one hotel in Aue, the *Blauer Engel*, and very few trains in or out of the station. Most visiting fans get the bus from the nearest main stations in Zwickau or Chemnitz, where I got on this morning. After an hour or so, as the main road dips down into the valley and the Ore Mountains start to loom above, we pass under a footbridge where someone has spray-painted huge violet-coloured letters on the side: *GLÜCK AUF.* The road drops down further on to the floodplain, through Lauter-Bernsbach, Bockau, Zschorlau, Schneeberg, Lößnitz, Bad Schlema. This is Europe.

'It's a really small place,' says Heiko, 'but when you think about the club you have to consider the whole, wider area. It's a club for the region.'

The region is a cluster of small villages and towns in a 30 or 40km [20-25 mile] radius which football puts on the map. In 1954 when Empor Lauter, a club based in another small town just a couple of miles from Aue, was moved wholesale to Rostock at the far northern end of the country on the Baltic coast – later becoming Hansa Rostock and later still the last ever DDR champions – the local space was left for Aue's club to try to establish a singular identity in the region. This modest club of the meadow and mountains soon became the dominant force in East German football, winning the cup in 1955 and three Oberliga titles between 1956 and 1959; but all this while still fighting to preserve that identity under a different name: the name of Karl Marx.

This club of the Erzgebirge is no stranger to resistance. The DDR's first strike in 1951 involved 3,000 Wismut workers, and three years later when the authorities were attempting to relocate Wismut Aue an hour down the road to Karl-Marx-Stadt the miners threatened to down tools again. The planned move came about after it was decided that Karl-Marx-Stadt, the *Bezirk* (county) capital, lacked a team good enough to compete at the top level, and that the miners' side from the meadow in the mountains was just such an outfit. Understandably the locals weren't happy about this, and the players threatened to strike. The Wismut *Kumpels* (workmates) stood firm. 'We are Wismut. We are invulnerable. We are Aue,' they said. The authorities eventually abandoned the plan, but while the Aue team would be able to stay in their home town they would have to take on a new name, SC Wismut Karl-Marx-Stadt.

It was under this name that they became the first East German side to play in the European Cup. In the first round of the 1957/58 competition they were drawn against Dutch champions Ajax. As if the underdog status as a team from a small town in the mountains on the other side of the Iron Curtain wasn't enough, even despite the weighty connotations of their new name, the economic challenge soon became striking too. On the way to the second leg in Amsterdam the travelling squad missed a connection and found themselves stuck in West Germany without enough money. The coach Fritz Gödicke pawned his watch to pay for a cheap meal for his team and managed to find three-to-a-bed accommodation. The next day they headed on to Amsterdam where Ajax won the tie as expected, 4-1 on aggregate. Still, the inventors of total football were kind enough to sort out their visitors' hotel bill and to buy back Gödicke's watch for him.

They never quite got back to the Netherlands to repay the debt, though nearly did 28 years later. Heiko remembers it well, 'When the draw was made for the 1985/86 UEFA Cup there was huge excitement. Everyone was listening to the radio; not like today when you can just look it up later on the internet. We were hoping for a big name, a Spanish or English team … And we were drawn against Dnipro Dnipropetrovsk. A tough opponent yes, but not what we wanted. They are from the Soviet Union.' Wismut Aue (as they now were, having got their home town name back in 1963) lost the tie 5-2 on aggregate but, as Heiko says, 'If we'd beaten them we would have played PSV Eindhoven in the next round!'

In contrast to Eisenhüttenstadt, where the vast new factory town housed a relatively small town team, Aue is the small town with a decidedly big club. For 40 years Wismut Aue established itself firmly in the top flight, an almost permanent fixture in the Oberliga. There are similarities here too, as just as Eisenhüttenstadt was linked to a grand Soviet plan, in Aue the iron-ore mining was supplanted by the search for uranium for Soviet weapons.

Heiko worked for the Wismut company, as just about everyone here did, but not underground. He worked in a factory making drills and when he clocked in each morning he called out heartily *Glück Auf.* And then again when he got home to his family or followed the waft of malt into the Blue Angel Hotel later on. It's what they say round here, in the post office or at the bus stop, a simple greeting like *Hi* or *Ciao*. But it's charged with something else too. It's what miners say to each other, here and elsewhere, as they're descending into the dark. *Glück Auf.* Its roots are in the danger of going underground. It means: *I hope you're lucky enough to come back up again: I wish you light.*

Heiko has been supporting Wismut Aue since 1974. He can't quite remember huddling round the radio to listen to the World Cup match in Hamburg that summer but he thinks his family must have done. He was too young to take in the *Bruderduell* when East met West, too young to understand *We* against *Us*. But a few years later when he *was* old enough he started to cheer quietly for whichever team was playing against the DDR. He didn't support the team of the country he was living in and was born in, because of a state machine he didn't believe in. 'I don't think I was an exception,' he says. 'To cheer for the others was another kind of protest, I suppose. At least it was our silent one.'

'Wismut Aue is a very local club,' Heiko continues as we sit in the stands of the Erzebirgsstadion (until 1991 called the Otto-Grotewohl-Stadion, named after the DDR's first Prime Minister). 'The stadium feels like home. Still nowadays when we play against teams from big cities, from Hamburg or Cologne, it feels like David versus Goliath.'

Despite this small-town club's regular high achievement, Heiko says, 'We still don't see ourselves at the same level as the others and it makes us very proud.' We skip back and forth as we talk, from the early days to the 1980s, forward then back again. In 1956 in the Zentralstadion in Leipzig, the East German champions, Wismut Karl-Marx-Stadt (Aue), played the West German champions, Kaiserslautern, in a friendly in front of 110,000 people. They were the lucky few who witnessed live the 'forgotten goal of the century' – Fritz Walter's back-heeled overhead volley from 15 yards. This is another of the ghosts on this trail. I look up to the mountains above us and try to picture it from 60 years away, a tantalising image of the impossible. Heiko goes on, 'It was a tight bond back then, in the '50s and '60s, a bit closer than now maybe. But there is still a real connection between players and fans today.'

The town was once dominated by the mining industry, and had a football club attached. Nowadays the industry is diminished and the town led by the football club alone, proudly holding their own in 2. Bundesliga. For the club at least the stadium lights are still shining bright.

Wismut Aue played more times in the DDR-Oberliga than any other club (1,019 matches) and held a place in the top division for every season but one: the last one. They were relegated for the first time in 1990, finishing second from bottom and so missing out on the chance to play for a Bundesliga place, but success and stability has continued into the new world post-reunification, as FC Erzgebirge Aue.

Having spent the 1990s in the third division they have now been a fixture in the 2. Bundesliga since a memorable promotion in 2003 (save for three seasons back at the third level) and are regularly the highest-placed of all the 14 clubs of the turning season. Of the 17,000 population of Aue, just a few months ago 1,700 travelled away to support the team in Hamburg against St Pauli. Ten per cent of the population on a 600-mile round trip for a league match is impressive. In 2015, having slipped to the 3. Liga and in recognition of the importance of their supporters the club decided to eschew the usual corporate sponsor on its violet shirts and replace it instead with an image of a group of miners and the word *Kumpelverein* – *Kumpel* is an informal word for friend also associated with mining, so something like *Pit pal's club*. Under this were the words 'because we're different'.

Our conversation turns back to that night in October 1989 – what I'd come to see as Aue's own, private violet revolution, running somehow alongside the gathering momentum of the Peaceful Revolution across the country in the autumn of that year. Players and fans together, Heiko remembers it as clearly as if he had walked down the dark tunnel with his footballing heroes, like Wismut star Harald Mothes. Mothes played over 300 games for the Violets and once for the DDR. Others were absent though, like Jens König, André Köhler and Thomas Weiss, who had defected to the west on an away trip to Sweden for an Intertoto Cup match three months earlier, as more and more people left the country. Heiko isn't an Aue player, and has never been one, but he's worked for the club since 2008 as a supporter liaison representative. Fan clubs are one of the lasting legacies of East German football and now Heiko has a key to most of the doors at the Erzgebirgsstadion, including the ones at the far end of the tunnel. He gestures me forward, and as I walk towards them I think back to my own life in October 1989, when I was 16. I'd broken my leg the year before so that was pretty much the end of my own unremarkable but cherished playing days. I stop, not quite ready to go through and because I want to share a memory with Heiko of something equally unremarkable, but still cherished.

The team I played for as a boy was Hurley Daw Mill Kings. We were one of many teams in different age groups connected to the Daw Mill Colliery, at one time the biggest coal producer in Britain. We'd always played in thick green and black stripes and then one year we got a new strip which had thinner stripes in green and white. We loved the old kit but the new kit looked brilliant and we couldn't wait to start wearing it the following season. But before that we had a cup final to play. We begged Jim, our coach, to let us wear the new kit in the final, arguing that it would give us the extra something we needed to beat whoever our opponents were. But Jim refused, saying the new kit was for next season and 'that's that'.

We went out to warm up then came back into the changing room to put on the old green and black kit. Once we were ready Jim gave us a few final instructions and sent us out. We started to trudge towards the wooden door but just as we were pushing it open he stopped us. 'Hold on lads,' he yelled. He threw a bin bag towards Andy. 'I think you'd better put these on.' We raced out on to the pitch in our brand new green and white kits and won the cup 1-0. Though thinking about it now, I did nearly score an own goal.

Heiko tells me a story in return. To reach the first round of the European Cup in 1957 (and that penniless trip to face Ajax of Amsterdam) his Wismut team had beaten Gwardia Warsaw in the preliminary round. The first leg in Warsaw finished 3-1 to the home team, then back at the Otto Grotewohl Stadium the score was reversed, with Wismut Karl-Marx-Stadt winning 3-1, to set up a play-off match two days later at the Friedrich-Ludwig-Jahn-Sportpark in Berlin.

Gwardia Warsaw were leading 1-0 from the third minute before a Willy Tröger strike right at the death took the match into extra time. There was still nothing to separate the teams, when ten minutes later (and after a total of four and a half hours of football), the match was abandoned.

Wikipedia has it that this was the result of floodlight failure, but there were no floodlights at the Jahn Sportpark until 1964. While it's likely there were a number of reasons for the match abandonment, the main one was probably poor light. On a gloomy day in Berlin, the match had kicked off late after the Warsaw players' boots had been sent to the wrong stadium and by extra time it was already getting dark. In the end Wismut qualified for the next round on the toss of a coin.

'It was a total surprise,' says Heiko. Back in the tunnel we're turning back to the turning season, before pushing open the doors. On 8 November 1989, the eve of the fall of the Berlin Wall, Wismut Aue played a local derby away at FC Karl-Marx-Stadt. That's the FC Karl-Marx-Stadt actually from Karl-Marx-Stadt (now Chemnitz), not the Karl-Marx-Stadt from Aue. Karl-Marx-Stadt won 1-0. 'That night, at the match against FCK no one thought about it,' Heiko says. 'It was a normal football day, a derby in Chemnitz. You never thought about anything like the *Mauerfall.*'

Under the lights, there were normal football nights right across the country that Wednesday: Jena hosted Bischofswerda; Erfurt away at Halle, a 3-3 draw for Rostock and Leipzig. Players and fans going about their business on the eve of the unknown, the cracks unseen on the terraces, but already irreparable in the structure of the state. The following day, 9 November, East Berlin district head Günther Schabowski called an evening press conference to announce new travel regulations as part of the government's attempt to stem the growing protest. A journalist asked when the new regulations would take effect. Schabowski, not sure how to respond, looked at his slip of paper but couldn't find an answer. He turned it over but still couldn't see one. 'Straight away,' he said.

Following Schabowski's *Zettel*, his slip (of paper as well as slip-up), people immediately started to gather at checkpoints. At Bornholmer Straße the first few began to cross the Bösebrucke at 9.20pm. More followed and at 11.30pm word was spread among the people to flood the gates. Twenty thousand people crossed the bridge into the West. The Berlin Wall fell.

The two aren't directly connected, of course. And football itself is insignificant in this story. But they are linked in so far as the Berlin Wall didn't fall. It was pushed over. By normal people. Alan McDougall has suggested, 'Kicking a ball around, or watching a ball being kicked around, was never likely to bring down communism by itself. But it was an essential part of keeping alive expressions of *Heimat* [homeland], *Resistenz*, and individualism that stubbornly resisted the SED's dictatorial goals.' (McDougall, 336)

Of the possibility of protest at a match, Heiko reflects, 'There was a stage where you could do this, among the masses. Flags sometimes had messages or symbols, so there was the possibility of a small kind of protest. I think of the games against BFC Dynamo. In my mind BFC was the representation of the state and so when we had a chance there was a kind of political protest. We used it as a platform, but only on a small scale because it was still very dangerous.'

Alan McDougall goes on to say, 'Football supporters did not cause the gentle revolution of 1989. But the world that they inhabited, the fan clubs where *Eigen-Sinn* [self-will] meant drinking beer with friends, fare-dodging, obscene chants, and keeping an eye out for the *Bundesliga* results, formed part of the crumbling backdrop for the momentous events that autumn.' (McDougall, 200)

On the Saturday two days later there were no Oberliga matches scheduled as the DDR national team prepared for a World Cup qualifier in Austria (needing only a point to make it to Italia '90, they lost 3-0). Heiko went to Nuremberg in the West. There were no Bundesliga fixtures that weekend but 2. Bundesliga games proved popular. Another fan remembers, 'We just went *somewhere*. It felt so strange to have the possibility to do so, but we just travelled. It was very hard to understand what had actually happened. It was unreal. So we lived in the moment. But if Aue had had a game that weekend maybe we would have stayed in the east, or maybe not. I don't know.'

I look through the edition of *FUWO* (*Fußball Woche*) newspaper from 14 November, and across its 16 pages there is extensive coverage of that imminent World Cup qualifier, a round-up of the previous midweek results and a brief report of Diego Maradona's recent wedding. There is about one page in total covering football matters in the light of the 'process of social reform' and 'democratisation', but I can't find a single direct mention of the fall of the Berlin Wall just five days earlier. The 'theme' of the weekly column is the retirement of Dynamo Berlin goalkeeper Bodo Rudwaleit. Though Bodo will later change his mind and turn up in Eisenhüttenstadt.

Meanwhile, in its small way, Aue's own gentle revolution had happened a month before. The doors Heiko's brought me to are made of heavy carved wood, sloping away at the base and rimmed with a strip of violet light to emphasise the effect of daylight beyond. The miners' crossed hammer and chisel are carved into them. The Erzgebirge Stadium is known locally as *Der Schacht* (the shaft), and the doors at the end of the players' tunnel are its entrance. They seem immovable.

The Wismut club has been part of Heiko's life for 45 years and one particular night remains a highlight. The visitors were high-flying Magdeburg, then top of the Oberliga, and the game finished 0-0. Here in the darkness Heiko puts two hands on the handles of the shaft doors and pulls them firmly. They creak to, slowly at first, then swinging faster as the weight of the heavy wood gains momentum. Into the dark shaft where we're standing comes another type of shaft, narrow then widening brightly. Heiko is caught in it for the first time in his life. It isn't sunlight now, reflecting snow on the hillside on a February morning in 2019. It's Friday, 13 October 1989, kick-off 6pm. *Flutlicht-Premiere*. He's back there and I'm standing by his side. The world is changing. Gathering strength, there in an instant the lights are on.

At the stadium in the shadow of the Ore Mountains the light is powerful and artificial. It is the 1,000th match in Wismut Aue's history and it's the first home game to ever happen under floodlights. Heiko can't believe his blinking eyes. The sky is painted violet for the colour of his club. Though now certainly dimmed, a month later the rest of the country was briefly lit by the dazzling, sudden turn of the *Mauerfall*. Revolutions happen on the wide streets of Berlin, Leipzig and Dresden. But they happen on the new boulevards of Eisenhüttenstadt and the slopes of Saxon hills too. On allotment plots overlooking a football ground where one night in 1989 the miners came safely out into the light. And their team played football at night.

# A spy in Sonnenberg

I MEET Mike at the Marx Monument in the centre of the city. It's a bronze head of Karl Marx. Not a bust but an enormous head the size of a garden shed on a plinth. The *Nischel* they call it here, shortened further to *Nischl*, meaning head in old Saxon dialect.

Before the 2014 World Cup finals in Brazil there was controversy when part of an advertising campaign saw black, red and gold streaks painted across the socialist philosopher's cheeks, and the plinth dressed in a large replica Germany shirt. The dressing up was removed by an anonymous group the next day.

Mike himself cuts a melancholy figure, but with a cheeky smile behind his glasses and short greying hair. I notice the silver chain hanging from his belt then the St Pauli sticker in his car, and from behind his quietness another side slides into view. He's a punk undercover. As I'd waited for him under the Nischl, I'd thought back to the last time I was here in Chemnitz. It was nine years ago and I too was undercover that day. I felt like a spy in a Cold War thriller, albeit bordering on farce. The set snow-covered then, I was on a mission.

* * *

*Fresh snow under foot. A cold wind blowing in from Bohemia. Agent Weggel has arrived in the East, in the city once known as Karl-Marx-Stadt. His mission: Operation*

*Salesman. His target: Wittig. Weggel volunteered for the mission. He had a choice and he leapt at it.*

* * *

Mike was born in 1967, the year FC Karl-Marx-Stadt won their only Oberliga title, in fact in the very same month of May. He walks me through the city centre before we jump into his car for a whistle-stop tour of the historic football sites of Chemnitz. We'll flit from ground to ground for the next two hours and I sense Mike could go on for much longer.

He doesn't follow Chemnitzer FC anymore but is steeped in its history. Born in Sonnenberg, the working-class area north-east of the city centre which is still home to the Chemnitzer stadium on Gellertstraße, Mike says he was a 'long-hair' in the 1980s, then later turned punk. He moved away from Chemnitz briefly in the early '90s but soon came back and has stayed put ever since. Sonnenberg is his patch. Still a punk at heart, the stuff of his youth and his city has changed so much that it's left him alone with only the traces of it, lines on a map or a park pitch. It's these lines that he wants to show me and many of them cross the route he takes every day as he drives his bus, 'a small minibus for pensioners and school children mainly'. When he gets home he looks after his cats, and some rats and guinea pigs too.

* * *

*Suitable footwear required after snowfall. Agent Weggel flies in to Leipzig-Halle from London Gatwick on an early flight after a late night briefing in a pub called The Capitol where the beer is cheap. As the plane lands visibility is poor and the man next to him turns conspiratorially and says 'Neblig.' To which he smiles, not having the foggiest.* He phones the target* *from Leipzig as planned, declaring his position just south of where two hills meet in south-east London, SE22; this to establish the alibi of a football match at the home of a team that play in pink and blue. But Weggel is not in SE22. He's in Leipzig, at Deichmann, buying new boots.*

* * *

Mike has an encyclopaedic knowledge of the history of the numerous incarnations of sports and football clubs in Chemnitz and of the sites of their various grounds. Off we head through the drizzle to see them. From pitches still in existence but without their stands, now used for school games, to a garden centre car park where once there was a stadium.

From another modest ground with a brand new clubhouse now used by Blau-Weiss Chemnitz, to a pitch near a university building with its original 1920s clubhouse and a large painted mural of local boy Michael Ballack watching over us. Ballack was born in Görlitz on the Polish border but grew up here in Chemnitz. He spent his youth and the first two years of his senior career playing for the Sky Blues of Chemnitzer FC.

* * *

*Leipzig's magnificent Hauptbahnhof. The new boots are beginning to rub even as Weggel boards the train. The mission is a prickly one, but he knows he's the man for it and he even trimmed his beard before he left the west. He arrives at Chemnitz station at 1300 hours and feels for the small box in his breast pocket. He sips coffee at the station kiosk then buys a bottle of sparkling white wine at the Spa shop. The wine is dirt cheap. Weggel's first task is to make contact with a local guide who will show him the lay of the land. Code name: Mike, he knows the lines that run deep through this city from pitch to pitch. Snow here in Chemnitz, five inches deep, but Mike is the man to clear a path. He's looking for a bearded head the size of a milk float, casting its long shadow from the 50s, tough and granite-like.*

* * *

In this 'Saxon Manchester' the rich history of Chemnitz football and the sites where the game was played here spread out before us. Mike is saddened by the decay of much of it, by the loss of industry and points out each disused factory as we pass. He loves to point to the workers' housing too. Sonnenberg and its neighbouring corners of the city are Mike's plot now and he rarely ventures to the city centre, unless his bus route takes him there. He has no truck with the Monopoly board version of Chemnitz I saw in a bookshop earlier, and little interest in the new Stadion an der Gellertstraße and the financial chaos surrounding it and the club currently, nor with modern football in general. But still he can reel off the history of the club as if he were still there now, a youngster on the Südkurve bathed in sky blue.

Chemnitzer SC Britannia was founded by students from the nearby town of Mittweida in 1899 and was a founding member of the German FA in 1900. After changing its name later that year to Chemnitzer BC 1899 and some successful seasons in the Central German Football Federation, which included a passage to the National Championships in 1927, the club went bankrupt in 1933 and reformed soon after with *1933* in its name.

Post-war the club was reformed again as SG Chemnitz Nord, before more name changes in the early years of the

DDR: first to BSG Fewa Chemnitz, then BSG Chemie Chemnitz. After that it wasn't just the name of the club that changed but the name of the city itself. The city of Chemnitz was renamed Karl-Marx-Stadt in 1953 and the club soon followed suit as SC Motor Karl-Marx-Stadt. Then in 1966 it became FC Karl-Marx-Stadt and remained so until 1991 when the city reverted back to Chemnitz and the club back to Chemnitzer FC, and almost back to square one.

The DDR-era football club with the Marx moniker spent all but one season in the Oberliga, commonly finishing mid-table and losing in the cup final three times. But two seasons stand out. In 1966/67 they won the league title, becoming DDR champions just as Mike was born a stone's throw from the stadium. Then in 1989/90 not only did the Saxon Sky Blues reach the last 16 of the UEFA Cup to set up a famous foggy tie with Juventus, but they finished runners-up in the league, over 20 years after that first and only title. Since reunification Chemnitzer FC have spent most years at the second or third level, with a spell in the fourth tier in the late 2000s and again for this season, 2018/19, as I take my tour with Mike.

* * *

*Agent Weggel leaves by the side exit then turns left at the corner with Schillerplatz and the Omnibusbahnhof. It's a wide road so he stops and thinks again. In an attempt to keep his cover he crosses diagonally through Schillerplatz, where it's dimly lit and not a soul about. 'Neblig,' he ponders, still in the dark. He passes the underground garage of Theaterplatz and notes there's a theatre here as well as a Stadthalle. His final rendezvous is at the city hall and he can't afford to mix them up. The rendezvous is hours from now so nor can he afford to get too close, too soon. Wittig and her team could be in the city centre at any time and he must avoid them at all costs. With this in mind he slows down and adopts a slightly lopsided gait, which has nothing to do with the fact that his new boots don't fit.*

*Weggel's at the corner of Richard-Tauber-Straße now. The sign says Richard Tauber was a theatre director and his son a tenor at the Chemnitz Opera House. Weggel turns left on to Karl-Liebknecht-Straße and heads down through an underground passage. He can't help but test the acoustics with a few notes, but rather than a model of Richard Tauber's son, he sounds a bit like he's at the dentist.*

*He blames the boots pressing on his ankles, and as he comes back up again he's keen to get off the beaten track. But two figures appear out of the darkness. They are completely still and staring at him. They're clearly not fans of his rich baritone he thinks, so quickens his pace and turns left towards the main road. But main roads are a recurring problem. He needs to find some narrower streets. Even then he could be spotted, so he'll start checking each corner before he rounds it and keep tight to the buildings. This feels good and the sort of thing an agent should do. He remembers it from* The Detectives Handbook, *his favourite book when he was about seven years old. It was a thick blue paperback and he read it from cover to cover. Though he can't remember reading anything about comfy shoes.*

* * *

Mike reminisces about his younger days. 'I was a weekend rebel,' he says. 'Finish work on a Friday and go to a gig, then to the match on the Saturday, more beer and more music. Then back to work on Monday. It was the only option.'

He remembers the protests in the city centre around the 40th anniversary of the DDR in October 1989, but not much else about the growing movement. On 9 November he remembers not really believing what had happened. Soon after, he bought his first Ton Steine Scherben LP on a trip to watch his first Bundesliga match, Bayern Munich v Borussia Mönchengladbach. He picked it up in Hof on his first step over the border, and was pleased he didn't have to listen on his cassette player anymore. He was buying records now.

When FC Karl-Marx-Stadt only drew with Stahl Brandenburg, after leading 2-0, on the penultimate day of the season they missed their chance to go clear at the top of the league, and Dynamo Dresden went on to win the title on goal difference. 'That was the wound,' says Mike. On the same day local rivals Wismut Aue were relegated. 'That,' he says, 'was the plaster!'

* * *

*Weggel suspects his ankles are bleeding, so he's stopped for a rest. He's examining posters for shows at the Stadthalle: Thriller Live: Die Show über den King of Pop. Bibi & Tina: Das Konzert. Nothing for Death of a Salesman. He heads off slowly passing Käthe-Kollwitz-Straße and up a pedestrian ramp. It feels good to be out of sight. Incognito in Chemnitz. He sends another text message, saying that the pink and blues have just scored in London, SE22. He chuckles to himself like a schoolboy rebel. 'I'm not even there,' he thinks, 'I'm here, in Chemnitz!'*

*Weggel is beginning to feel like the agent he was when he read* The Detectives Handbook *as a seven-*

*year-old, an agent of change in a turning season. He looks up to the sky and rolls the words 'Himmel Blauen' round his mouth. Then he starts to whistle a tune he's never heard before. It is by Ton Steine Scherben and it's called 'Zauberland'. There is magic in the air.*

* * *

Mike and I are walking round the site of the second ground of the Chemnitzer club, but the first that was their own, the Sportplatz an der Bernhardstraße. It's now a school pitch with large heating pipes all around it. Mike used to work in a factory at the far end. Our next stop is the car park surrounded by DIY shops and a garden centre. Here where the cars now jostle for space was the Sport und Exerzierplatz: deeply significant ground Mike says, but it's hard to see. Then we head to the Sportplatz next to the stadium at Gellertstraße, where the police team play.

But we don't stop here at Gellertstraße, not yet. Instead Mike whisks me off again, this time to the scene of romantic ties in Europe. *Neblig* dreams, in the foggy days just after the fall of the Wall. It's still drizzling, making it equally hard to see through Mike's windscreen but we've reached as far out as the Sportforum, a vast sports complex to the south of the city centre. Its main football and athletics arena was built in the 1920s to accommodate 60,000 spectators and was called the Großkamptbahn pre-war, before it was renamed the Ernst-Thälmann-Stadion in DDR time.

It's hard to picture but international football fixtures were played here, as well as Chemnitzer FC home games during their 2. Bundesliga years in the early 1990s, and before that European matches for FC Karl-Marx-Stadt. Today it's an empty bowl, rain-beaten and run down. Three boys throw a big stick like a javelin, water ponds on the home straight and a busted umbrella trips in the wind. Mike tells me about the European adventure when his FC Karl-Marx-Stadt reached the last 16 of the 1989/90 UEFA Cup, the furthest they ever got. They'd beaten Boavista 3-2 after extra time in the first round and then saw off Sion of Switzerland 5-3, to set up a clash with Juventus. The first leg in Turin was shrouded – in *Nebel.*

The Alpine Stadium was engulfed in a winter fog that made it near impossible for the crowd to see the players let alone the ball, and it was just as difficult for the referee. But we have to take the official's word for it that after Lutz Wienhold's 70th-minute opener for the visitors, Totõ Schillaci and Gigi Casiraghi both netted late for the Old Lady. For the second leg here at the Sportforum the view was clearer and despite, impressively, only trailing by one goal from that first leg, the Karl-Marx side conceded an early De Agostini goal and went out 3-1 on aggregate.

Mike was there in the Sportforum on 6 December 1989 to see it, just weeks after the Wall fell, watching his home side take on the might of Juventus who went on to win the UEFA Cup that year. 'I was on the Südkurve, just over there,' he points to broken seats among the moss. I ask what he remembers of that night. He looks blank then shakes his head. 'Nothing,' he says, and mimes a pint glass to the lips. He wasn't able to go to the first leg in Turin because it was too expensive, costing around 800 marks which was a month's salary. Only the Stasi and the rich could go, he says. But it was so foggy in Turin, 'it was a better view on the television'.

* * *

*Weggel pops his head round the corner of a flower shop. His face is reflected in the window where there's a wreath with sky blue ribbons. On the ribbons it says 'Deutscher Fußball-Mesieter 1966/67'. Now on Straße der Nationen he's ducking from one side of the road to the other looking for cigarettes. Secret agents smoke, don't they? These days they probably vape, but still. He finds a kiosk and stands puffing away in front of the Chemnitzer Hof. He kicks a ball of snow over a bin. He'd love to sit down and rest with a coffee or a beer but he doesn't want to get too agitated, or too pissed. Plus Wittig could walk in at any moment and he can't risk that. He has to keep moving. Keep checking round corners. Keep trudging through snow in painful boots and a biting wind. It's hard being a secret agent, he thinks.* The Detectives Handbook *never mentioned that either.*

* * *

Finally we arrive at the house where Mike was born and spent his first ten years. We look up to the attic room with a small window in the eaves which was his bedroom. Now derelict, the house stands on a corner where it's the only one of its kind still left. There would have been others like it on either side. It has a broken grandeur like much of Sonnenberg. Like much of what I've seen on this journey. The Stadion an der Gellertstraße (the *Fischerwiese* as it was) is just along the road, about 100 yards away and we can see the modern version of the stadium from where we stand on the pavement outside the house. Mike remembers riding his bike and roller skates on the cobbles right here before he was old enough to go to the game himself. He remembers the crowds in the street on matchdays and hearing the roar of a goal – before rushing in to watch the replay on the TV. He remembers the songs of the crowd reaching into the house and dragging him down the street.

Last night's match at the Stadion an der Gellertstraße started with the torch song ballad of the modern Chemnitz club, rousing the Sky Blues to another win. I was there to see

Chemnitzer FC take on Rot-Weiß Erfurt in a Regionalliga Nordost tie: top versus bottom. Among the Chemnitz ultras there's a flag with the head of Karl Marx on it. In front of 6,600 fans, including a healthy 300 or so travelling from Thuringia, Chemnitz brushed aside struggling Rot-Weiß 2-0, both goals coming early in the first half from Daniel Frahn after excellent work from left-winger Rafael Garcia. Chemnitz are currently far too good for this league and will go on to win it comfortably.

Later I slipped into the VIP lounge unnoticed, not sure whether I was allowed or not. I'm certainly not a VIP but I did have some sort of pass and I am, of course, a highly skilled secret agent. I enjoyed being incognito as I sipped a beer and watched the press conference feed, but felt uncomfortable too. I feel it in my feet now, a spy in ill-fitting boots.

* * *

*It's freezing cold, he's tired and his feet hurt. Weggel's on the corner of Brückenstraße at the foot of the tallest building in Chemnitz, the Congress Hotel, 24 storeys high. That's where Wittig and her team are staying. That's where he'll spend the night, if all goes to plan. He checks his breast pocket and feels it there still. He still has the cheap bottle of sparkling wine he bought at the station Spa. Broken feet, too many cigarettes, but at least he's not drunk.*

*He starts to head round to the stage door of the Stadthalle.* Death of a Salesman *is well under way on the small stage, and the Dutch magician Hans Klok is making people disappear in the Big House. When he arrives it's half-time at Klok's show and outside half a dozen magicians' assistants have popped out for a fag themselves; a fog of sequins and tassels. He'll need to find a way past the stage door keeper, who will almost certainly be a fierce dog of a guard.*

*But Weggel has been here before, he's played this stage, so once he gets past the keeper he'll be able to jink his way down the corridors. He decides not to explain what he's doing, not to appeal to any sense of romance. What's romance to a stage door keeper? He'll simply say that he's 'with the team'. She'll tell him to sit and wait. And once she turns her head he'll run for it. Into the wings. Run like hell to deliver the box ... it would be nice to have a sit down though ... No, he's going in.*

* * *

Mike doesn't go to the matches at Gellertstraße these days. He's a roller hockey and ice hockey fan now. At home with his cats he has an archive of rare material relating to hockey history in Chemnitz. The football he follows is from St Pauli, mainly on their travels. He didn't get drawn in to FC Karl-Marx-Stadt until his teens in the early 1980s, and followed them passionately from then. He shows me an old picture from the local newspaper of him holding one corner of a red banner: dark beard, long hair; the young left. That's not to say he was a party-liner, he says. He was a rebel, from the left wing. He still loves Karl Marx. But he stopped loving FC Karl-Marx-Stadt around 1992. They were renamed Chemnitzer FC by then, but he was finally fed up with a sway among the support. 'There were too many right-wing fans,' he says. 'And that has only got worse.'

He explains if he went there now with his St Pauli badge proudly sewn on to his jacket he would probably be on the receiving end of violence, miming a fist pushed under his jaw to make his point. He feels this club is not for him anymore. Last night's goalscorer Daniel Frahn will go on to cause controversy by, among other things, holding up a t-shirt in tribute to a deceased known far-right hooligan, during a match in March 2019. In August the club captain is dismissed for 'club-damaging behaviour' connected to his alleged links with far-right fan groups.

Before we part we think back to where it all started for his Chemnitzer club. The students from Mittweida in a photo from the book Mike has shown me, smartly dressed, smoking their pipes and drinking beers. Who knows whether it's post- or pre-match, but they have it all ahead of them, all the history and mystery of this sky-blue football town. One of the students, Mike says, went on to play for Barcelona – Udo Steinberg, who was the first scorer in the first El Clásico.

He looks back up at the house. His dreams are different now. One day, he says, he'd like to buy back the house on the corner where he was born, restore it to its former glory and live there with his cats. It's very unlikely he knows, but Mike the gentle punk still dreams. I wish him well. I wish him his corner of Chemnitz. Mike is a really nice man and as we leave he gives me a gift of the same cloth patch as the one he's wearing with 'St Pauli Brigade Chemnitz' under the head of Karl Marx. We go our separate ways; stepping over the romance trapped under concrete slabs in Sonnenberg.

* * *

*She said 'Yes.' Wittig did, I mean. I popped the question during the curtain call. Well, I mean, Weggel did.*

*He tried to catch her between bows but each time he was on the wrong side of the stage, like a poor farce. Wittig came off stage-left and Weggel was on the right. Then he dashed round the back to the left and Wittig come off on stage-right. Once when he ran round he tried to cut the corner and found himself briefly on stage. If any of the audience had been looking in that direction they would have seen a strange, agitated man clutching a small box. He eventually asked the question in a dusty corner by some brooms and stacked chairs. She said yes, but that they'd have to clear up quickly to get out of the way of Hans Klok and his magic boxes.*

*Later they raised a toast in Schnitzel Paradise. There was no one else there except Weggel, Wittig and her team. They asked the waitress for some glasses for the cheap fizzy wine, explaining the mission. She smiled and offered a corkscrew. 'No thanks,' he said, 'it's a screw top,' and finally kicked off his boots. Blood on the carpet.*

*A year later they were married in the centre circle at Champion Hill, SE22. She wore his mother's wedding dress from 1967 with a muddy footprint still on its train. The sun shone on Weggel and Wittig from a sky-blue sky.*

* *Neblig* means foggy.

** Walter Weggel and Herbert Wittig played for the Chemnitzer Ballspiel Club in the 1920s. Weggel was a goalkeeper known for wearing a cap and his high-spirited trips outside the box. The word *Wittig* means funny as well as referring to a chemical reaction involving coupling. Walter and Herbert never got married (as far as I know) – I just really like their names.

# Sparwasser shoots

I'M STANDING in a car park with Paul Heaton. It's not what I'd expected from my tour of east Germany, but this is a bummel and what's round the next turn is usually surprising, like *elf* men in bath robes. So standing in a car park with Paul Heaton is as apt a way as any to kick off a Saturday afternoon on the banks of the River Elbe.

I used to live in Hull and I love The Housemartins so I'm happy to be with this Paul Heaton if not with the other one, though both would be better. This Paul Heaton is not singing 'Happy Hour' or 'Caravan of Love' but is a man called Martin from Magdeburg, and he might just be the world's best fan. Let's call him Paul Heaton though.

Fanatical about many things, including The Housemartins and The Beautiful South and hence taking on his nickname in tribute to the singer (he's also sometimes referred to as HouseMartin), Paul Heaton's other obsessions include Borussia Mönchengladbach, his western club; Depeche Mode, who he's seen live over 70 times; and his beloved 1. FC Magdeburg, where he's an attendant at the VIP car park every matchday. Later he'll take up his position as a stadium steward, as he has for 20 years, right next to the home team bench, and next week he'll be back running the ticket office for the club's youth academy. He'll also find time to add to his large collection of autographed player-cards. Brilliantly bonkers, his is a mix of diehard dedication, encyclopaedic knowledge and wide-eyed wonder at his two favourite things, football and pop music.

There are different types of club legend and you don't have to have won the European Cup Winners' Cup to qualify. Though I am starting to think that everyone in Magdeburg is a legend. In the half-hour I've been standing with Paul, as he stewards cars into his rough patch of ground outside the Heinz Krügel Stadium – named after the legendary coach – at least three *Europapokal-der-Pokalsieger-Sieger* have breezed up and greeted us. These winners of the Cup Winners' Cup are woven into the fabric of FC Magdeburg, as are many of the generation that came after them. I ask Paul Heaton if Jürgen Sparwasser will be the next to pull his car up alongside us. But the most fabled of local lads, Sparwasser is absent. Paul smiles, 'He is from Halberstadt though. Like me.'

Jürgen Sparwasser was born 30 miles from here in 1948. A promising young striker, by the age of eight he was picked up by the youth team of Lokomotive Halberstadt. He moved on to the FC Magdeburg youth team at the age of 18 and made his debut for the first team in 1966. Three hundred appearances in white and blue and 133 goals followed. He'd arrived at just the right time, reaching his peak perfectly in tune with Magdeburg's golden generation of the mid-70s. Sparwasser was part of a side that won three Oberliga titles and four FDGB cups, as well as playing his part in the greatest of all achievements for a club from the DDR. While 1966 is a pivotal year for East German football in general, it's a brief period eight years later that is the pinnacle: spring and summer 1974.

Germany, of one sort or the other, won just about everything in 1974. Across the border Bayern Munich lifted the European Cup before West Germany became world champions for the second time. But for their relations in the

East, '74 was their own *annus mirabilis*. In the season leading up to that summer the DDR was very much on the map: Lokomotive Leipzig had taken on Tottenham Hotspur in the semi-final of the UEFA Cup; Dynamo Dresden had beaten Juventus and narrowly lost a thriller against Bayern Munich in the European Cup; and then there was Magdeburg. Journalist and author Uwe Karte, then a seven-year-old Leipzig lad, remembers thinking 'it would be like this every year!' It wasn't, but it was the town on the banks of a river that roars westwards on to Hamburg and the North Sea whose moment stands out; and Magdeburg's Jürgen Sparwasser is inextricably linked to two tales, one of club and one of country. Over three months in 1974 a drama played out in three acts, followed years later by a jig, as after a Shakespeare play. A merry dance we might call *Sparwasser shoots*.

## Magdeburg, Saturday, 6 April 1974

The last day of the Oberliga season. Axel Tyll on ten minutes, Detlef Raugust midway through the first half, and a second-half Pommerenke penalty see Magdeburg beat Vorwärts Frankfurt/Oder in front of 35,000 people in what is then the Ernst Grube Stadium. Heinz Krügel is the trainer. Meanwhile, third-placed Jena beat second-placed Dresden to cancel the chances of either of them catching Magdeburg at the top. The club known by its fans simply as *Der Club* is crowned champions of East Germany for the second time in three years.

The previous year *Der Club* finished third behind Dresden and Jena, its focus perhaps distracted by that season's European campaign, which was the reward for their first league title the season before. The European Cup run of 1972/73 proved a short rehearsal for what was to come as Magdeburg beat Finnish side Turku Palloseura 9-1 on aggregate in the first round to set up two legs against Italian giants Juventus. They lost 2-0 and bowed out in the second round, but a domestic cup final win – 3-2 against Lokomotive Leipzig in Dessau – later that season set up the next European campaign and the very faint chance, against equally formidable Italian opposition, to reverse that score. It was Jürgen Sparwasser who scored the 80th-minute winner in the domestic cup final, his second of the game, and a year later, a mere month after securing the league title again, the European stage was set.

## Rotterdam, Wednesday, 8 May 1974

By the end it was a very strange sight indeed. Eleven men in matching white dressing gowns wandering round a field in Rotterdam on a mad May evening. Never mind the state's ideal of 'diplomats in tracksuits', these were *elf* men in bath robes. Here they come, not an outing from the local old folks' home but:

Schulze<br>
Zapf<br>
Abraham Enge<br>
Tyll Pommerenke Gaube Seguin<br>
Raugust Sparwasser Hoffmann

These youngsters had just beaten AC Milan 2-0 to win the European Cup Winners' Cup Final. Where the gowns came from is a bit of a mystery, but the images of the victors in their hooded white bath robes are iconic and strangely haunting, as if the *elf* were already ghosts of the game they'd just played, costumed now and parading around a near-empty stadium in a Dadaist pantomime. They look really daft, which is why I love them. After Lanzi's first-half own goal it was Paule Seguin's strike past Pizzaballa in the 74th minute, appropriately, that clinched it. No need for Sparwasser to shoot. Extraordinary scenes followed, but as Alan McDougall has pointed out, 'one of the great moments in East German football history went almost unnoticed'. (McDougall, 49)

The passage to the final at *De Kuip* had seen Magdeburg knock out the Dutch, Czech, Bulgarian and Portuguese cup winners, but very few people were there in the flesh to see them crown the glory in Rotterdam, the first European trophy for a DDR team. An Austrian commentator called it 'the final nobody wanted'. Just 6,461 souls in a 70,000-seat stadium is the second-lowest ever crowd for a European final. It seems most of the Milan faithful didn't fancy the trip north to see their team trounce the unfancied minnows from behind the Iron Curtain, while Madgeburgers were in even smaller number, with just 288 supporters, hand-picked, travelling on the four chartered planes to the Netherlands, plus a few sailors and lorry drivers who happened to be in Rotterdam anyway.

Most real fans from both sides stayed at home in dressing gowns of their own, but Magdeburg's feat was nonetheless unique. Carl Zeiss Jena came close to equalling it in 1981 in front of a similarly small crowd, as did Lokomotive Leipzig in 1987; both reaching the Cup Winners' Cup Final and both losing by a single goal. But thanks to the *Gown* Princes of Europe, Magdeburg remains the only East German team to win a European club competition. A cold and rainy night in Rotterdam, the legend says the gowns were borrowed for the lap of honour, apparently a long-standing tradition in the Netherlands for cup-winning teams to wear them. While the East German officials planned to use the prize money for the national team's training camp, so clearly weren't going to waste it on bath robes. The story goes that what there was of a party that night was paid for by a Dutch hotel owner.

It was a very young side and a very local one too. The average age of the Magdeburg team that season was 22 years and three months, and each of them was born within the Bezirk Magdeburg (one of the DDR's 15 counties), roughly 30 miles in any direction from the city. The Halberstadt Prince, Sparwasser, was among them, already preparing for the next act of the drama, as was midfielder Axel Tyll. Tough-tackling and dynamic, Tyll wasn't short of flair or cheek either – watch him with two minutes left of the final as he flicks the ball up and proceeds to do six keepy-uppies on the edge of his own box.

Tyll tells me, via Paul Heaton's translation in the car park, that the celebrations that night didn't last very long at all, at least not for some of the squad. Half of them were to head straight off to join up with the national team at a training camp for the DDR's first and only appearance in a World Cup finals. But after that daft and glorious night in Rotterdam, those Magdeburg youngsters would stick together in the years to come. *Elf Freunde* in bath robes. There are more of them pulling in to the dusty car park now, 45 years later, pulling Paul Heaton closer to their hearts and ever-expanding waistlines. But has anyone seen Sparwasser?

## Hamburg, Saturday, 22 June 1974

Axel Tyll, Martin Hoffmann, Paule Seguin, and the two Jürgens, Pommerenke and Sparwasser, all joined up with the national team direct from Rotterdam ahead of the World Cup in the other Germany. Tyll didn't eventually make the final squad of 22 to travel across the border, and of the other four Magdeburg heroes Seguin didn't make an appearance and only Sparwasser started all of East Germany's games. The draw for the 1974 tournament had been made in January at the Radio Für Hessen Salon in Frankfurt am Main, where the second slip of paper pulled out of the pot for Group 1 read *BRD* – the third *DDR*; setting up the first and only real German football *Bruderduell*. We against Us.

Croy
Kische Weise Bransch Wätzlich
Lauck Irmscher Kreische Kurbjuweit
Sparwasser Hoffmann

But maybe more significant than that, the DDR had actually got there. It was to be the first and only time the country appeared in a major football tournament. They missed out on qualifying for the 1978 and 1986 World Cups, as well as the 1976 European Championships, by just one point; and at numerous other attempts at qualification by just two points, earning the national team the nickname 'the world champion of friendlies'. This is a little harsh as a DDR *elf* did win Olympic gold in Montreal in 1976. But with no professional footballers allowed to enter the Olympics before 1988 and Eastern Bloc athletes, nominally at least, amateur, it is not surprising that teams like the DDR's were able to enjoy a level of success in the Olympic Games, while struggling to replicate it in the established international football tournaments.

Still, the newcomers started their first World Cup well and defied some expectations throughout. A 2-0 win against Australia in Hamburg was followed by a 1-1 draw with Chile in West Berlin, Magdeburg's Martin Hoffmann with the goal. Later in the tournament a narrow defeat to Brazil in Hannover, a loss to eventual finalists the Netherlands and an impressive draw with Argentina, both in Gelsenkirchen, frame the big night. Hamburg, 22 June.

A different Jürgen, then a 17-year-old HSV fan from Hamburg, remembers the build-up. He and his friend had managed to get standing tickets for the three group matches at the Volksparkstadion. They saw first East Germany, then West Germany beat Australia, before the third of their matches which would be, he says, 'a little tricky'. Still as they headed off to the stadium, and in the early exchanges of the match, Jürgen remembers it feeling 'like a typical Hamburger SV game against a lower league team, with everyone expecting a win for West Germany'.

But the longer 0-0 stuck on the scoreboard the more the balance seemed able to shift, the favourites maybe having to hope for a draw. But even that wasn't part of the DDR plan, at least not among the leadership watching on, and Jürgen remembers looking around the stadium. 'The group of DDR supporters didn't look or act like football fans to me,' he says. 'They wore strange suits and were waving small flags.' Meanwhile, on the pitch the East Germans had potential match-winners, and on the bench too.

Throughout the tournament Joachim Streich would add two goals to Hoffmann's one, but was a substitute for the *Bruderduell*. Streich was a star striker at Hansa Rostock but was set to join the Magdeburg youngsters the following season and would go on to become the all-time leading goalscorer and appearance-maker for the DDR. A huge picture banner of him in the rich blue of Magdeburg, receiving a bunch of flowers as the 1979 Oberliga footballer of the year, decorates the Heinz-Krügel-Stadion today. His goals are legend and many: 229 in 378 appearances for Rostock and Magdeburg; 55 in 102 appearances for the national team. He won his 100th cap for the DDR against England at Wembley in 1984. But there is one goal that is scorched into the East German sporting consciousness and it's not one of Streich's strikes. It's a ghost of a goal.

Midway through the first half Jürgen Sparwasser is booked for dissent, but he keeps out of trouble for the rest of the half and into the second. Hansi Kreische misses a sitter for East Germany, while West Germany dominate possession and have a few long-range shots that don't trouble Jürgen Croy's goal too much. The hand-picked East German fans wave their flags and occasionally break into a polite chant of '*DDR, DDR*', maybe distracted by the pitch-side boards advertising Martini, TicTac and 'Nuts, Nuts, Nuts'. There are far more photographers behind the East German goal, still expecting the action to come at that end, like the young Jürgen in the stands did on his way here, or Dresden-born West Germany manager Helmut Schön. West German striker Gerd Müller does hit the post at one point but honours are very much even as the game seems to be heading to that diplomatic 0-0. Then it happens.

The pass is from substitute Erich Hamann, who receives a throw from goalkeeper Croy midway inside his own half on the right-hand side and runs with it into space. Reinhard Lauck ahead of him makes a run to the right, taking a defender with him and creating space through the middle. Hamann plays a long sweeping ball into the oncoming striker's path. In the TV footage as Hamann collects the ball you can just about see Sparwasser in the bottom right-hand corner of the screen sprinting from his own half faster than anyone else. The ball bounces up and hits Sparwasser in the face. That's the difference. This is enough to nudge it just beyond the two chasing defenders. A second touch as the ball rolls off his chest and on to his thigh takes it further away from them, and seemingly from out of nowhere the shot is on. Sparwasser shoots.

The commentary from either side of the border seems to mirror each other's in a strange reflection of fraternity. The East German commentator Heinz Florian Oertel's voice rises in disbelief, 'Sparwasser … Sparwasser?' His West German counterpart says the same. Oertel's volume rises more, 'Und … Tor!' The West German voice, though slightly more restrained, says exactly the same.

Describing the scene, translated here roughly in order to keep the figures of speech, the West German commentary continues with, 'A lightning-fast counterattack bridging the midfield in a wind-rush. And below me a forest of black-red-gold flags with a hammer and compass. The replay: beautifully played in free space. Even Berti Vogts can't reach it. And then the considered shot by Sparwasser. There's still about 12 minutes to play.'

Still with some echo as if not fully separable despite the ideology, the East German voice goes with, 'Jürgen Sparwasser from Magdeburg. Here, have a look: our tourists … and our players! The replay: a brilliant action by the Magdeburger. See how he retains an overview. And now, how he manages to get in a position to shoot – considers – and finishes. A masterly action. Twelve minutes before the end.'

You can just about hear Oertel's 'tourists' – those carefully chosen fans now chanting '*Heja, Heja, DDR!*' as Sparwasser veers off to the right and, out of character, gambols into history. His team-mates in blue surround him but he's now lying flat and face down so they hug each other instead. Erich Hamann, who'd only been on the pitch for 12 minutes before popping up on the right to play the long pass into Sparwasser's path, was normally a central defender.

He played only three games for the DDR. This was the second of them, with the third, perhaps the reward for this significant assist, coming against Brazil in the next round; while his first appearance had been in 1969, a full five years earlier, in Magdeburg and in a bizarre coincidence on the very same date, 22 June. Since that time Erich Hamann had also been an IM (*Inoffizieller Mitarbeiter*) of the Stasi, informing from his club in Frankfurt an der Oder. Alan McDougall has noted, referring to Hanns Leske's research, that 'one-third of a typical Oberliga squad (i.e. six out of 18 players) were IMs

– a far higher rate of collaboration than the DDR average' with the number higher at clubs that participated regularly in European competition. (McDougall, 125 & 143)

I mischievously imagine IM Hamann having just released his long-range pass, reaching down and taking a small camera from behind his shin pads and taking a shot of his own for the file.

In the shadowy photograph, snapped just before the ball crosses the line, Sparwasser is frozen in the statue of just having struck: both arms extended behind him to his left, his right foot planted, his left about to follow through with what will be his first step as the man who scored *that* goal.

Elsewhere, Sepp Maier is already on all fours and turned to face his own goal. If we could see his face we'd see the grimace forming. One defender in white slides on his knees, eyes fixed on the ball he will always be too far behind. And then the ghostly figure of Berti Vogts, his left leg extended high in a can-can, swinging a boot at thin air. It is part of the phantom dance that Massimo Furlan will re-enact years later in Halle and Munich and elsewhere. Free public art.

Yet even here, with the major players all still in place and time, attempting to change the course of this Cold War history, there is a spectre at play. As if only Sparwasser is left, already a lone figure. One man in an empty stadium with an invisible ball. Face down. Spotlit.

* * *

Paul Heaton points out the curse of Magdeburg: that it is, or rather was so close to the West. Neighbouring town Braunschweig, in what was West Germany, is just 60 miles away, the distance to the old border half that. The magnetic field between the two towns, and between east and west, has been part of the club's story. At the time of the *Wende*, for

Magdeburg as much as all the Oberliga clubs, there was a liminal period during the 1989/90 season, between the Wall being opened and reunification. It was an uncertain time, like a transfer window into a new world mid-season, that Paul Heaton describes as 'half DDR, half no-man's-land'.

But despite the temptations in touching distance, the Jig which was later to conclude Sparwasser's story is rare among those of the young heroes of FC Magdeburg. There's a more common tale I found here on the River Elbe today; a story if not of remaining at least of coming home.

'Friendship.' Back in the car park Axel Tyll pinpoints the one quality the 1974 Magdeburg side had. 'We were friends,' he says. And that spirit seems to have been passed on to the next generation as well as on to the terraces. Joachim Streich had joined the Cup Winners' Cup champions in 1975 and by 1985 was Magdeburg's manager, coaching the team through the turning season. At which point he headed west to take over at Eintracht Braunschweig just down the road. The Braunschweig effect exerted a strong pull even on Streich but it's clear that the Magdeburg resistance was equally strong.

It sees Streich back here now 30 years later, also pulling into the car park and stopping for a chat with Paul Heaton. He's followed by Frank Siersleben, one of his players at that time, a solid defender who's now a social worker and organises the Christmas Legends tournaments at the club, making the phone calls to rally the ageing troops. The troops of 1989 include the two Dirks, Stahmann and goalkeeper Heyne, and Frank echoes Axel Tyll's sentiment as he passes by, 'We'd been together for many years. We knew each other well, Dirk Heyne, Dirk Stahmann and me. Uwe Rösler is still one of my best mates, too. I've many friends here.'

With Streich in charge Magdeburg went into 1989/90 after a fairly typical sixth-place finish to the previous term, and not having picked up a trophy since they won the domestic cup in 1983 (which set them up for a 7-1 thrashing at the hands of Maradona's Barcelona in the first round of the Cup Winners' Cup later that year). But despite this and their recent league record of hovering outside the top three the troops did rally, trying to keep focused on what was to be a real title challenge this time round, amid the uncertainties of the *Wende* and the growing pull of the west.

'In 1989 we had a good team,' says Frank Siersleben, 'we were at the top of the league and were able to keep focussing on the sport.' While his friend Dirk Stahmann – now a clean-shaven car salesman, back then the strikingly bearded sweeper and captain, a one-club man – acknowledges the new influence on the fans: 'As soon as the Wall was opened interest in football declined. It was the first time people could go to the West, so on Saturday they went shopping instead. They didn't come to the match.'

Joachim Streich goes further, seeing the influence spreading from the terraces to the pitch, or maybe pulling in both directions at once. 'In '89/90 we were half-time champions,' he says. 'But after the *Wende*, after the winter break, we were not so focussed anymore. The players were looking west.' To Braunschweig and beyond. It's not surprising their heads, and those at other clubs, were turned. If the momentous events in Berlin weren't distracting enough, western football agents moved fast to try to sign the best of the talent from the east. Less than a week after the *Mauerfall*, in the DDR's crucial World Cup qualifier against Austria one agent is said to have sat down on the bench to talk to players *during* the match.

After the fall of the Wall and heading into the winter break Magdeburg were top of the league, with current champions Dynamo Dresden breathing down their necks. Then after the first match of the season's return Dresden had edged them off the top spot. Magdeburg did keep up the title challenge, even managing to get back to the top briefly, and they kept pace right until the end, but ultimately fell short. There was another factor to this, beyond the political upheaval of the time and the Braunschweig effect, a simple footballing one, explains Paul Heaton.

Young striker Markus Wuckel had been prolific in the first half of that season, alongside Uwe Rösler, and Paul Heaton believes he was the difference, crucial to Magdeburg's own turning point. Up until the winter break Magdeburg had won nine games and lost just two. When the season resumed in February they would go on to win only four more, lose three and draw six.

Between the match with Lokomotive Leipzig in late March, and the next one away at Bischofswerda in early April, Wuckel was injured in a car accident, and heading into the run-in his absence was felt. With three of the six draws coming in that period, a Wuckel winner in just two of them might have been enough. Still, Magdeburg went into the final matchday on equal points with Dresden and Karl-Marx-Stadt and even at half-time were still top of the league. But in a nail-biting season's end it wasn't to be.

Many of the generation of the turning season did move on to other clubs sooner or later, but many of them also now return, turning up at the Heinz-Krügel-Stadion, season tickets and VIP parking passes in hand, pulling into Paul Heaton's car park. Tyll, Hoffmann, Streich, Stahmann, Siersleben, the line goes on. 'It's passed from generation to generation,' says Niels Mackel outside the stadium after today's 1-1 draw with high-flying Paderborn. Mackel was a youth player here in 1989, making an appearance from the bench on that final day of the season, before setting off a few years later on his own journey westwards, stopping off at Eintracht Braunschweig on the way.

In the Bundesliga qualification season of 1990/91 Magdeburg finished tenth, their lowest league finish since 1967. Their DDR story is that of a regular top-six side, a club that reached seven East German cup finals and won them all, but this sudden new low meant they started reunified German football life at the lowly, and then non-professional, third level. Since then they've flipped between the third and fourth divisions (with relegations being the result of restructurings of the league system or, in one case, financial insolvency), and finally gained promotion back to a fully professional league, the current 3. Liga, in 2015 – 25 years later. It's been a long time coming, and promotion to the 2. Bundesliga last year, for the 2018/19 season, is a new, long-dreamed-of high. By the time the 19/20 season starts they'll be back down again, but at least for now the terraces for today's match with Paderborn are jumping for joy.

However, Paul Heaton explains that this will be the last chance for a while to enjoy that sort of thing, 'When we got promoted four years ago attendance increased and the supporters kept jumping during the match. So the concrete started to crack on the terraces. They wanted to shut the stadium down, but in the end the council of Magdeburg, the club and the ultras made a deal which stated, "no jumping anymore"!'

They'll start rebuilding measures next week which will increase the capacity to 30,000 and strengthen the terraces. 'So hopefully we'll be jumping again before too long,' he says. Before today's last bounce begins, I ask Joachim Streich if he'd like to turn back the clock, to 1974 maybe, or to 1989. 'In football terms it was better then,' he admits. 'More quality, playing in the first division, and we were at the top. But in life? No. For me it's good now. Here.'

Talking of which, has anyone seen Sparwasser?

## Saarbrücken, January 1988

Uwe Karte tells me his theory. 'The Football God had an idea,' he says. 'What should the scorer of this goal for east against west be called? *Sparwasser. Wasser* is water. *Spar* is save. Save-water. In the DDR you had to save everything: save water, save money [save energy, save glass, save paper], everything was saved. It's a brilliant name for the scorer of the most famous East German goal.'

Sparwasser wore number 14 on his shirt that night in Hamburg. And 14 years later he would shoot again. He hung up his boots in 1979 after nearly 300 games for Magdeburg and 49 appearances for the DDR. The daily chore of having to talk about Hamburg '74 and *that* goal followed him into retirement and continues to this day. I'm sure he's fed up with talking about it. There's even a book called *Where were you when Sparwasser scored?* (or literally 'when Sparwasser's gate fell').

Meanwhile, the Magdeburg youngsters of 1974 remained familiar faces around *Der Club*, and now retired would play in veterans' or *Tradition* tournaments at Christmas time, happy to try to relive those barmy (not balmy) nights in the spring and summer of '74. These tournaments were increasingly popular in the 1980s and soon invitations came from abroad too. In 1988 Magdeburg and Sparwasser were invited to play at one such event in Saarbrücken, near the French border in West Germany. His wife travelled too.

The autobiography section of Sparwasser's website has plenty of detail about his life and career pre- and post-1988, with statistics and honours, notes on his work as a coach for young footballers and the training books that accompany it, but at this point the story becomes sketchy and brief. It's as if the protagonist almost rubs himself out, 'He then decided in 1988 to attend a traditional tournament in Saarbrücken together with his wife, who was visiting her aunt at the same time in the Federal Republic of Germany.'

There's a full stop. But an unspoken ellipsis too maybe, like that which follows the commentary to his famous goal, printed on postcards still today. '*Sparwasser? Und …*' The Berlin Wall would fall the following year but Sparwasser's own turning point had already happened. Some 14 years after scoring the fateful goal in Hamburg he defected to the West and left Magdeburg and the East behind him.

* * *

Sparwasser is not here today, but Paul 'Martin' Heaton is and he's the spirit of 1. FC Magdeburg just as much as any of the stars in his car park or the absent ghosts of 1974. Without him and those like him, at clubs of all levels and whatever the colour of the kit, the terraces would surely crack and stop all jumping for joy at goals far and wide. It's a thankless task being a football fan sometimes, but he isn't asking for thanks. There's work to be done.

Kind and clearly loved by all at the club, he extends me a very warm welcome to Magdeburg, a city of friends, and sees me off again the next day at the bus station. As we wait for my delayed bus back to Berlin he tells me about another project he has on the go: to record the exact kit colours – shirts, shorts and socks – worn by both teams in every single Bundesliga, German Cup, German European cup, World Cup, East and West Germany and Germany international match in history. Goalkeepers and all. It's a mammoth task, untold kits to colour in. But Martin will do it, I'm sure. Selflessly, joyfully, hopelessly devoted to them.

EUROPAPOKALSIEG
08. MAI | AC MAILAND–FCM 0:2
1974
UNSER ZUHAUSE IST MAGDEBURG.
UNSER TRAUM IST EUROPA.
Humanas

# Hinterland: a fiction

*Ralf leaves in good time. He doesn't like to rush on matchdays. He wants to be able to take it all in, the build-up, the warm-up, the loosening of limbs. Today he's taking Lisa with him so it'll take longer. Lisa dawdles. She likes to run her hand against the concrete slabs as she walks and stop to look at the colourful signs. They'll pass school where her teacher, Miss Taube, says she daydreams. But she listens too, especially when Miss Taube tells them the story about the balloons. It is 1963.*

*Inge's always rushing and today's no different. She has about ten minutes to get changed and add some extra layers. It took longer than normal at the station. A particularly dry desk sergeant liked the sound of his own voice. She needs the extra layers as there's a sharp wind blowing up there on the Prenzlauer hill; there always is at the Sportpark no matter the weather elsewhere. It's as if the wind gets trapped in the stadium, swirls in anger until the Abpfiff.*

*Now Inge's rushing again and she even thought about cycling. But she decided against it. Walking is the way. It's more respectful. It recognises the lack of distance between them or some old-new sameness. She will cross lines, from Wedding to Prenzlauer Berg, but these are just districts once again, and ignorable. Unless you need to complain about a missed rubbish collection and then you need to know which side you're on. Apart from that you step over from one to the other without fuss. And if you can, you must. Inge thinks of Wedding and her Uncle Klaus, who did cycle to the match. It is 1991.*

* * *

It's Tuesday, 5 March 2019. I start at the north-west corner of the Friedrich-Ludwig-Jahn-Sportpark. The sun has just come out. I can't see where I'm heading from up here, there are too many cranes in the way, but I'll be able to see my starting point from there, looking south, back to floodlights on Prenzlauer hill. I want to know how many steps it takes. Not how long but the number of footsteps. I'll walk in two halves. First to the eastern end of the Behmbrücke. Then across the bridge to the place where the pumps once were. Ignoring east and west, I'm measuring the distance in footsteps between two *north* Berlin clubs. Between Dynamo (in the old East) and Hertha (in the old West).

* * *

Andy jumps the tram and rarely pays. We meet in a pub called Panenka close to Normannenstraße, where the Stasi is now shut up in a museum, and the Frankfurter Allee. This wide street heads east in a straight line towards Poland. Panenka is Czech. He took a kick once that we're still talking about now. In the Panenka pub they talk about it almost every day. One kick. Some still try it, the kick. But it often makes them look stupid.

Andy knows the line of this city runs east to west as much as the other way, it always did, so separates the north from the south roughly along the line of the Frankfurter Allee. This wide road changes its name: Frankfurter Allee – Alexanderstraße – turns a sharp left at Alexanderplatz – Karl-Liebknecht-Straße – Unter den Linden – Straße des 17 Juni – Bismarckstraße – Kaiserdamm – but it's the same street cutting through the heart of the city. As the crow flies the Panenka pub is closer to Prenzlauer Berg in the north than Köpenick in the south (of the old East!), but it's a pub for Union Berlin who play in Köpenick at the stadium at the old forestry. Andy is from Prenzlauer Berg, Dynamo territory, but like all good football fans he's contrary. That's why we're drinking a beer in the Panenka pub. It gives him grief every time. But at least he has a choice.

* * *

*Ralf and Lisa's walk to the ground would take no more than 30 minutes if they paced it out but he knows that's not going to happen, so they leave the apartment two hours before kick-off. From their block on Rykestraße they turn left on to Sredzkistraße, then pass the Anne Blume café. Lisa likes the Anne Blume café. She likes the name and sometimes wishes she was called Anne too. She thinks of a girl like her but made completely of flowers.*

*She asks her dad what their Kiez is called. Ralf has explained this before. Each Berlin neighbourhood is a particular Kiez. She repeats the word. Later she'll tell someone at the match that her Kiez is Kollwitz-kiez. Miss Taube told her in class who Mrs Kollwitz was but she's forgotten. 'Come on. Forwards.' Ralf pulls gently on her hand as Lisa lingers outside the café. There's a big tree outside and someone has scratched a letter into its trunk. She doesn't know why, but it's an 'A' with a circle round it. Opposite Ernst is emptying ashtrays outside the Kollwitz bakery. It is 1963.*

* * *

I've reached the eastern end of the Behmbrücke bridge. It is 1,071 footsteps from the north-west corner of the Friedrich-Ludwig-Jahn-Sportpark to here. There's not really a corner to the Jahn Sportpark, it's a vast bowl shape with a gale blowing inside, but at least from where I started, at the Max-Schmeling-Halle-end, I've taken 1,071 steps. I don't know the exact point of the border line here on the bridge but I can only be a few paces away, maybe 11 metres. The distance of a penalty kick.

The course of the old wall has confused me before. I have to try to print a map in my mind and sometimes swivel on the spot to reorientate. It's easiest to think of it running from north to south, dividing the east from the west. But from the corner of the Jahn Sportpark along Bernauer Straße it ran, while dipping southwards, essentially from east to west, dividing north from south. The same again at the top of Chausseestraße, which is why the Walter Ulbricht Stadium, later renamed the World Youth Stadium, was in the East when it feels like it's far too West. The line runs horizontal again for a longer stretch south of Potsdamer Platz, again dividing north from south. The Wall turned sharp corners and teased with diagonals. But from here on the Behmbrücke I can map my mind fairly clearly. I guess that the checkpoint was at the eastern end and the rest of the bridge still in the East but part of the *hinterland*.

This is where they must have stood to listen to the match. Human radio waves blowing across the bridge. It took me eight minutes to get here. At the start of my walk I reached the line of the old wall within less than a minute, just a few steps like a referee pacing out from the spot of a free kick to the players forming a wall. From here on the bridge the site of the old stadium is in view. It's not a long bridge. It must have been possible to feel like you were there. In *Die Plumpe*, the nickname of Hertha's ground. But you weren't there. You weren't allowed to be. I imagine Inge coming the other way rushing across the bridge, past the ground, bumping into Uncle Klaus from 30 years ago.

* * *

*Inge is heading east through Gesundbrunnen. She doesn't think of it now but she's retracing Uncle Klaus's steps but in the opposite direction. Following Osloer Straße she'll cross the bottom end of Wollankstraße but she won't stop there, where Uncle Klaus had to stop. She'll continue on to Bornholmer Straße. It runs parallel with Behmstraße and the blocks of flats eight storeys high which now sit on the site of Die Plumpe, where Uncle Klaus delighted the crowds on a Sunday; and before that where the pumps were, delivering water to the people of Wedding and Gesundbrunnen. She's running parallel. She approaches the Bösebrücke on Bornholmer Straße but there's no one on the bridge. Not a soul. It is 1991.*

* * *

*Sunday, 13 August 1961. Klaus Taube packed his bag the night before. Boots, tie-ups, tracksuit, hair wax. It was a big game, a Sunday game. Twenty thousand people maybe. The bag strap on the back of his bike had come loose so he fixed that then allowed himself a small beer in the stübchen opposite his block on Pasteurstraße. He got into bed early. He's a stickler for routine on the morning of a matchday: coffee, start the crossword but don't finish it – save it for the stübchen later – a wash in cold water, stretch the hamstrings, an early lunch and carry his bike down four flights.*

*He heads off in good time, cycling towards Greifswalder Straße, crossing over at Christburger Straße, which becomes Sredzkistraße. He doesn't stop for a quick coffee and a chat with Ernst at the Kollwitz bakery opposite Anne Blume café like he might do. He'd surely be held up by telling Ernst some of the stories he's told a dozen times before and which he really doesn't mind telling. Some of the detail behind those games Ernst was in the stands for. Why else would you work in a small bakery on a quiet street in Prenzlauer Berg if not for the chance for a local footballer to drop in on his way to the game and tell you about the day he played against Pelé? Yes, just last year he'd played for Hertha Berlin in a friendly at the Olympic Stadium against Pele's Santos from Brazil.*

*Despite being a citizen of the DDR. Part of the team crowned Berlin champions in 1957, Klaus is a Hertha hero and he always has time for the fans. You find them on both sides of the line. The division of the city means little to his routine and he crosses there and back again on his bicycle every day, pausing whenever he's got time to speak to Ernst. Today he rides past and rings his bell on his way to the Wackerplatz. Ernst is inside trying to get his head round what they've been saying in the café this morning about crossing lines. He can't take it in. It is Sunday, 13 August 1961.*

* * *

It's rare, but sometimes someone comes into the Panenka pub who doesn't know who Panenka is. They're normally tourists heading to the Stasi Museum on Normannenstraße, stopping in for a local beer. The barman likes it when they do because then he can describe it afresh rather than continuing the endless discussion of Panenka penalties through history: Totti in 2000; Zidane in 2006; Aaron Ramsey a couple of years ago in the very same place the kick was coined, the Red Star Stadium, Belgrade.

That west of here they don't call them 'Panenkas' is no surprise. The final of the 1976 European Championships finished 2-2 and went to penalties. West Germany were the holders and the world champions; Czechoslovakia were from this side of the line. Two years earlier Jürgen Sparwasser had chipped a shot over Sepp Maier on his knees to win the *Bruderduell*, and now Maier was up against it again.

Uli Hoeneß missed the seventh penalty which left Antonin Panenka with the chance to step up and finish it. But instead of striking to the goalkeeper's left or right or blasting it down the middle, he slowed his run, let Maier dive to his left, out of the picture, and chipped the ball into empty space. A ghost of a kick, struck so gently it took time for the ball to cross the line. Arcing and spinning, it seemed so easy once Maier had fallen, foxed by the feint of the kick. Panenka's *Elfmeter* is a poem: *the audacity, the wit, the cheek of it.*

* * *

*Heading up Schönhauser Allee, Ralf and Lisa pass Konnopke's Imbiss, selling the 'best wurst' in town, and then the place under the train line where the youths gathered to dance and make trouble in the film* Ecke Schönhauser. *The opening scene was filmed at this very spot and Ralf saw it soon after it came out six years ago. Lisa hasn't seen it. She's too young to get ideas about dancing in the street and making trouble.*

*That's the street lamp there, just across the road that they smashed with a stone for a bet. 'Behave yourself,' Ralf jokes as they walk on, 'or you're nicked.' A man in a uniform passes but he doesn't notice them. He's an army man on his way to watch his team Vorwärts Berlin at their home ground, the Jahn Sportpark.*

*They'll be moved on before long, exiled to a place at the far invisible end of the Frankfurter Allee, to a place called Frankfurt on the Polish border. In their place the secret police will come, but today they're still playing at the Walter Ulbricht Stadium on Chausseestraße in the west of the East. But that stadium in turn will be torn down to make way for the offices of the Federal Intelligence Service. 'They're watching you.' But Lisa's not worried by the army man or the police. She's dreaming of balloons and swinging on the railing just like the big kids in the film. At the corner of Eberswalder Straße there are two railing bars next to each other with a gap in between. She tries to swing from one to the other. It is 1963.*

*Friedrich Ludwig Jahn invented the horizontal and parallel bars. He's the Turn-Vater, the father of modern gymnastics, and Inge's heading to the place named after him right by the old wall in the east, now home to Dynamo Berlin. Jahn was influenced by a man called GutsMuths who was an early pioneer of PE in schools. Jahn has a stadium named after him and numerous sport and football clubs, and GutsMuths got his name in a club too, Guts Muts Dresden (with the lost h), but 'The Lillies' haven't played since before the war.*

*Inge doesn't know it but Lisa is swinging on the bars outside the Jahn Sportpark nearly 30 years ago.*

*Parallel bars conceived by Jahn. Either side of the Bösebrücke, the Bornholmer Straße has two roads running in parallel, separated by a narrow island, one heading east to west and the other back again. Inge reaches the bridge and looks to the right. There's no one about. Without moving her head the view takes in both at the same time: the floodlights of the Jahn Sportpark and the block of flats on the site of Die Plumpe. They're so close. In striking distance. She closes her eyes. It is 1991.*

* * *

It takes me 209 steps to cross the full length of the Behmbrücke from the east end to the west. The sun's still shining. My walk across the bridge is easy. Just ahead I can see the site of *Die Plumpe*, the centre circle somewhere down there among the blocks of flats by the children's playground, and if I turn 45 degrees to my left I can see the floodlights of the Jahn Sportpark too, just across the train tracks. In striking distance. Up ahead, in front of the flats on the roadside, abstract statues remember footballers in action but with limbs missing: one missing a leg here, another both arms from the elbow. Where the limbs remain they're exaggerated in form, bulbous boots lunging forward. Two bodies horizontal, mixed up in the moment of tackle. Across the road the site of the original pitch where it all began. A pub landlord encouraging the drinkers to drink. To spur them on he made a football team. The crowds will come, he thought, and they will roar. One day. Ten, twenty thousand.

*We're flooding the gates.*

On the bar beside his mobile phone is the book Andy's reading. *Die Angst des Tormanns beim Elfmeter*. It's dog-eared; he's read it many times before. *The Goalie's Anxiety at the Penalty Kick*. The walls of the pub are covered with pictures of Antonin Panenka that night in Belgrade and shirts hanging in the colours of the clubs he played for – Bohemians of Prague, Rapid Vienna. There are scarves of other clubs too from around the world, left by football tourists on their way to the stadium by the old forestry. Andy applied for papers to leave East Germany in 1986. I ask him where in the West he wanted to go. To West *Berlin*, he says.

* * *

*We're flooding the gates. It is 1961: Klaus Taube is pedalling fast, from his home in the east to his team in the west, before he has to stop. It is 1991: Inge is rushing across the bridge, from her home in the west to her team in the east. It is 1963: Ralf is dragging Lisa forward, from their home in the east to as far as*

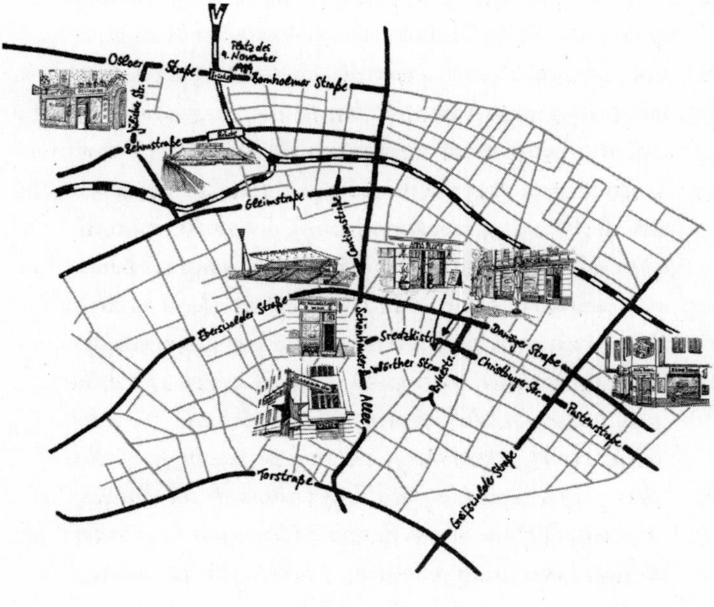

*they can go. Until they have to stop. He's telling her the story of the pump. They'll get to the bridge and from there they can hear the roars of the crowd. Human radio waves on the wind. The same wind swirling round the Jahn Sportpark, 1,071 footsteps away.*

*It is Sunday, 13 August 1961. If Klaus Taube had stopped for a chat with Ernst at the Kollwitz bakery as usual he might have known earlier. There was nothing on the streets around the Ecke Schönhauser to suggest anything was different. A normal Sunday matchday as he headed to the Wackerplatz ground for the clash with Wacker 04. He heads off down Cantianstraße on the eastern edge of the Jahn Sportpark which he ignores as usual. His Hertha Berlin played there until 1904, but today it's the army side Vorwärts who call it home. And later the secret police will move in, his niece's team in wine-red.*

*He turns left on to Gaudystraße, cuts diagonally across the Falkplatz and on to Schwedter Straße. It isn't until he's closer to the railway tracks approaching the bridge at Behmstraße that he notices anything at all. A turning in the stomach. A flick of nerves before a big match. But the nerves don't usually start until about 30 minutes before kick-off, when he can hear the crowd gathering. Ten, twenty thousand of them.*

*Inge opens her eyes. In her mind she's been back in 1989, two years ago. The first brave few went through at 9.20pm. They were given a stamp which officially meant they couldn't return, but they shouted 'We'll be back!' At 11.20pm the guards are increasingly afraid that people will use force to get through the border. The chief officer of the Passport Control unit decides to stop examining passports. Then at 11.30 word is passed around, here on the east side. The message doesn't change as it's passed from ear to ear, from voice to voice, a wave of it: We're flooding the gates. And 20,000 people crossed the Bösebrücke. The scenes are incredible. People are all saying the same word. 'Amazing!' 'It's amazing!' Walking from the East into the West. Walking to another country. What will this freedom mean, 30 years from now? It is dizzying to think of it. The wind picks up. Lisa spins on the railings 30 years ago.*

* * *

I squint through a gap in the wire fence on the Bösebrücke, over the allotments to the inverted triangles of the top of the floodlights at the Jahn Sportpark. If one of them uprooted and started to walk towards me it would take nine, ten, maybe 11 steps to get here. I imagine the floodlights of all the east Berlin sports grounds – the Jahn Sportpark, the Sportforum, the World Youth Stadium, the Stadium at the Old Forestry – kicking off their foundations and stomping, giant metallic memories, into the centre circle of a new Berlin. Wherever that is.

* * *

*They flooded across the Bösebrücke and Inge was there to meet them. She remembers those first few who had no idea what was in store for them, their cards marked but crossed the bridge anyway. The surprised and overwhelmed guards made hectic phone calls, but it was too late. There were no pickaxes here, no wall to climb and push at. That was for later. For now, one foot in front of the other. 209 steps. Footsteps marking east to west with the sheer weight of walking. But so much more than that. Such guts flowing across the Bösebrücke. Such footfall. Inge met the first dizzy few and then more and more came. They walked on for ten minutes before turning left. It was thirsty work changing the world. They shared a first beer in celebration a short way down Julicher Straße in the pub that is now called Offside. It is 9 November 1989.*

*It is 1963. As they cross the footbridge over the railway lines Ralf tells Lisa the story. She likes to hear it again and again. The Tale of a Pump. There was a man who owned a pub, where people go to drink and tell jokes and fall over. He wanted more people to come to his pub so he decided to put a fence around a patch of grass beside it and make it into a football pitch.*

*Some teams played there for a while but he soon wanted a bigger and better football pitch that he could call a football ground. There was a patch of grass over the road where there used to be lots of pumps to send water to the people of Gesundbrunnen and Wedding. So he made a football place there and it became known as Die Plumpe. 'The pumps' in Berlin speak. A few different teams played there at first but then a really good team which had been playing their games at a ground on the other side of the railway tracks decided to come and play and make it their home. They are the best team and they play in blue and white, Lisa adds.*

*Hertha's roots are in Prenzlauer Berg too but now they played at Die Plumpe. And then when they divided up the city the line which separated Wedding in the Western zone with Prenzlauer Berg in the East was very near Die Plumpe, which was just inside the Western part. The football club didn't want to lose their fans from the East, like Lisa, so they made a special doorway,*

*Stahl Brandenburg in UEFA Cup action against Coleraine, 1986*

*Brandenburg*

*Ernst-Abbe-Sportfeld, Jena, 2019*

*European Cup Winners' Cup Final 1981, at Rheinstadion Düsseldorf. Carl Zeiss Jena v Dinamo Tbilisi*

*Rot-Weiß Erfurt's Steigerwald Stadium, under reconstruction, during a 3. Liga match with Energie Cottbus in 2015*

*Erfurt. Author's translation: 'Only when the umpteenth major investor has created a plastic club, the last traditional club has gone bankrupt, the last real fan has disappeared from the terraces and every game has been scheduled to suit the television industry – only then will you find that football, the people's game, has become part of the daily grind you originally went to the stadium to escape.'*

*Lokomotive Leipzig captain Karl Drößler holds aloft the Rappan Cup at the Bruno-Plache-Stadion, 1966. What became known as the Intertoto Cup was the first international trophy for a DDR team*

*1966: Eusébio before the Inter-Cities Fairs Cup, third round, first leg in Leipzig*

*Line-up for the 1987 European Cup Winners' Cup Final, Lok Leipzig v Ajax, in the Olympic Stadium, Athens (plus pre-match buffet before Lok Leipzig v Union Fürstenwalde, Regionalliga Nordost, February 2019)*

*East German champions Wismut Karl-Marx-Stadt (i.e. Aue) against West German champions Kaiserslautern, at the Zentralstadion Leipzig in 1956. Willy Tröger (9) has just scored for Wismut. This is the match of Fritz Walter's 'forgotten goal of the century'*

*Floodlight masts being installed at the Otto-Grotewohl-Stadion, Aue*

*Stadion der Hüttenwerker, Eisenhüttenstadt, February 2019*

*December 1989: FC Karl-Marx-Stadt v Juventus in the UEFA Cup*

*Captains Bernd Bransch and Franz Beckenbauer shake hands before the* Bruderduell. *Bransch was a Halle player for his whole career apart from the single season before the 1974 World Cup when he played for Carl Zeiss Jena*

*Sparwasser shoots*

*Meeting Streich, February 2019*

*The Friedrich-Ludwig-Jahn-Sportpark, Berlin, March 2019*

*The Jahn-Sportpark, November 1989, showing the Berlin Wall with the inner wall on the eastern side close to the stadium*

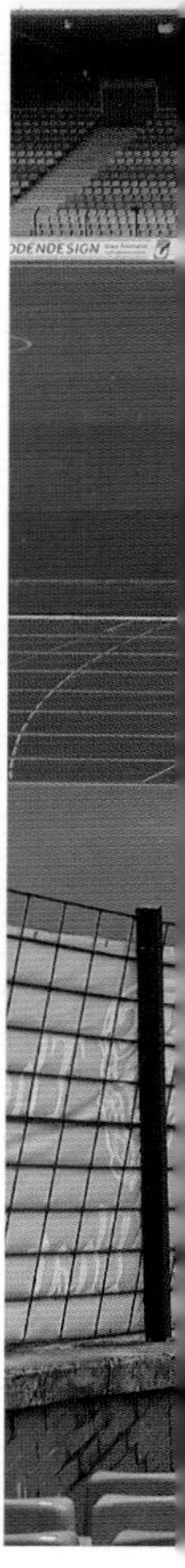

*The Jahn-Sportpark, March 2019, with DDR flag*

DEBAG
KMAB
FACON
energiekonzepte-valentin.de
JAKO
DWB HOLDING
HIER regiert der BFC. 1966. Auf gehts - WEINROT-WEISSE Jungs!
TOR
2

*Third division Energie Cottbus beat Karlsruhe of the Bundesliga to reach the German Cup Final in 1997*

*Bischofswerda: an outsider's view of the Wooden Goods Stadium*

*An Olympic qualifier against Iceland in 1988. Damian Halata shoots for East Germany. This match actually happened in Bischofswerda*

*Magdeburg v Dynamo Dresden in the turning season*

*Meeting Ulf Kirsten and Hans-Jürgen Kreische, March 2020*

*Jörg Stübner against France*

*The Jahn-Sportpark, Berlin: Hansa Rostock beat Stahl Eisenhüttenstadt in the last cup final after the last Oberliga season. Rostock win the double, 1990/91*

UHU

*Rostock's Axel Schulz tussles with Berlin's Andreas Thom in the cup semi-final, 1988*

*Montreal 1976: the DDR face Brazil in their first match, and go on to win Olympic gold*

*a Tor, with a bar that turned round and round, and a place where you could pay with Eastern money and still go inside and cheer on Hertha with everyone else. There was a fence there already, separating them, but you could still get through the special Tor.*

*That was before the people who made the decisions about where they were allowed to go in their city got anxious. They put some bricks in the entrance hall at the Nordbahnhof station, so there are two entrance halls now. They wanted to keep us safe. That's why today we're not allowed in. That's why we meet on the bridge and listen to the crowd from a short distance away. We close our eyes and hear the voices. From about the length of a football pitch away.*

* * *

Andy was born in Berlin. He has lived in dozens of apartments since, moving often but never far. Every flat he's lived in, apart from the *gap* years, was in Prenzlauer Berg. He draws me a map. At the centre of it is the Jahn Sportpark and reaching out from there all the streets he's lived on. On Danziger Straße now, near the Willy Bresch pub, but before that on Gleimstraße bordering the Falkplatz and what is now the Mauerpark; before that just round the corner on Schwedter Straße, linked by the footbridge to the Behmbrücke. And before then Torstraße, named for the north-east gate to the city: a secret door, a goal. It was on Cantianstraße, right on the eastern edge of the Sportpark and practically in it, where his mother was born and where his ex-partner lived. He wonders if his son was conceived there, in touching distance of the home of Dynamo, and maybe he was too.

He thinks back to the 1980s, the good-bad days with big crowds on European nights, and tells me he's looked out for the Aston Villa scores ever since they came here for a European Cup match the year the Villa won the competition. The secret police versus the Villains, reversed. The fact that they have wine-red on their shirts helps. Lines drawn across the maps of Europe, linked by the colour of a kit. *Wein-rot Leidenschaft* means claret passion. He thinks of matches out at Lichtenberg 47, the pitch loomed over by the offices of the Stasi on Normannenstraße. Then his mind skips to the strange 1990s, lawless days when Dynamo played out there at the Sportforum in Hohenschönhausen, past the allotments, near the prison. From the highs of ten Oberliga titles in a row to the lows of the lower leagues, small crowds and scraps.

Weeds grow there now and Andy has grown up. But there was another good time about five years ago when the fanzines were taking off and the Oi! bands – Turbolover and Bierpatrioten – kick-started a new scene. Andy used to write a fanzine for Dynamo. He called it *Zugriff*. It means 'You're nicked'. Some of that crowd still go to the Sportpark. Punks in sensible coats and warm hats. Last week he took a sticker with him which his friend had given him. He stuck it to a metal sign in Block A inside the ground. Someone has drawn a circle round the A. The sticker was of Laurel and Hardy. They're both wearing bowler hats and on the hats a D for Dynamo. Stan and Ollie seem pretty pleased about that. Beside them the text says, 'Don't trust the police.'

* * *

> *Lisa remembers now. Mrs Kollwitz was a painter. She made etchings and woodcuts and statues. Her best one was* The Weavers *which was about the workers' misery, hope and courage, Miss Taube said. When she was a young girl Mrs Kollwitz was sometimes very sad and she had bad headaches. They said she had Alice*

*in Wonderland syndrome because she saw things that weren't there. When she grows up Lisa wants to be a footballer and score goals so that the crowd cheers so loud that you can hear it in Kollwitz-kiez. If she can't play football or do gymnastics she thinks she'll join the police force.*

*The closer Klaus gets to the bridge more and more people are gathering: one group on the corner of Kopenhagener Straße, another outside Frau Krüger's. He feels another flick of nerves so decides to turn back to Gaudystraße. He'll cross the tracks on Schönhauser Allee. That way he can meet the top of Wollankstraße at the Rathaus Pankow and avoid the crowds. He pushes hard on his pedals to try and make up the time. Heading north he glances over towards Hohenschönhausen and thinks about the allotment. He needs to get out there tomorrow if he's got the legs for it. Approaching Pankow, ahead on the other side of the road he can see a larger crowd, much more than at the bridges. The allotment still on his mind, he quickens up again, veering left and heading towards Reinickendorf and the Wacker ground just beyond. He's approaching Wollankstraße which is just north of where the Offside pub is today. It is Sunday, 13 August 1961.*

* * *

I order another beer. Above the bar is a pennant, a *Wimpel*, made by the DFV to commemorate the 1989 season, the crests of the Oberliga clubs floating on a wine-red background. There's a D for Dynamo in the crest of the reigning champions, but they're not from round here. They're the Dynamo from Dresden; the Dynamo that was moved wholesale to the capital in 1953 just as they'd become champions for the first time. They fought hard to get back to the top and had managed it by the '70s, but then had another ten-year wait before they could knock the pesky Berlin lot off their perch again. There's another D for Dynamo for the cup winners though, under the letters BFC.

I tell Andy that I have the same pennant hanging above my desk at home in south London. My friend Jan gave it to me to help me on my way. Above the bar there's another wimpel, there are loads of them. I spot one from the 1960s with the D again and alongside it 'The Ernst Thälmann Schalmei Orchestra'.

Andy's friend Nick tells me a schalmei is a traditional workers' instrument, like a bugle or trumpet but with loads of horns. It looks really strange and is good for marches. They were popular in East Germany, particularly in Thuringia, as well as in Saarland in the West where Erich Honecker was from. In Wuppertal in 1987 Honecker gave the West German singer Udo Lindenberg a schalmei, in exchange for a leather jacket. Nick likes the idea of the schalmei.

He's planning to make a banner with the face of Ernst Thälmann on it alongside the Dynamo crest. It makes him laugh because in the picture Thälmann looks like a 'typical' Dynamo fan of today. He means he looks like a right-wing hooligan, when in fact he was a revolutionary communist. Andy asks if I'd like to walk with him to the next match so he can show me the streets of Prenzlauer Berg. We can take a *Wegebier*, a beer for the way, he says.

It's 1,596 steps. I'm standing as close as I can get to the centre circle of the Plumpe pitch. As close as my guess will take me. It took 13 minutes to get here. I'm standing beside a sandy children's playground with swings on wooden frames, horizontal and parallel bars. The play park might mark the middle of the old pitch, surrounded by blocks of flats eight stories high, grey chunks with faded orange balconies.

To the south the railway tracks cut off Wedding from Prenzlauer Berg. One of the old pumps is there too in the cobbled courtyard. The flats were built after the stadium was taken down in 1973 so they're the same age as me. A few yards further north is the Bösebrücke running from Bornholmer Straße, the station on the bridge, where the people streamed over in the early hours of a November morning. My phone says, '0.71 miles. 13 minutes walking time. 58.9 Kcal burned. 1,596 steps. Paused.'

* * *

*Klaus Taube has come to a stop. It is Sunday, 13 August 1961. 'It was so unreal. I stood at the border and didn't understand what was going on.' At Wollankstraße Uncle Klaus has got himself as close as he can to the front of the crowd and then he sees it for the first time. Barbed wire. Hectic phone calls were made but the star striker couldn't get through. The border was closed. They'd have to kick off without him. He'd go to the allotment on Monday as planned. And Tuesday too. He might get a game out at Hohenschönhausen or for Lichtenberg 47 at Normannenstraße in the shadow of the Stasi. But he'd never play for Hertha again. 'My career at Hertha was over in a matter of minutes.'*

* * *

If we've time, Andy says, we'll walk to the other side of the train tracks, to Wedding and the Plumpe place. We can do that. We can have a drink in Offside. Afterwards he'll show me *Zur Insel* where they have toys in cabinets from the DDR and *Lenin's Collected Works*, and maybe the old pub Willy Bresch where Klaus Taube used to drink. Later we should go to Baiz bar. On the other side of the piece of paper where he's drawn the map is a photocopied flyer for Mountain Energei: An Unacademic Symposium for Mark E. Smith. But we think it's karaoke on Saturday.

The map is expanding in front of me. Andy extends the lines up and to the left, from Schwedter Straße across the tracks and over the bridge. He marks Old Hertha Village. It's all connected in his eyes. Then Hanne-Sobek place.

Johannes Sobek was a German international who played for Hertha Berlin before the war. He died in 1989 and never saw November. Andy marks the 'football place', the original site of the pub landlord's pitch: the 'small house' next door which was the pub and is now a hostel and the 'big house' which stands where the pumps once did. For Hertha Plumpe place he marks A and B and writes '20,000 visitors'.

Later I look up his scrawled notes for A and B. They're hard to make out but in brackets next to A he's written 'Clock', and beside B, 'The Magic Mountain'. I've no idea what he means but I love this map. I think Lisa would love it too. A football ground with a big clock at one end and a Magic Mountain at the other.

Later still I see pictures of the massive stone terraces behind each goal, filled up on matchday to make a mountain made of people. Andy draws me another map. He's got so close to the detail of Prenzlauer Berg and Wedding that he needs to show me some perspective, a footnote as a bird's eye view of Berlin. In one corner he draws an oval. The left side of it is blank but on the right side smaller circles, each a slightly different size, squashing up against each other: Köpenick, Friedrichshain, Hohenschönhausen, Pankow, Prenzlauer Berg, and Wedding too, the eastern city. It looks like part of a brain. But just one half of it. Each of the lobes sharing space in the head. If one part stops working life becomes very hard. It is Andy's brain. It is Inge's too.

* * *

*When she was younger Inge had trials for Turbine Potsdam. She was always a Dynamo fan first but still she went out to Potsdam, to the Karl Liebknecht Stadium in Babelsberg. And she liked Turbine's nickname. Torbienen: the Goal-bees. She didn't get picked for the team but she wasn't disappointed. Turbine had only just started playing then.*

*On New Year's Eve 1970 a piece of paper was found stuck to the notice board at the local energy company. It said a women's team was to be started for Turbine. No one knows who put the notice up. Inge didn't know they'd go on to be the best. Six DDR championships from 1981 to 1989 is not as many as Dynamo but still pretty good. She wonders how the Turbine women will fare in the Bundesliga, in the new world. Pretty well, she thinks.*

*She's reached the other side now. She stands on the north-western corner of the Jahn Sportpark and looks back at the bridge to Wedding. She's home, from home. BFC Dynamo is her team. But it is hated. Everyone hates Dynamo and that's the fun of it. It is the Stasi club, Erich Mielke's club. Dynamo won ten Oberliga titles back to back from 1979 to 1988. They say the referees favoured them. Everyone says that. No one says they had good players too, and good fans.*

*People love to travel. Referees love to travel too. If you get picked to referee a European match you can travel. As long as the Stasi will allow it. Dynamo are the Stasi team. If you do well by Dynamo the Stasi might let you travel. People love to travel. Dynamo are the over-underdogs. Everyone hates Dynamo. But Inge loves them. Wein-red.*

*This is where she first met Andy. This is where they fell in love. On a hill in Prenzlauer, tucked up against the wall. They're separated now. But that is a choice. On her way back from the match at the Jahn Sportpark Inge will stop again on the Bösebrücke. She might hold on to the railing as she crosses. She might swing on it. Inge is not exactly Lisa but she might be. She runs her hand against a stone plaque. It says, 'Berlin will live and the wall will fall.' Further on someone has written on the wall of the Bornholmer Straße station in chalk. It's already rubbing off but she can see what it says: There is a light that never goes out.*

*Abstract statues remember footballers in action, but with limbs missing, one missing a leg here, another both arms from the elbow. Where the limbs remain they're exaggerated in form, bulbous boots lunging forward. Two bodies horizontal, mixed up in the moment of tackle. Uncle Klaus among them.*

*On the Behmbrücke a small group of people stand in silence, listening. It is 1963. Ralf is there. And Lisa too, listening while she swings on a metal railing. The swinging helps her concentrate. She knows you have to listen really hard to picture the action in your mind's eye. The sounds of the crowd inside Die Plumpe. The murmurs, the cheers, the groans, the gasps, the roars, carried on the wind. Each sound means something different. And the silences too. You have to know what they mean, you have to learn the language and listen really, really hard. Ever since they blocked up the special door with its metal bar that turned round and round. Ever since Ralf and Lisa had to stand here with the others on the Behmbrücke, a huddle of people from just over there, even when it's raining.*

*It's a deep sort of listening. The people of the football ground called The Plumpe send radio waves to their family on the bridge. When she gets home Lisa will write a story. She'll read it out as clearly as she can like a radio announcer on the air waves. The story will have balloons in it, lots of them. It will be called Twenty Thousand Radios in Wedding.*

* * *

Two days later on 11 November 1989, 10,000 east Berliners crossed into the west over each and every bridge and headed for the Olympic Stadium to watch Hertha Berlin play football. We're in Baiz bar. There's a Kicker table football game with three players on each side. I'm here with Andy and Nick; with Haydn and Duncan and Fouldsy from London. Ralf's in the corner finishing the crossword. There's karaoke on.

'Shall we sing one?'

'Yeah, why not.'

'We'll need a schalmei,' says Nick.

It took three years for Andy's papers to come through. He first applied to leave in 1986 and the papers came through in June 1989. So he left, for West Berlin.

Whatever they say, no one knew it was coming.

They asked him if his application was for political or family reasons. He said he wanted to express himself.

'What shall we sing then? "There Is A Light That Never Goes Out"?'

'I hate Morrissey.'

'Yeah, me too.'

'Great song but he's a twat.'

'Let's sing something else then.'

'Like what?'

'What about "99 Red Balloons"?'

'"Neunundneunzig Luftballons"? Yeah.'
Yeah, I think, for Lisa, swinging on the railings.
Then we sing another, and another and another.
'Goodbye Horses' time and again.
Fouldsy does 'Transmission' by Joy Division.
We're on our feet now. We're not leaving. We're staying.
*Dance, dance, dance, dance, dance, to the radio …*

# Lauzi: singular

I MEET Lauzi at the corner of the West Stand and the North Wall. He's busy but has time to stop for a quick hello and to pose for a photo. I ask him where he's from. 'I was born in Görlitz,' he says. 'It's the eastern-most city in Germany, about 100km [62 miles] south of here, famous for Landskron beer and the 15th meridian east.'

Lauzi seems very proud of this last point but I don't know what he's talking about. So I quickly look it up and discover it's a line of longitude that runs from the North Pole, through Europe, Africa, the Atlantic and Southern Oceans before reaching the South Pole. Its journey through Germany is brief, running just 16km [10 miles] near Görlitz on the Polish border. There are lots of meridian lines but this one is special as it's the axis for Central European Time.

'Wow,' I say. I'm impressed, but Lauzi hasn't time to dwell on the fact that he hails from the axis of Central European Time. He's busy posing for more photos with children and their parents, all thumbs up and wide-eyed wonder – Lauzi and the dads, that is. He wears the home strip of FC Energie Cottbus, with a red and white scarf around his neck and another on each wrist. His red and white baseball cap is set on sideways and under his button nose his huge mouth holds a permanent grin. I'm not being rude, that's what he looks like. I ask him how old he is, not wanting to appear ruder but trying to get the measure of this Cottbus star. 'Well,' he says, 'Lauzi is 16. But inside I'm 52. My name's Jens and I'm an electrician. Pleased to meet you.'

## Cottbus, or Kottbus

It sits on the banks of the River Spree, just south-east of the Spreewald forest. The river starts as a small pond near the Czech border, flowing through Saxony, Brandenburg and Berlin before joining the Havel, which then joins the Elbe and into the North Sea. There are lines running through this region growing ever more weighty. Despite its seeming singularity, not only is there still debate over whether the city name begins with a C or a K, but there are two languages here.

The first street sign I pass on my way to the ground says 'Friedrich-Engels-Straße / F.Engelsowa droga', and I soon see that all the street signs are bilingual: in German and Lower Sorbian, a West Slavic minority language of the Sorbian people from the region of Lusatia or, in German, Lausitz. Lauzi, I learn, is named after the region in which Cottbus (Chóśebuz in Sorbian) sits. This is *Lauzi*-land. Lauzi stands for Lausitz and for Cottbus too. A singular place with a double life.

Lauzi, I should clarify before we go any further, is the FC Energie Cottbus mascot, in the form of a broad-smiled and wide-eyed seven-foot-tall teenager. He's been the mascot since 2003 when during its third season in the Bundesliga the club realised it was one of the few top-flight teams not to have a cuddly character to jolly the crowd. The fans voted for the name from a long list of suggestions. In February 2017 Jens officially took over as Lauzi. 'I thought I could play the role well,' he says, and has been bounding round the touchline ever since, a bundle of matchday *Energie*. 'My first assignment was against Carl Zeiss Jena. That day there were 13,120 fans in the stadium.'

A sizeable crowd considering there are about 5,000 here today for the clash with lowly Bischofswerdaer FV. Lauzi led the cheers then and today, but there's another cheerleader who's trod this path too, encouraging a bumper crowd of 18,000 to share the *Freundschaft* (friendship). That was in 2008 and this other rabble-rouser was no less distinguished than the smiling giant schoolboy.

Angela Merkel is an honorary member of FC Energie Cottbus. Though born in Hamburg, when she was three months old the Chancellor's family moved to the DDR, to Templin, north of Berlin. She went to university in Leipzig and later lived in East Berlin. But for some reason she's an adopted Cottbusser, cheering on the Crayfishes (the city's coat of arms includes the crustacean) in their Stadion der Freundschaft on her visit for a Bundesliga match against Borussia Dortmund. The German Chancellor was given the membership card number 2008. I look up an online report of her visit and though the translation may be deceptive, I fear not. 'She said thank you and said that she is firmly convinced of our relegation,' said club spokesman Ronny Gersch.

Merkel's conviction is heart-warming and not surprising, as singularities abound in Cottbus. And I bet she's seen the footage of Tomislav Piplica's bizarre *Eigentor* too. Affectionately known as Pipi, the Energie Cottbus goalkeeper's own goal against Borussia Mönchengladbach in a Bundesliga match in 2002 is a singular joy. With four minutes to go and his side 3-2 up, Pipi carefully watches the ball take a deflection and loop high towards his goal, before allowing it to bounce on the top of his head and straight into his own empty net. Giving him the benefit of the doubt, he presumably thought it would loop over the crossbar, which would explain the fact that his feet are firmly planted to the spot throughout.

I half-expected to see a statue of Pipi in the town centre or outside the Juri Gagarin Space-flight Planetarium near the stadium. But that's for the future. Today I was searching the streets for Pipi and more, and after a long trek trying to find the Fürst-Pückler-Passage where I'm told there's a *Stammtisch* (a regulars' table) in McDonald's on the first Monday of the month, I resign myself to the fact that the McDonald's is long gone and the *Stammtisch* elsewhere. I fear I'll never find it, nor enjoy a slice of the Neapolitan-style ice cream dessert named after the visionary landscape gardener, Prince Pückler.

Still hungry, my tour of the town takes me past the magnificent, imposing Art Nouveau state theatre on Schillerplatz, built in 1908, a century before Merkel's 'Let's be 'avin you' moment. I once played Winston Smith in *1984* in this theatre, hanging upside down for the duration of a goalless second half. Tonight it's offering *The Visit* (*Der Besuch der alten Dame*) by Friedrich Dürrenmatt.

Behind the theatre is the Wendisches Haus and Serbski Dom housing the Sorbian institute for language and culture. Then past the Elektrizitätswerk, the electricity works that puts the 'Energie' into Cottbus, and further on past small half-timbered factories to Goethe-park and the modern art museum housed inside a huge, old power plant. There is definitely energy here, round every turn. Now thirsty, I pause at a ten-pin bowling bar then continue on along the banks of the Spree. I'm hoping to have a look inside the Juri Gagarin Raumflugplanetarium, but it's closed and there's no sign of life, cosmic or otherwise, so I cross a bridge over the railway tracks and arrive at the Friendship Stadium. Time for a Landskron beer.

## What's in a name?

If I've learnt nothing else so far on my bummel through the Oberliga, it's that nothing is straightforward in East German football. Questions as simple as when a club was formed, or what it was called pre- and post-war, signal a head-scratching trip through a maze of names. Alan McDougall has noted the most extreme example:

'The army team founded as VP Vorwärts Leipzig in 1951 underwent no fewer than thirteen name changes and two relocations (to Berlin in 1953 and to Frankfurt/Oder in 1971) over the course of the following forty years, ending up with the post-*Wende* name Frankfurt FC Viktoria 91. Though remaining in one place, a further eight Oberliga clubs underwent either six or seven name changes during the same period.' (McDougall, 157)

In this respect the history of the Cottbus club is one of the knottiest among my 14, save perhaps for the tangled map of Halle. I'm sure there are other more mind-blowing football family trees across the region, but considering Cottbus let's just pause and marvel at its naming evolution: FSV Glückauf Brieske-Senftenberg was founded in 1919 (For *Glück auf* see Aue).

After a name change to FV Grube Marga, in 1924 the coal miners whose team it was left to form a new club called FV Sturm Grube Marga. After the war the club re-emerged in 1949 as BSG Franz-Mehring Grube, and then in 1950 became BSG Aktivist Brieske-Ost. Renamed SV Aktivist Brieske-Senftenberg in 1954, it played in the top flight until falling down to the fourth tier, at which point the first-team players formed a new club called SC Energie Cottbus while the reserves reformed BSG Aktivist Brieske-Ost but renamed it BSG Aktivist Senftenberg, a club which still exists today as FSV Glückauf Brieske-Senftenberg, the name, you'll remember if you're still awake, they started with in the first place.

But that's not it and the maze tightens its peculiar grip. A wholesale transfer, ordered by the authorities, of players from BSG Aktivist Senftenberg to SC Energie Cottbus assisted its climb back up the leagues, with 'Franz Mehring' being reattached to the name, and after a brief period playing as BSG von Bodo Krautz (don't ask, but it's something to do with another coal mine), the club was renamed BSG Energie Cottbus in 1966. That's the club which played in the 1989/90 Oberliga and is now, since 1990, FC Energie Cottbus. Lauzi, I need a lie down.

BSG Energie Cottbus spent most of the period from the 1960s until the late 1980s in the East German second division. Throughout the '60s they commonly finished towards the top of the table without doing quite enough for promotion. In the 1970s the story stayed the same, although twice they did earn a place in the top league (for the 1973/74 and 1975/76 seasons) only to go straight back down again both times.

The contrast is stark between the Energie effort and that of the high-fliers at the top of the table at that time: while Magdeburg were winning a momentous league and European Cup Winners' Cup double in 1974, Cottbus finished the season bottom of the table with just one win and a joint-record fewest goals scored, 16 in 26 matches. Things didn't get much better for their next stab in 1975/76. By February of that season they were on an 11-game losing streak, with a record zero points from a possible 22. They didn't find the net at all for nine matches and finished bottom of the pile once more. These are singular statistics in Oberliga history. (Thanks to @FussballDdr for consistently digging them out.)

Things were looking up by the late 1970s and early '80s though, when Cottbus won their second division league three times; though they only managed to get back up to the top division once, for 1981/82, only to hurtle straight back down again at the end of the season (there were five leagues at the second level at the time and a play-off group for the two promotion spots).

And nothing much changed into the mid-'80s with the pattern repeating itself in 1986 (promotion) and 1987 (relegation). Until something clicked. In 1987/88 they won their second division title by 14 points and reached the top table once again. Finally they stayed there. In 1988/89 they finished tenth in the Oberliga, and then the following year, 1989/90, reached a peak and solid mid-table seventh.

However, singular as the Crayfishes are, in the scramble for places during the reunification season of 1990/91 they finished second from bottom and so started life in the new Germany back at the third-level Oberliga Nordost. Their position in the Eternal Table of DDR-Oberliga points was set at 24th – the lowest of all the turning season clubs save for Stahl Eisenhüttenstadt and today's opponents Bischofswerda, (though I'm not sure they even exist). The regular yo-yo between the bottom of the Oberliga and the top of the second division meant there were no chances for Energie to enjoy European competition at that time; this despite their status now as one of the better-known and more successful clubs from the east. This was because the best was yet to come.

'During the first 20 years of post-unification *Bundesliga*, only two East German clubs, Energie Cottbus and Hansa Rostock, survived in the top flight for any length of time.' (McDougall, 326)

After six seasons playing at the third level of a united German system, Energie Cottbus won promotion as champions to the 2. Bundesliga in 1997, where they played for three years. In that same season, while still a third-tier club, they also miraculously reached the cup final, another (almost) singular achievement for a team from the DDR. After seeing off Stuttgarter Kickers after extra time, followed by Wolfsburg, then Duisburg and St Pauli both on penalties, and Karlsruhe; they faced Joachim Löw's VfB Stuttgart in the final in front of 76,000 at the Olympiastadion in Berlin. Cottbus lost 2-0 with both goals from Brazilian striker Élber, but they remain one of only two teams from the former East to reach a *DFB-Pokal* Final; the other was Union Berlin in 2001.

Things got even better after that. A third-place finish in 1999/2000 saw Energie Cottbus qualify through the play-offs to reach the Bundesliga for the first time, and to play in a first division of any kind for the first time in ten years. Three seasons in the top flight (2000–03) were followed by three seasons back in the second division, and then another three back at the top table (2006–09): yo-yoing once again but this time among the big names from the west.

Their record in the Bundesliga was a fairly consistent one (finishing 14th, 13th and 18th in their first spell; and 13th, 14th and 16th in the second), but considering Cottbus's unremarkable league history during the life of the DDR, their survival among the elite of German football was another singular achievement. It is shared only by Hansa Rostock in a similar period of time, and currently by Union Berlin. After Cottbus were relegated in 2009 there was a ten-year gap before any former East German club made it to the top flight. Cottbus is not altogether singular then but among a select few, of the five clubs from the DDR to have played in the Bundesliga, and Lauzi has a lot to shout about. No wonder Angela Merkel wears the scarf.

Still, despite the Chancellor's support, since 2009 the Crayfishes have been on a slow but steady slide back down the leagues to take up another yo-yo space between the third and fourth tiers. And despite their two significant, heroic spells in the Bundesliga, the highlights of a history that lacks

European adventure, today in 2020 they play in the fourth division Regionalliga Nordost.

## The Stadium of Friendship

The players' cars are lined up in the car park outside the clubhouse: a Mercedes, an Audi, a BMW, another Audi. This is modern football. Professional, slick and fast. This despite the fact that these are very different days for the club; its players semi-professional, its competition regional. Today's Regionalliga fixture is against Bischofswerdaer FV 08, sitting second from bottom with only one win all season. Cottbus are fourth. Life for much of the past 30 years has been very different for these two clubs, despite sharing a place in the Oberliga season of 1989/90. That time round, either side of the *Wende*, Cottbus beat Fortschritt Bischofswerda as they were, twice: 4-1 away and 3-0 at home. There are hints at those days today. A banner pitch-side reads *Betriebssportgemeinschaft Energie Cottbus*: celebrating the BSG of a previous incarnation as a 'company sports community'.

Today it seems the community of Bischofswerda didn't much fancy the trip north up the River Spree, across the state border from Saxony to Brandenburg. There are 15 of them here in the Guest Block in one corner of the South Stand, few enough for me to be able to count them a number of times to check if everyone's back from the loo. I wouldn't be surprised if Lauzi, who has paraded out with the players to a rousing club anthem, doesn't welcome each of the Bischofswerda fans personally – this is the Friendship Stadium after all – but for now he's working hard geeing up the crowd from the touchline. All 5,604 of them (minus 15).

The match is particularly one-sided, as expected, but it takes almost an hour for Energie to break through. A free kick on the left is headed home by captain Dimitar Rangelov on 55 minutes before Jonas Zickert claims a second 15 minutes later, when a cross from the right is deflected over a helpless Mika Schneider in the Bischofswerda goal. I'm not yet convinced the town of Bischofswerda really exists and on this evidence their defence, at least, is certainly lacking. Energie should win by far more, but can't quite match the result of July 1990 and have to settle for just the two.

At the *Abpfiff* (a lovely word for the final whistle) the players line up in front of the fans in the *Nordwand* (another lovely word for the standing terrace: the north face or wall), then bend down on one knee. The official flag wavers do the same, as does Lauzi, while the fans who have been standing all sit down. Then on cue, encouraged by a Lauzi still bursting with *energie*, they leap up together as one. The singular energy of Cottbus.

It's not all singular though, as after things have calmed down I meet another Jens at the fan shop selling stickers and badges. This second Jens is not dressed as an over-sized schoolboy but is a fanzine writer. He makes the Cottbus-based international ground-hopping fanzine *Auslandsjournal*. Jens tells me that most Energie fans are too young for 1989 to mean a great deal to them, and even he, who is old enough, doesn't think about it too much. 'Today,' he says, 'it doesn't matter if you're from east, west, north or south – or Poland! You're just a person and a football fan.' He goes on to add, 'I'm not from East Germany – I'm from Germany and I'm from Cottbus. We all love our clubs.'

Jens clearly does, and so does the other Jens. Just past the cars parked across the practice pitch I bump into Lauzi again. He's still hard at it almost an hour after full time, posing for photos, forever thumbs-up. He's surrounded by friends outside his Friendship Stadium. For him the connection is more recent, 'I've been a fan of FC Energie since 2004. That was the first time I was in the stadium. Three years later I bought my first season ticket. I was a flag waver for eight years and have now been the mascot for three years. I don't get into the players' changing room much but I'm close to the fans.'

He wants to talk more about Lauzi, reluctant I think to drop the mask, but I want to know a bit more about who's on the inside. 'I'm an electrician, I told you,' he says. 'I've worked on assembly since 2000, so I'm only at home at the weekends.' Perhaps to humour me, but I think more so out of kindness he goes on, 'Work led me to England for four months. I stayed in Chester. Then later I was in King's Lynn for another two months. Both jobs were in a paper mill and it was a nice time for me personally as I'd always dreamed of going to England once in my life.' I ask him if he follows an English club. 'No, I don't have a favourite club there, but my sympathies are currently with Liverpool, which probably has a bit to do with the German coach!'

I feel like I'd better let him go and de-Lauzi. He's worked his socks off as the cheerleading lad for four hours or more and he probably wants a glass of Landskron. Lauzi might not be old enough for the beer but Jens is. I tell him I've enjoyed meeting him and visiting Cottbus. I want to say that it feels like a unique place, somehow out on a limb, and with an energy all of its own, but I don't for fear of sounding like a prat. Still, I do say I've long wanted to come back here as I went to college in Nuneaton, in Warwickshire, a town of a similar size which is twinned with Cottbus. He tells me Cottbus is also twinned with Saarbrücken and Gelsenkirchen, both cities in Germany. I think again about singularity, and how this one country was once two.

# The myth of Bischofswerda

1) *Do you know anybody from Bischofswerda?*
2) *Have you ever been to Bischofswerda?*
3) *Do you know anybody who has ever been to Bischofswerda?*

Or is *'its existence merely propagated by an entity known only as SIE ("they" in German, always in block capitals), which has conspired with the authorities to create the illusion of the city's existence.'*

THE ABOVE is in fact the Bielefeld conspiracy: the likelihood that most people answer 'no' to each of the three questions thus confirming the non-existence of the city. It was first suggested in 1994 on Usenet, a precursor to internet forums, is used in the city's marketing and was referred to by Angela Merkel in 2012 when she said she had been to a town hall meeting in Bielefeld, adding, 'If it exists at all.' The Chancellor of Germany went on to wonder, 'I had the impression that I was there.'

As my journey went on I was starting to have a strong suspicion that the same was the case with Bischofswerda: that it might be the eastern equivalent of this mythical place from North-Rhine-Westphalia. Whenever I told football followers, from home or in Germany, of the 14 places I was heading to on my bummel through the Oberliga, it was only when I got to Bischofswerda that they glazed over, stared ahead quizzically for a moment then turned to me and asked one of two questions: 'Where?' or, more often to be fair, 'Why?' I started to think of the place as Bischofs*where*?

Bischofswerda had become for me not only a potential conspiracy – an invented place, once entered never returned from – but an existential crisis. Bischofswerda as the Albert Camus of lower league football. I even started to consider I'd been chosen, admittedly by myself, to establish and promulgate the myth of Bischofswerda, an equivalent conspiracy from the east: that just like Bielefeld, Bischofswerda doesn't actually exist. So I set out bravely to prove it one way or another. Not an easy task when considering that even proving that the place does exist would merely further the position that 'anybody claiming knowledge about Bielefeld [or Bischofswerda] is promptly disregarded as being in on the conspiracy or having been themselves deceived'.

Not being in on it, I was surely setting myself up for a deception, or at best a profound lack of understanding, which was fast becoming a theme on this bummel of mine. But Bishchofswerda *does* exist.

Doesn't it?

I check the tourist board website. This is the 'Gateway to Upper Lusatia' it says. 'The medieval town centre of Bischofswerda lies on a flat hill made of ice-age sands and gravel, which slopes slightly on all sides.' Explaining its name, 'It is likely that around 600 AD this Sorbian hill, located in the middle of an inhospitable swamp, was settled. The spot was called "Werda" – river island.'

The *Bischof* in the name is likely to refer to a Bishop called Benno, and Bischofswerda became a city in 1361. Then it got busy, 'After the bakery trade had already been confirmed in 1379, the guilds of shoemakers, furriers, cloth-makers, locksmiths, blacksmiths, wheel-makers, linen-weavers, bricklayers, butchers, tailors and needle-makers followed.'

The wheel-makers are significant, as are the slopes, as this is also the City of the Sliding Block. Not only its football team but the townspeople as a whole are known as *Schiebockers*. A Schiebock, I discover, is a pushing or sliding block or trestle, most commonly a wooden, single-wheeled platform for delivering and displaying goods at market.

Basically it's a wheelbarrow which doubles as a table, and each year in June there's a race with them through the streets. I couldn't wait to see the sport. The tourist website goes on to point to various other attractions of the town including the Carl Lohse Gallery, named after the Expressionist painter who lived in Bischofswerda for many years; and its large Tierpark which is home to 300 animals of 60 species, including bears.

'The central challenge,' it proclaims, 'is for us to preserve the quality of life of the city and its towns and to make them equivalent for all residents. We are always guided by the principles of sustainability and quality.' It doesn't go on to say that they're also trying to pretend Bischofswerda doesn't exist (which is encouraging), nor to suggest hiding down holes. But I'm getting ahead of myself.

Yesterday I got off the tram at the stop called Bischofsweg, but I wasn't in Bischofswerda. Not yet. I was in Dresden, all set to make the short trip by train 30 minutes east the next day. Then Tommy Klotke e-mailed. It had been hard to get in touch with Tommy in the first place. Hard in fact to get in touch with anyone from Bischofswerda, further suggestion perhaps that the place only exists in the imagination.

I tried not to take it personally, but my e-mails to Tommy Klotke, the club's head of marketing and communications, had failed to get a response; nor when I decided to take it to the top did my plea to the club president, Herr Neumann. Similarly my messages to the faithful fan club called *Die Treuen* (The Faithful) fell on deaf ears, and my dream of joining them in an imaginary five-a-side faded fast. It seems *Die Treuen* are faithful only to the idea that there's nothing to see here. They're in on it too presumably, I thought.

But keeping the faith I e-mailed Tommy one last time as Dresden, the Florence of the Elbe, approached, and my heart leapt as he replied, with an invitation to the match against Germania Halberstadt on Saturday. Surely, I thought, my heart now racing, Bischofswerda exists if its football team, Bischofswerdaer FV 08, is taking to the field against Germania Halberstadt on Saturday. Assuming Halberstadt exists that is; I'm pretty sure its team does as I saw them win 2-0 away at Rot-Weiß Erfurt at the beginning of my journey. But then again Rot-Weiß Erfurt currently doesn't exist itself so that's not necessarily helpful. Still, surely at least I could get to the game and see the reality of Bischofswerda for myself (unless of course the football club is at the frontline of the conspiratorial effort and resolutely pushing the myth like a wooden wheelbarrow). For now I replied to Tommy saying I was on my way.

The football ground I'd be heading for was the Sportpark an der Wesenitz, otherwise known as the Holzwaren-Simundt-Kampfbahn: a brilliant name translating as the Simundt 'Wooden Goods' Stadium. I'd zoomed in to it on Google Maps, tracing the perimeter and spotting a gap in the fence should Tommy Klotke never materialise. As I panned and zoomed I was trying to imagine Oberliga clashes here 30 years ago. It was a very hard thing to imagine and nor was there a wood product in sight. But I couldn't wait to see the place in action, to see a competitive match here and try to picture those scenes of yesteryear, the Oberliga glory days – the highest of which was an improbable 2-0 win against Dynamo Berlin in 1987 – and now was my chance. I was in Dresden and ready and raring.

I did some research, believe it or not. Bischofswerdaer FV are currently bottom of the league – the Regionalliga Nordost table only further propped up by the name of Rot-Weiß Erfurt who became insolvent a few weeks ago. Rot-Weiß actually don't (currently) exist, but what of Bischofswerdaer FV? At least as far as the league table suggested they were holding up the now 17 clubs with just 11 points out of a possible 60. Germania Halberstadt were sitting just three places above, but with a far healthier number of points. Before the winter break the Bischofswerda *Schiebockers* (think wooden wheelbarrows) had lost 4-0 away at Dynamo Berlin – now playing in the same division 30 years after battling it out in the top flight – and since the restart had lost away at Fürstenwalde and drew with Chemie Leipzig.

The Wooden Goods Stadium doesn't seem to cope too well with the weather and there had been no matches there since early December last year, further proof of its lack of substance I thought. Home friendlies during the winter pause had been played on the out-of-town Kunstrasenplatz, which could cope better with the weather being an artificial pitch. I wanted reality. Confident of finding it I arrived in Dresden, a major European city with a rich history and a vibrant present, but for me merely a prelude to my trip to Bischofswerda. I was ready. Were the Schiebockers? Was the Wood Stuff stadium? I thought I'd better get serious. Never mind where, or even why: *who* is Bischofswerdaer?

The answer is at first glance straightforward as the history of the club's name is relatively simple compared to the norm in eastern Germany. The original Germania Bischofswerda club was founded in 1908, disbanded and reformed after

World War II as SG Bischofswerda. It became BSG Industrie Bischofswerda, then BSG Fortschritt Bischofswerda in 1972, by which it was known throughout the rest of the DDR period and during its Oberliga heyday. Fortschritt literally means 'progress', but here refers to the company the team represented. Approaching reunification it played one season as FV Fortschritt Bischofswerda before becoming the Bischofswerdaer FV 08 of today, but er … is it just me or is that additional 'er' somehow suspicious? Or should I just let it go and revel in the so-called reality?

The Bischofswerda-*er* heyday was quite something. In fact there were two heydays. It is incredible that this small tractor town (Fortschritt is better known as an agricultural machinery company) in the middle of, well nowhere, managed to reach the heights of the DDR-Oberliga, and unbelievable that they did it not once, but twice. Think something like Tring Athletic getting to the Premier League. In 1986 and again in 1989 Fortschritt Bischofswerda won their second division title (Staffel B) to reach the top flight. Both times they then finished bottom of the league and went straight back down again, but still these were exceptional years. And in between their two seasons at the top Bischofswerda even reached the quarter-final of the 1988 East German Cup.

That first spell in the top flight also included perhaps the most remarkable result in the club's history, that 2-0 win against Dynamo Berlin in front of a capacity-bursting 10,000 fans (their average that season was around 8,000) at what was then the Youth Stadium. Dynamo Berlin, with Thomas Doll, Andreas Thom, and Bodo Rudwaleit in goal, were eight-times consecutive league champions at the time, and were about to make that nine, then ten titles in a row.

But the Wheelbarrows beat them with goals from Tino Gottlöber and Karsten Petersohn. And whoever the

Bischofswerdaers are they do have a sense of humour. They must have as a year later they signed Jens Ramme. It doesn't look like the hapless Dynamo Dresden reserve keeper ever got off the (wooden) bench, but more of him in the next chapter.

In the turning season of 1989/90 there were some fairly outstanding results too. At the top table Bischofswerda beat Wismut Aue, Stahl Eisenhüttenstadt, Lokomotive Leipzig and Rot-Weiß Erfurt at home; and Wismut Aue, Stahl Brandenburg and finally Hansa Rostock, away. The season included a run of five wins out of six in February and March 1990, before that final win away on the Baltic coast. This last ever top-flight victory in the club's history, 2-1 against Hansa Rostock, is also quite some result when you consider that Rostock would go on to play in the Bundesliga for ten years; and that the population of Bischofswerda is about 12,000, roughly 20 times smaller than that of Rostock (which incidentally is a lot smaller than Bielefeld, which also doesn't exist), and is similar in size to Tring. Much of the relative success in this late 1980s heyday is apparently down to the support of a man called Dr Bernhard Thieme, the Director General of Combined Agricultural Machinery in nearby Neustadt. Dr Thieme didn't just love tractors, he loved Fortschritt Bischofswerda too.

Post *Wende*, Bischofswerdaer FV played for a few years at the third level and since 1996 have bounced between the fourth and fifth tiers, with a foray down to the sixth, and very local, Bezirksliga Dresden. The club doesn't have quite as dramatic a history of variation in levels played as Lokomotive Leipzig, nor as bumpy a fall and rise as big brothers Dynamo Dresden, but it is a club which has played up and down the tiers and even reached the play-offs for the 2. Bundesliga in 1993. In that same year they reached the third round of the now reunified German Cup, losing to Bundesliga club Karlsruhe after extra time. Those wheelbarrow races are apparently good training for matches against the big guns. So I couldn't wait to see them play on home turf. Then Tommy e-mailed again.

But before I read it I wanted to try to summon up the spirit of 1989 and that final season in the sun. Though there is little sun here at the moment, in chilly Dresden, and even less across the country 30 years ago. On the Eternal Table of the DDR-Oberliga, of the 14 clubs of the 1989/90 season Fortschritt Bischofswerda sit forever at the lowest spot, in 35th. Nonetheless I try to warm up by watching some of their footage, as close to this date 30 years ago as I can find, and in comparison it's positively tropical here. I find a brief video of highlights on Sport Im Osten's series remembering the turning season, this one from February 1990 called *Chances, Chances, Chances*.

It seems all the games in that round of matches, the first after the winter break, were played in the same conditions: bright orange balls on seriously snow-covered pitches with everyone involved sporting thick gloves and leggings. Of the highlights I can make out through the mists of weather, technology and time, in most cases the big round orange bobbles about in the snow for a while, with players slipping this way and that, before one of them inevitably slices it just wide. Chances come and go but of all the teams on show it is Bischofswerda who seem most able to cope with the conditions.

This was the day they beat fellow promotion newbies Eisenhüttenstadt 2-0 with goals from Heiko Löpelt and André Merkel (no relation, as far as I know): the latter a fine guided header after a move of genuine quality considering the surface. The wheelbarrow boys in blue slide across the carpet of snow in celebration like kids on a homemade wooden sledge. In those conditions it's a wonder this or any of the matches were played that weekend. I'm lucky though, 30 years on, as despite the Wooden Goods stadium's slightly dodgy surface there's no chance of a match postponed tomorrow, surely.

The game's off. That's what Tommy's Klotke's e-mail said, in a nutshell. He sent 'sporting regards' and attached a letter from the city administration of Bischofswerda which I couldn't fully understand, but gathered that after a pitch inspection the grass was deemed unplayable. I guessed at waterlogged, but the peeping sun and mere light drizzle here in Dresden increased my suspicion, despite the pitch's recent history of being incapable of hosting any sport. Surely this was all part of the conspiracy. Still I replied and thanked Tommy for letting me know and went about my business in Dresden still considering other theories. Match abandoned. In March. On a sunny day. Surely this was further evidence that there was never going to be a match played in the first place; that the wheelbarrow town was a figment of my own, and most other people's, imagination. I considered my Bischofswerda story to date.

On this journey so far I'd now seen Bischofswerdaer FV 08 play twice away from home: in a 2-0 defeat to Energie Cottbus at the Stadion der Freundschaft in November 2019, with that 15-strong support in the guest section; and before that in a clash with Hertha Berlin under-23s in the shadow of the Olympic Stadium in the grounds of the vast Weimar-period Sportforum – where 289 people turned out in the damp capital to see Bischofswerda lose 2-1. For that match there were about half as many travelling fans as the faithful 15 in Cottbus.

In both games there'd been plenty of huffing and puffing from the wheelbarrow boys, and a good deal of effing and jeffing from the crowd, but despite hitting the crossbar once in each match at times when the tide could have turned,

Bischofswerda never really looked convincing. What I *was* convinced of, however, was that the 11 players, and roughly the same number of fans, were actually *there.* I'm pretty sure of that. The nature of the deception was coming into view, led by its football club: namely that Bischofswerdaer, the football club, does exist but only *outside* Bischofswerda; and only if Bishchofswerda, the town, exists in the first place.

I couldn't find recent evidence of them touring further afield though, and my inclination that they might have played an overseas friendly against Streatham Rovers, for instance, reached a dead end. Disappointed but delighted to be closer to cracking the case, I wondered what to do with my free time. Whether to see a Dresdner SC match at the historic Heinz-Steyer-Stadion or to take a swirl around the Erich Kästner micro-museum. I decided to think about it over a Lübzer Pils in Katy's Garage in Dresden-Neustadt, the best decision I'd made for some time, convinced now as I was that even if Bischofswerda does exist on some plane – a wooden one presumably – its football club surely doesn't exist at all, unless it's outside Bischofswerda. Or does it? It was driving me mad.

So after watching Dresdner SC play out an exciting 2-2 draw in an icy wind (the weather was changing by the second!) on an artificial pitch in the shadow of the Heinz-Steyer-Stadion – the Dresdner SC who, incidentally, Germania Bischofswerda knocked out of the German Cup in 1942 at a time when the Dresden club was one of the most successful in the country; the Schiebockers seeming to have a habit of popping up periodically to match the big guns – I got on the train heading east. I'm going there anyway I thought, game or no game. To Bischofswerda.

* * *

I'm in the market square. It seems to exist. I'm sitting drinking a Radeberger Pils brewed just down the road, in the afternoon sun (this weather!) I passed Radeberg on the train ride here, at least I'm sure of that. The streets around me are cobbled and sloped, surely not easy for that wheelbarrow race. There's no race today but this small town still has some bustling life. People going about their business briskly through the market square, nonchalantly pretending it doesn't exist. I feel fairly incognito among it all too. As if as much as the town might not actually exist, nor do I. Or maybe it's just me who is the fiction?

I need something to cling on to, something concrete, so I finish my beer and take a walk. I pass the Kulturhaus 'Bertholt Brecht', wind-lashed and broken down. There's not much culture to be had here anymore, at least not at Brecht's House. It too has ceased to exist. To make matters worse at the Freibad, the open air swimming pool, there's a man in a hole. He's digging the hole and is now inside it up to his chest. He shouts at me to bugger off. Whether that's because the Freibad has been closed since September or whether he wants to be left alone to dig a hole for himself is unclear. I shout back trying to explain that I just wanted to have a quick look as I'm visiting the town from England and testing whether it actually exists or if its existence is a myth, or in fact whether it's my own existence which is a myth in the face of an existential – but he shouts at me again, a lot more aggressively, and I realise I'm just digging myself a hole.

At the Simundt Wooden Goods Stadium all is very open despite being deserted and distinctly closed. There's a metal fence round the whole of the ground but you could easily watch the action, if there was some, from outside without going through the turnstiles. I test this theory as I walk the outer perimeter and find a spot where it's possible to see the full pitch and both goals from a grassy bank outside. Even if you were inside there's no cover and basic terracing on two sides: behind one of the goals for away fans and in two blocks down one touchline for the locals. There's no match on today obviously. I'll have to come back for that, but things are looking up. The stadium is real.

I continue my bummel around Bischofswerda and start to read the signs. This is the Oberlausitz region, Upper Lusatia, and it says so everywhere. Curiously, Upper Lusatia is south of Lower Lusatia, home to Energie Cottbus, in the north. There must be mountains somewhere beyond these cobbled slopes. The town feels far more connected to the Lausitz region and the town of Bautzen further east than with Dresden, the big city I've come from. But then in the bookshop the only football books available are covered in the yellow and black of Dynamo Dresden. No books on Bischofswerdaer FV here, which makes me wary of the football club's credentials once more.

Those credentials are hard to prove, but there are flickers of clues if you look behind the patchy elegance and small town charm. A peeling sticker on a lamppost here, a poster for a match with BFC Dynamo there. I finally find the football club shop housed on one rail in a clothes boutique on the market square called *Colorado Fashions*. Here you can grab a team strip, t-shirt or a soft toy of the mascot Rocky. Rocky might be a racoon but he looks like a dog.

But beyond the soft toys and wooden wheelbarrows, it's in the actual fabric of the buildings here, pressed into their crumbling brickwork that the ghosts of the place start to reveal themselves. This is a textile town and a tractor town too. The Fortschritt company associated with BSG Bischofswerda through its late DDR era was a manufacturer of tractors and combine harvesters based in Neustadt, 10 miles to the south. The Fortschritt connection with textiles I can't quite fathom, but I'm glad to have had a swirl round *Colorado Fashions* nevertheless. And as I move on down the street the fading patches of ghost signs glimmer in the brickwork beside me: E. LEHMANN: TEXTILREINIGUNG. KLEMPNEREI. HG TEICH, a fruit-seller for 30 years.

There's an even older-world feel here too, as if it could be 30 years ago beside the Milk Bar on Schmiedegasse, and at the same time it might still be 1908 when the original Bischofswerda club was formed. Today the place is getting busier, the people briskly criss-crossing its circular centre, round and back again. No one bats an eyelid at me, a clearly confused Englishman who's slowly coming to really like this place. The myth of Bischofswerda, I realise, is that it has just got on with things, equally unnoticed, for centuries. Even when its football club was playing in the big league of the DDR-Oberliga, no one really noticed. The place is like a child or a clown with a hand over their face, saying, 'You can't see me.' It does exist, I'm pretty sure, but it's incognito. Like me, wandering around wondering whether I actually exist myself. I soon realise its circularity too, as I find myself right back at the Freibad where I started. 'Mate. Sorry to bother you again. But I was wondering if I could borrow your spade.'

My mate shouts at me again, and I scarper back towards the train station and the reality of Dresden. I've got to come back here though, I think, one day. I must see a match and prove once and for all that even if Bischofswerda doesn't quite exist, at least not in the same way as other places, then Bischofswerdaer does, with that extra er.

But what of the reality of the Oberliga years? The spirit of 1989 and the peaceful revolution? That really did happen, just maybe more quietly here than elsewhere. On the eve of the fall of the Wall on 8 November, Fortschritt Bischofswerda travelled to Carl Zeiss Jena. They lost 1-0 to a 13th-minute

Jürgen Raab header despite having chances to level in front of 2,400 people, and remained firmly bottom of the league. As ever. Fred Wonneberger was on the bench that night and came on after 75 minutes. Today he's the head coach of Bischofswerdaer FV 08, the team I never got to see. But *Progress* goes on, discreetly, in Bischofswerda's own understated way. Just a year earlier the fruit shop opened; the one I passed on my walk. And it's still going strong today more than 30 years later. I know that's no myth. I went in there the day I went to Bischofswerda. I know it's real because I spoke to a man and I bought a plum.

I think.

# The loss of Jörg Stübner

EAST GERMANY missed out on qualifying for the 1986 World Cup finals by just one point. On the way to disappointment they beat Yugoslavia away and Bulgaria at home, but in the attempt to make it to Mexico one match stands out, and one player. Officially, 78,000 people (but there were many more) were at the Zentralstadion, Leipzig in September 1985 to see the DDR beat France 2-0. France were European champions at the time and among their classy midfield the current European Footballer of the Year (alongside the runner-up for the award, Jean Tigana). But that night in Leipzig, as Rainer Ernst and Ronald Kreer scored the goals, Michel Platini was outclassed by the man tasked with keeping him quiet. Platini was played off the park by Jörg Stübner, *Der Rasenmäher*.

Stübner was nicknamed The Lawnmower for his work rate, the fact that he invariably covered every blade of grass. At other times he was known as *Der Staubsauger*, The Vacuum Cleaner, for the same reason. Everything cleaned up; Platini in his pocket. 'I was in the stadium when East Germany played France with Platini,' says author and journalist Uwe Karte, who grew up in Leipzig. 'No one thought the DDR would win this game, but it finished 2-0 and Stübner was the best player on the pitch. At that time he could have played for any club in Europe, he was that good.'

The DDR team for the qualifier against France was an even mix of Dynamo Berlin, Lokomotive Leipzig and Dynamo Dresden players, plus one rogue from Rot-Weiß Erfurt; and as well as Stübner's club team-mate Ralf Minge (now sporting director of Dynamo Dresden) included Ulf Kirsten.

Uwe takes me back to their early days together, 'At first Jörg and Ulf fought for the same position in the team. Ulf joined the youth sports school one year after Jörg. He played in midfield at first but after four or five years he became a striker and Jörg, who had been by far the best striker in the youth team, moved to midfield. For Jörg this was difficult. Later, when he played for the national team his role involved less creativity, only one goal: his job against France was simply to stop Platini. He did this brilliantly but it was difficult mentally for Jörg to get over this switch.'

This was just one of the changes Jörg found difficult to cope with in his life. There would be another major change in 1989.

* * *

Jörg Stübner died of a heart attack in June 2019, at the age of 53; just four months before a book about his life as the reluctant pop star of DDR football was published. The man writing the book, alongside Jörg himself, was Uwe Karte. They'd set out together on a journey to tell his story in 2015 and now, just as they were about to finish the book, Jörg passed away, after a long struggle with addiction and financial problems. 'Every day now I get e-mails from people who've read the book and who are happy to have been reminded of Jörg,' says Uwe. 'But I just wish I could have given him a job: the job of sending parcels to the people buying it. To actually wrap up the books and post them. It would have been a wonderful job for him, I think, to help him realise that people really were interested in him and cared about him.'

'I was a worker, but Stübs was the talent.' This is how Ulf Kirsten described his old friend Stübner to me, and it's high praise indeed considering who it comes from, but more of Ulf later. We were standing in the entrance hall of the Dynamo Stadium after Dresden's 2-1 win over Erzgebirge Aue in a 2. Bundesliga clash. The hard-fought Saxon derby with a crowd of 30,000 had seen Aue's early lead (after a seven-minute VAR delay) equalled and bettered by two strikes either side of the break from Patrick Schmidt; but I was looking in the wrong direction twice and missed them both.

I should have taken note of the trumpet-accompanied Dynamo ultras' rendition of 'Can't Take My Eyes Off You' earlier. I was however concentrating late on when, with the visitors pressing for an equaliser, a young Aue player snatched the ball out of the Dresden assistant manager Heiko Scholz's hands and scattered his notepapers in the process, to a mock roar from the Aue fans. Musing on how the next generation must always come along to scatter the dreams of the old guard, I quickly look up Heiko online (risking missing a late equaliser) to find that he played for Lokomotive Leipzig in the 1987 European Cup Winners' Cup Final against Ajax, before joining Dynamo Dresden for the final Oberliga season and then moving westwards to play for Leverkusen, Bremen and Cologne in the Bundesliga.

I learn later that Heiko's move to Dresden in the summer of 1990 marked the first one million East German Mark transfer deal between two DDR clubs. Times change. I'd wondered who the stout coach was yesterday when I watched him barking orders to his young strikers on the park pitches of the 'Big Garden' where Dynamo Dresden train in full public view, just across the road from the club's historic stadium.

The Rudolf-Harbig-Stadion, named after an Olympic middle distance runner, was opened in 1923 as the Dresdner

Kampfbahn and renamed after Harbig in 1951. It was called the Dynamo-Stadion from 1971 to 1990, before reverting back to Rudolf-Harbig-Stadion from 1990 onwards, with some variations for sponsorship. But I discover many still call it the Dynamo-Stadion today, in a nod perhaps to the golden generations of the 1970s and late '80s.

SG Dynamo Dresden was formed in 1953 as a sports club affiliated to the police force. Its predecessor as the city's successful club Dresdner SC was a founding member of the German FA (*DFB*) in 1900, whose origins go further back – to the Dresden English Football club formed in 1874. Dresdner SC won the national championship in 1943 and '44 and was reformed as SG Friedrichstadt after the war, but following a riot at the championship final in 1950 was dissolved by the communist authorities who regarded the club as too bourgeois. Its players were sent off to play for BSG Tabak Dresden, but many of them fled to the west.

The current Dresdner SC was formed after reunification in 1991 and today plays amateur football in the Saxony League at the seventh level, though did briefly play in a higher division than Dynamo Dresden at the turn of the 20th century. The period between SG Friedrichstadt's dissolution and the forming of Dynamo Dresden involves a series of complicated threads from various clubs reaching back and forwards from that point. But in simplified form a club called Volkspolizei Dresden, which was formed in 1950 out of 11 police-affiliated clubs, was developed into SG Dynamo Dresden and now became part of the central Dynamo sports society associated with the state security services rather than the regular police force, in 1953. It's more complicated than that, but for the sake of all our sanities let's call this the Dynamo Dresden we know today. They won the DDR-Oberliga title that same year.

But things took a turn for the worse soon after. The president of the SV Dynamo organisation was Erich Mielke, at that time also deputy head of the Stasi. Mielke wanted a successful club for his capital city – not least as football fans in East Berlin were clearly drawn to teams such as Hertha, a stone's throw into the West – and so ordered the relocation of most of the Dynamo Dresden players to Berlin to become Dynamo Berlin. The remnants of the Dresden club, mainly youth and reserve players, regrouped in the second division but within four years had fallen to the localised fourth level. It wasn't until 1962 that they managed to get back to the Oberliga and another ten years before the club finally re-established itself at the top. With the 'Little General' Walter Fritzsch's team, known as the Dresden *Kreisel* (spinning tops) they won the Oberliga title five times in the 1970s, including two league and cup doubles in 1971 and 1977. (Dynamo Berlin and Hansa Rostock are the only other clubs to win a DDR double, and only once each.)

In European competition they had notable wins against Juventus and Benfica and reached four quarter-finals, the pick of the thrills being a 7-6 defeat to Bayern Munich in the last 16 of the 1974 European Cup. They also reached the semi-final of the 1989 UEFA Cup, beating AS Roma on the way to a famous and narrow defeat to Stuttgart.

Meanwhile, domestically Mielke was plotting his revenge to knock Dynamo off the top in favour of his other Dynamo in Berlin. He would succeed, with the help of plenty of questionable refereeing, with Dynamo Berlin winning ten consecutive titles from 1979 to 1988, but it was Dresden who had the last laugh; by 1988/89 they'd finally knocked Berlin off their perch by winning the Oberliga title again, and then followed this up with a third league and cup double in 1989/90. After that they played for four seasons in the

Bundesliga and since then have bounced between the second and third divisions, with two seasons at the fourth level when local club Dresdner SC (remember them?) briefly had the city bragging rights once again. Throughout the DDR period Dynamo Dresden was the best-supported club in the country, its Rudolf-Harbig regularly packed to the 'giraffes'.

The stadium was redeveloped on the same site in 2009 and the scoreboard of the old stadium is still standing outside the boundary of the current one, and now sits in the grounds of the Georg-Arnhold swimming pools next door. I went for a swim there a few days ago, the back of the old scoreboard right beside the outdoor pool. On matchdays I imagine splashing about gaily in the heated bubbles while the crowd above roars me on.

The old scoreboard that watches over my swim was installed in 1979 and at the time was a technically innovative and expensive addition, '4,333 incandescent lamps could light up a total of 120 letters and numbers on six lines,' the club website explains. A bit more hi-tech, I think, than Mr Schmidt's current apparatus at Stahl Brandenburg, but still there was a rudimentary aspect even to this fancy new board. 'The 20-watt bulbs were initially controlled by an electronic typewriter, from which every letter was sent directly – a typo and the whole line was ruined.'

I look at pictures from 2008 when the stadium was being rebuilt, with matches continuing to be played in what is still half an old stadium and already half a new one; with its remaining, now much-missed, 'giraffe' floodlights wondering which era they're in. While the stadium today is big and finished and full of the future, under the giraffes' gaze and the lens of '89/90, which is permanently stuck to my own eyeballs at the moment, these images stand as a symbol of that strange space between the old world and the new – a bit like Heiko and his papers, upset by the young Aue upstart.

Heiko's busy after the match, presumably still picking up his papers, so he's not standing here with me and Uwe and Ulf Kirsten at the players' entrance, but another man is. I'm not sure who he is though, embarrassingly. He's tall, in his 70s with balding grey hair and a leather jacket. He points to a black and white photo on the wall behind him and smiles. I smile back. The photo shows a young player in a 1970s kit with long hair combed neatly, kneeling with the ball at his feet. I look closer. The caption underneath says, 'DDR-Oberliga Player of the Year, 1973.' The man points to himself. 'Me,' he says.

Hans-Jürgen 'Hansi' Kreische spent his entire playing career with Dynamo Dresden, from the mid-1960s to the late '70s, won five Oberliga titles and three domestic cups, and was the Oberliga's leading scorer four times. He was in the East Germany team in June 1974 for the World Cup match with West Germany (and missed a sitter from five yards after 20 minutes), after winning a bronze medal with East Germany at the 1972 Olympics. He won the double with Dresden in 1971 and 1977 and scored 143 goals in total for his home town club.

But it wasn't all highlights for Hansi and he had his fair share of run-ins with the authorities. While he would surely have turned the Olympic bronze medal into gold with his national team-mates in Montreal in 1976, he was left at home as punishment after the Stasi got wind of a bet he'd made. It was a friendly bet, of five bottles of whisky, made after the 1974 World Cup match with West Germany. But the problem was who the bet was made with: the West German Finance Minister. Kreische said that West Germany would win the World Cup, and it was agreed that only the Finance Minister would have to honour the bet in any case, as Kreische didn't have the means to find or send whisky across the border. Of course West Germany did win, and the Minister sent the whisky as promised.

Kreische was aware he was in a bit of trouble at the time, seen at the least to be fraternising with the ideological enemy and maybe even considering worse, but the matter was soon over. Meanwhile, Kreische wasn't picked for the national team squad travelling to Montreal. It was only years later, when he was able to read his Stasi file, that he realised that the bet was the reason he was blacklisted and permanently expelled from the national team. His club career came to an end two years later after a number of further disputes with club officials, but Hansi remains a Dresden idol.

He has no regrets, explaining to the BBC in an interview last year, 'That I could be part of that 1974 World Cup was overwhelming. And that we could prove we could play good football on the other side of Germany was wonderful.' Of the whisky bottles he adds, 'I shared them with my friends. It was good whisky. Black & White.'

By the turning season Kreische had long retired from playing, worked as a Dynamo Dresden youth coach and, briefly, as the first team manager. Ulf Kirsten meanwhile went on to an illustrious career in the west with Bayer Leverkusen, playing with a reunited Germany in two World Cups and one European Championships and appearing in the 2002 Champions League Final. He was still on the bench though when Zinedine Zidane struck his wonder volley in that final, so wasn't able to stop the talismanic Frenchman in the way his old friend Stübner had done Platini before him.

Kirsten made over 500 club appearances for Dresden and Leverkusen, played 49 times for East Germany, 51 times for Germany and is ranked seven in the all-time list of Bundesliga goal scorers. His career strides over the *Wende*. He even bagged a sponsorship deal with Braun, famous as he was for his beard growth as much as his marksmanship. But, as he says, Stübs was the talent.

Ulf and Hansi are among the Dynamo legends. There are others: Matthias Sammer, Ralf Minge, Torsten Gütschow – who was the league's leading scorer for each of its final three seasons and the last ever DDR Footballer of the Year. Before them Hans-Jürgen 'Dixie' Dörner, twice double-winning captain and three-time DDR Footballer of the Year, who straddled that era and the previous golden generation of Hansi Kreische and Matthias's father Klaus Sammer in the 1970s. But despite this illustrious list, I sense that it's still Stübner that stands out. Ulf and Hansi remember Stübs fondly today, as the talent in their team as well as a friend. But he was a friend who was hard to find, and becoming increasingly lost. His is a very different tale from the one which tells of opportunity and riches beyond the turning point of 1989. Jörg's life took a different turn after the turning season.

'The only reason I started writing the book was I wanted to try to help him.' I meet Uwe Karte in an Italian restaurant in Dresden-Neustadt the night before the Saxon derby. 'And my biggest wish was to see Jörg with the finished book,' he says. 'This was the last chance to help him.'

Originally from Leipzig, Uwe grew up a fan of Lokomotive. 'In my class there were four Uwes!' he says, all named after West German striker Uwe Seeler. He remembers being taken as a seven-year-old to the Zentralstadion to see UEFA Cup matches against Torino, Wolverhampton Wanderers, Ipswich Town and Tottenham Hotspur in 1973/74. Later he met Leipzig players of the '60s: Frenzel, Löwe, Geisler and Drößler. 'Wonderful boys,' he says, 'the heart of Lok.'

But in 1990 he moved to Dresden to work as a newspaper sports editor and these days hangs around with Ralf Minge, Heiko Scholz and Ulf Kirsten instead. One of his first assignments was to cover the *World Football* Gala in Cologne, where he was one of few journalists from the east to speak to Lothar Matthäus, the World Player of the Year for 1990, and so got his first big story. 'The DDR was a little country,' he explains, 'and that's part of my story. At that time when I spoke with people at the *DFB* I'd say I'm one of the few people here from East Germany. You, in the west, have the biggest success but we in the east have the better stories. The DDR was a crazy country. It was *other* from the rest of the world. And football in East Germany was equally strange.'

Uwe has gone on to tell many of those strange stories, chronicling his adopted Dynamo Dresden along the way, but perhaps the one closest to heart was yet to come and when the time was right he knew he had to help it be told. 'We were the same age,' he says. Uwe was born in 1966, Stübner in '65. 'I'd known him since 1990 and we'd occasionally worked together doing a piece about Dynamo for the stadium programme or something like that. Then in 1995 I made a little film with him, about him when he was playing for FV Dresden Nord in the fifth division. We met again in November 2003, at Ulf's testimonial.' Some 36,000 people turned out to honour Ulf Kirsten, and many of his former team-mates played in the match, including Stübs. Although in the days leading up to the match he'd been very hard to contact and it was a relief when he finally did show up.

'I saw him again in 2009 at the opening of the new Dynamo Stadium, and then we met again in 2010, when I was working on a story about Matthias Sammer.' Sammer had left Dresden in 1990 and gone on to a glittering career in the west with Stuttgart, Inter Milan and Borussia Dortmund, winning the Champions League and the 1996 European Championships where he was named Player of the Tournament. From 2006 he was technical director of the

German FA and credited with playing a major role in the resurgence of German football in the late 2000s. Sammer's career, post-*Wende*, is in stark contrast to that of Jörg Stübner. He was presumably a very wealthy man by then, working at the heart of world football. Jörg, by this time, was surviving with the help of social security and battling painful personal problems. Struck by the contrast, it was around this time that Uwe started to think about telling his story, trying to find the right way in to Jörg's world.

'In 2015 he turned 50 and I suggested to Ralf Minge that we do something to celebrate. So on his birthday we went to see him and Minge was wearing a Dynamo shirt with "Stübner" and "50" on it and I made a little film for him. We wanted him to see that the players who played with and against him had so many good memories of him. He wasn't at home but we left the shirt for him. He phoned a couple of days later to thank us, and said that we should auction off the shirt to raise money for the youth team. I thought that really summed up Jörg.'

It's clear that Uwe is referring to his generosity, but also to the fact that he never really wanted the limelight. He was alone and maybe also didn't know how to be helped.

'And then I really started to think about a book which would tell his story. It took some time to persuade him to do it. He was the sort of person who didn't say very much. After a few years of talking to other people about him eventually we met again, with Ulf Kirsten and Heiko Scholz. These three players had known each other since 1978 when they were at sports school together, but they hadn't seen Jörg for 15 years, since Ulf's testimonial game. It was after this meeting that I was able to speak to Jörg more freely about everything. I think after that meeting he thought maybe things could get better. In the December he came to watch a Dynamo game and then to every game. He even got a part-time job working at a football school.'

Now Jörg was talking, something he obviously found difficult to do, Uwe went back to the start, to the young Stübs with a bright future ahead of him.

'This crazy life begins in Mongolia,' Uwe says. Jörg was born in Freiberg. His mother came from a town nearby and his father had studied geology at Freiberg University. At the time the DDR was mining for gold in Mongolia and Jörg's father was asked to lead an expedition there, taking his family with him. Jörg was two years old and his brother a year younger. 'They were the only children on the expedition so it was difficult for them,' says Uwe, 'with no streets, no water – in the summer it was hot, in the winter cold.'

They stayed in Mongolia for four years until the children started school. Then later they went back for six-month spells during the summer. 'At that time they didn't know any other children. Jörg first went to school in Halle but after six years he moved to Dresden and his friends were left behind in Halle.' He was homesick. It was a pattern that would continue with 'no real group of friends, no friend for life by his side'.

'Maybe I was the only person who was close to Jörg in the end, I don't know,' says Uwe, talking of how they started working closely together on the book, 'I had to cross the river by ferry to meet him. I never went to his flat. We only ever met in the same café: always at the same table, at the same seats, with him on the left, me on the right. That was very typical of Jörg.'

The title of the book is *Stübner: Popstar against his will.* 'I thought about the title for a long time. Popstar is right. In DDR football there were two real popstars. The first one was Peter Ducke at Carl Zeiss Jena and the other one was Jörg Stübner.' You could perhaps add Hansi Kreische as a third, I think. But it's clear from what Uwe goes on to describe later, that Jörg wasn't cut out to cope with such stardom and that the subtitle is right too. 'Still it's good to have this book now,' he adds. It's good for the fans, who've never forgotten him.

No other club in the DDR had as many fans as Dynamo Dresden and Jörg was one of the reasons. I'd met up with Dynamo fans Andre and Bastian on my first night in Dresden in the clubhouse of SV Helios 24, a local club playing at the eighth level, and where the friendly host gave me an extensive tour of the facilities, including an immaculately kept *Kegelbahn* (bowling alley).

The Helios clubhouse and pitches are very near the racecourse where 10,000 people queued overnight to get tickets for that UEFA Cup semi-final against Stuttgart in 1989. In the desperate rush once the barrier was opened unexpectedly early some people sleeping in tents were injured and there were, now dispelled, rumours of deaths. Andre and his mates were in that queue, taking it in turns to bunk off school and swap in, before his dad took over for them. Andre remembers other school days as a Dynamo fan and of his frustration at not being able to follow his team to away matches – apart from those just about near enough in Riesa, Chemnitz or Leipzig – because they had school on Saturdays until 11am, which didn't leave time to get to the station and then to the match.

Of those that they could get to, Andre says, 'I told my mum and dad that I was being taken by my friend's parents but that wasn't true. We'd run off to the station with our school bags and get the train to Leipzig or wherever.' The point he's making, the reason he was so desperate to be there was to see his favourite player, Jörg Stübner.

'Jörg played his first game in the first division just the same as he played his 100th game,' continues Uwe. 'And all the young fans said "wow".' He was a fans' favourite throughout his career, a gifted and hard-working player who was good-looking too, giving him pop star appeal.

Mention the pre-*Wende* Dynamo team to anyone over 40 in Dresden and Stübner's name will come up quickly. I hadn't heard of him before my first trip to Dresden, unlike others of his generation whose names have travelled – Kirsten and Sammer from Dresden, or Thom and Doll from Dynamo Berlin. But Stübner's name hasn't. Of course this is largely due to his lack of a post-reunification Bundesliga career, but even throughout my own travels among the Oberliga clubs over the past two years, it was only once I got to Dresden that his name started coming up, with fondness and sadness.

Stübner started his youth career with Motor Halle in 1973 and moved on to Dynamo Dresden at the age of 13. He made his debut in the first team at 18 and over the next ten years made 182 appearances, winning back-to-back Oberliga titles and three cup finals – including the double in the turning season. He played 47 times for East Germany, scoring once in a friendly against Bulgaria, and was in the last ever line-up that played Belgium in September 1990, alongside Heiko Scholz. After reunification a month later he stayed on with Dynamo for their first two seasons in the Bundesliga, with no lucrative move westwards materialising for him as it did for others of his generation, but he played in just five Bundesliga matches, with injury and fatigue taking their toll.

Later he slipped back to amateur football – playing first for Sachsen Leipzig, then Neubrandenburg, Eresburg Obermarsberg, and FV Dresden Nord – and further and further into relative football obscurity. This, the man who once had Platini in his pocket. He scored his last goal at the Dynamo Stadium in Ulf Kirsten's testimonial in 2003.

I ask about Jörg's friends in the team, how he came to feel isolated even before the events of 1989. 'Every day after training he was the first to leave,' says Uwe. 'The other players wanted to spend time with him, he was a popstar after all, and at least when they drank together they thought he was their friend. One player told me that on a Monday he would ask Jörg to come for a drink that evening. The next day another player would say the same. On Wednesday a third player … and the result was sometimes Jörg was in the pub every night of the week. But the others were there only once a week. After four or five years of that you see that it's no life for a football player.'

It took its toll; he was tired and could no longer do what he used to on the pitch. 'That was one of the problems,' continues Uwe. 'The second problem was drink. And the third problem was painkillers. His dad had told him if he wasn't able to play he was a failure, so he took painkillers to get through the match. At first you only need one tablet, but then more and more to keep you going. Jörg's father was a dominating presence in his life. Good for the story. But not necessarily good for Jörg.' By 1990 he was burnt out.

'The stories of east and west are stories of the east.' Uwe had mentioned the rich strangeness of stories from the east side of the divide earlier. Dynamo Dresden is a big club which attracts big stories and big scores. If the 7-6 scoreline against Bayern Munich wasn't peculiar enough, in the quarter-final of the 1985/86 European Cup Winners' Cup Dresden faced Bayer Uerdingen and were subject to a notorious turnaround. Winning the first leg at home 2-0, with goals from Lippmann and Pilz, by half-time in the second leg Dynamo were 5-1 up on aggregate and cruising. The Dresden goalkeeper Bernd Jakubowski was taken off injured at half-time and replaced by reserve keeper Jens Ramme. It was Ramme's debut and it turned out catastrophic: he conceded six goals in 28 minutes and the tie finished 7-5 to Uerdingen. Poor Jens Ramme would make only 12 appearances for Dynamo over three years, before moving on to Bischofswerda (which doesn't even exist!). 'If East German football was a history of snatching defeat from the jaws of victory, the Uerdingen debacle was its nadir.' (McDougall, 55)

Not even Stübner could prevent the embarrassment. He was playing that night. 'It's also a story about Jörg too,' says Uwe. 'Before the second leg the Stasi thought he would stay in the west. The team were on their way to the airport in the morning to fly to Düsseldorf and then by bus to Uerdingen. The Stasi looked in Jörg's locker in the changing room. They were looking for a letter from a Polish woman who had gone to the west just weeks before. She'd written a letter to Jörg and the Stasi were looking for it. If they'd found it they would have stopped him travelling to Uerdingen and surely taken him to prison. We spoke about it in the café years later and he remembered everything. He remembered the letter and that he'd put it in his jacket pocket just before he left for the airport. "I'm not stupid," he said.'

I ask if Uwe thinks Jörg ever did consider defecting (*Republikflucht*). 'I asked him about that and he said no, he didn't want to stay in the west. He had a thousand chances to defect but he didn't take them.' But one man did flee. Frank Lippmann, whose goal in the second leg of the quarter-final would be his last for the club, defected to the west on that very trip to Uerdingen. 'I read Jörg's file,' says Uwe, 'and it said that the first person they thought would try to stay in the west was Stübner, not Lippmann. Lippmann maybe the second [he had his troubles with the authorities, including crashing his car into a police van on the way home from a party and fleeing the scene]. But they were wrong about that one.'

The *Wende* was a turning point for all aspects of people's lives and it's hard not to see it as a direct shift in Stübner's fortunes. 'At first in 1989/90 everybody thought about themselves,' says Uwe. And right from the start Jörg was left behind. 'Initially he had an agent, but he fired him after an argument and he didn't get a new one. It was the same problem for him: that it was hard for him to speak to people. He had a chance at Unterhaching and at Cologne but it didn't work out. He would have had to go to Munich or Cologne and speak to them but I don't think he even tried. It was really difficult for him to speak to strangers. He even tried to avoid speaking to taxi drivers.'

I think about meeting Ulf and Hansi at the Dynamo Stadium, seeing the ease with which they spoke to the fans flocked round them, consummate popstars. The contrast once again is stark.

'It was the old thing from his father,' Uwe goes on. 'He felt like a failure. Sammer and Kirsten had a lot of money, all the headlines, fans and followers. But Jörg didn't have any money. And when the time came he just wasn't prepared for life without football.' By the mid-1990s, so soon after the *Wende* and the end of his playing career, life was very hard for Jörg. His parents divorced and he cut off contact with his father. He had no job, disputes with his neighbours which led to him losing his apartment, and was drinking increasingly heavily. He attempted suicide in 1995. 'But at the same time he hadn't been prepared for life as a football star,' Uwe adds. 'He often said he wished he could have had a normal life. And by the end Jörg was very alone.' There was no one there to speak to, even if he'd been able to. Until he started talking to Uwe, I think, but then maybe it was too late.

I ask Uwe about Jörg's family, beyond the presence of his father. 'I met his mother, who's in her 80s, and his brother only after he died,' says Uwe. 'He didn't want me to meet them while we worked on the book. We spoke in the March [2019] about publishing in November. He was happy about that and wanted to lose 10kg [1.5 stone] by the publication day. The book was nearly finished. In May it was difficult for them because his brother was diagnosed with cancer around that time, and Jörg drank too much. By June it was a little bit better and we met up then. At that time he brought me some of his personal history: photo albums, documents. On 17 June he gave me some of his school reports and said he'd bring me more. That was in the café a week before he died.

'He passed away on 24 June 2019, and the next day I went to the flat with Ralf Minge and his mother and brother, and we spoke about what we might do. To think that Jörg had been sitting in this chair only yesterday.'

* * *

It's hard not to see the shifts of the *Wende* as inextricably linked to Jörg's own life, to the loss that he felt and ultimately his own loss. But the turn came and we don't know any other way. 'If the *Wende* hadn't come,' says Uwe, 'if the DDR had continued, maybe it would have been a little bit easier for Jörg; but the end, perhaps, would have been the same. In the old system he would have got a job at the club as a youth trainer, but with the drink problems maybe not even that. And to say he had problems as a result of the *Wende* – that the difficulties, like the fact that he had no money, were caused by that – is the perfect explanation for himself, yes. But it's only half the story. The other half is just that it hurts. The football was over for him, and it hurt.'

The world was changing fast and a young Uwe, who would fare better than Jörg, was there to see it in Leipzig. 'On 9 October 1989 I was at the first big demonstration. We were very afraid. But after that night things changed and it wasn't like before in the DDR. Normally at the end of the day there would be blood. But whereas one week before there were

20,000 people demonstrating, on 9 October they said there were 30,000–40,000, but it was more like 70,000.

'And from then on people's lives had a different tempo. Before life was slow and people had so much time, because the country was small and the borders were high. You knew what you'd be doing in 20 years or 40 years from now. But on 9 October it felt like the decision was made [a month before the *Mauerfall*]. Every day after that you wanted to read the newspaper to see what had happened: new people, new thoughts. From 9 October to 9 November was the best time in my life. Because during these four weeks I thought now anything can happen, anything is possible. At this time it meant a new type of DDR, not east and west together.'

But after 9 November, Uwe noticed another turn, 'It was a Thursday and the following Monday I heard a new noise: one I had never heard before. It was the sound of an empty beer can on the street. I had never heard this before because in the DDR there were no beer cans on the street. You either took them home or if you dropped them someone else would take them home, to make a pyramid out of them. I told you the DDR was special! I heard the sound of the beer can on the ground and I thought, now the world has changed.'

First the call was for a new East Germany, a new type of socialism. Later came the call for reunification – a shift from 'we are the people' to 'we are one people' – which signalled the end for the DDR itself. And Uwe goes on to sketch a third turn, perhaps a turning back, a 'wall in the head' that still exists today and can be seen among other things in football, 'In the summer of '91 Dynamo played in the Bundesliga. The first away match was in Hamburg and I remember my neighbour said to me "now we are together". But perhaps just five or six months later it felt other than that. Even by then the euphoria was dead.'

Football was just one part of the swallowing up of East German life that began in 1990 and, as Alan McDougall has concluded, 'What happened to football was a microcosm of the unification experience in the East. Initial euphoria gave way to disappointment, displacement, and – among some people at least – an embrace of the GDR past in all of its absurdities.' (McDougall, 324)

I think about that euphoria of just 18 months before, the borders already down, when for a brief period after the *Mauerfall* – initially aided by an international break – young fans all over East Germany headed to the west, on the very next weekend and the one after that, to buy records or go to a match. That meant going to the nearest interesting game or, ideally, going to see the western team that you'd always followed. It was normal for young fans in the DDR to have two favourite teams.

Like Andre: the Dynamo fan who'd spent his childhood Saturdays racing to catch a train to away matches, but only those nearby and only in the east. 'Most of us had a second team in the west,' Andre explains. 'My team was HSV and after the Wall came down, maybe two or three weeks later, we went to Hamburg to see them play. There were free tickets for people from the east.'

Andre was back in Hamburg two years later for that first Dresden away trip in the Bundesliga, and felt another turn, matching Uwe's description of the waves of them. Andre explains, 'I was wearing two scarves – one Dynamo, one HSV – and the Hamburg people looked at me and said, "You can't do that." But it was normal for me to have two teams before.

'Then later on I thought about it and realised they were right. So for the next Dynamo match I put aside the Hamburg scarf and I never wore it again.'

It wasn't just the season that turned. I think about Jörg Stübner, increasingly lost in a new place, and about stereotypes of life in the DDR: grey conformity, row after row of *Plattenbauten*. No stars. But Jörg was a popstar of the DDR. He was still only 24 years old when the Wall came down. I think back to standing in the World of the DDR museum yesterday, in a shopping centre just down the road from here, and how looking around I was reminded as I have been many times on this journey that the life of the country stopped suddenly at the end of the 1980s. By 1990 it was pretty much gone, a thing of the past to be disbanded, deciphered and made into a peculiar version of itself in museum-time.

So of course everything here feels to me like the 1980s, and the feeling is that of my own youth too, which I now often see through a filtered version of the football matches I watched back then. I choose to do that of course. I was 16 in 1989 and spent every possible waking hour kicking a ball about with my mates on local park pitches, usually until after dark. We'd drag ourselves home in the end, desperate for one more kick. The nostalgia of it, the looking back and not forwards, has its dangers; and there is certainly an increasing industry which taps into *Ost*algie, in positive and negative, connected to this. But I can't help thinking now that Jörg, or at least this version of him, was somehow stuck back then – not allowed or not understanding how to grow up – stuck in 1985, in a DDR shirt, mowing the lawn of the Zentralstadion, marking Platini. Trapped, not in the DDR, but in the *world* of it.

Back in the Italian restaurant in Dresden-Neustadt I thank Uwe for spending so much time speaking to me. 'I could tell you two thousand stories about football in the DDR,' he says, 'but you'd have to stay in Dresden for months!' I promise to come back. I sense Uwe loves talking about Jörg and loved the talking they did together. But it was sadly cut short before they were finished. His book stands as a tribute to the life of this talented and troubled man, his friend, whose eulogy he gave at the funeral.

'Jörg was not one person, not two people,' he says as we leave, 'he was three or four people, maybe more. The first Jörg was a very good person. The second Jörg was quite a difficult person. The third Jörg was a terrible person. And all the different people inside him fought with each other. But he was special. We had good times. We had many conflicts too, but the time we spent together was unforgettable. And in the end the book is the result of how well we spoke to each other: I to him, he to me.'

# Blue Monday

NEAR THE start of this journey I was in Aue, in the far south of what was the DDR, thinking back to the night the lights came on at their Otto-Grotewohl-Stadion in October 1989. And now, nearing the end of it I've reached as far as it's possible to be from there among the 14 clubs in my league. I'm in the far north and at the end of the road. Any further north beyond here, when the Inner German border existed, was a line in the Baltic Sea known as the 'Blue Border'. I've reached Rostock where at tonight's match, in opposition to the story of Aue, the lights will literally, and later metaphorically, go out. It's Monday, 9 March 2020. Blue Monday.

Sorry about the over-dramatisation. Basically Hansa Rostock play in blue, I arrived in Rostock on a Monday and the first person I met when I got here was a man dying cloth blue. But then the New Order song is a cracker, so I take the apology back. I'm referring to this chapter as my 'blue period' and I'm off to the match.

At the Ostseestadion, for the evening kick-off against Eintracht Braunschweig in the 3. Liga, there's a lot of talk, banners and chants about the fact that it's a Monday, and none of it positive. While 30 years ago Monday-night demonstrations meant a very different thing, today there are ongoing large- and small-scale protests against Monday night football, here and elsewhere across the country, aimed at the FA and TV companies. Accepting that European club competitions are played on midweek evenings, and the necessity to play some cup matches and rescheduled fixtures midweek, German football fans want their league football at the weekends, specifically on Saturdays, when fans young and old can be there, and where the schedules are not dictated by the TV broadcasters. There were similar protests previously against Friday and Sunday evening fixtures, and as well as for younger fans the concern then and now is for travelling supporters who struggle to get to grounds on time for, or home from, these fixtures.

Tonight as part of the protest the travelling Braunschweig fans remain entirely silent throughout the first half, adding to the eeriness of what occurred just after kick-off. But the bigger question for fans of German football, as for those of leagues around the world, is that of whom football belongs to if not to the fans? The global game is increasingly allowed to belong to corporate sponsors, broadcasters, and at best viewers watching at home on TV. This is wrong. The protests against Monday football have succeeded in the case of the 1. and 2. Bundesliga, but in the 3. Liga and fourth-level Regionalliga the fight goes on. To the point where tonight the mascots walking out of the tunnel with the players are not the usual shy or grinning children, but their shy and grinning grandparents, the older generation showing solidarity with the young and making the point very well that those who should be the mascots for this match are at home tucked up in bed with lights out, probably before half-time.

In the case of this evening's match though, with mid-table Rostock taking on sixth-placed Braunschweig, the youngsters' lights will be on for longer than ours. Less than a minute after kick-off two of the four sets of floodlights fail and the Baltic Sea Stadium is plunged into semi-darkness. I don't think it's part of the protest, but I wouldn't put it past the ingenuity of the average German fan who I've discovered on my journey is constantly protesting and is very good at it.

During the delay in play some Rostock supporters improvise a new addition to the protest, unveiling a hastily penned banner suggesting 'Even the floodlights aren't up for Monday night football'. But after 20 minutes the lights are fixed and have warmed up sufficiently to illuminate Hansa's first goal one minute after the restart – John Verhoek's toe poke past a still-napping Eintracht keeper. On 14 minutes Daniel Hanslik adds a second after a jinking run into the box, and right at the death Verhoek gets his second, the pick of the bunch after a flowing move, to see Hansa finish 3-0 winners. The Baltic blue is happy, sort of.

Earlier in the afternoon, having just arrived in this city of blue and waiting for my friend Jan to arrive from Hamburg, I had a stroll around the old town. I came across a lovely, small house painted blue and white. The only word I could understand on its sign was *werkstatt* so I gathered it was a workshop for some sort of art or craft. In front of the building was an elderly man with a big white beard sitting on a bench smoking a cigarette. He was wearing a yellow jumper, a red scarf and beret and looked every bit the picture. So I paused briefly, admiring the building and him, and then without really having thought about why, I went up to him and said the only thing I could think of, which was '*Kunst*' (art). He didn't seem as alarmed as he probably should have been and replied firmly, 'Ja.' He put his cigarette out, stood up and walked into the house, clearly expecting me to follow.

I spotted a name on the door as we went in, and later studied the sign outside more closely, 'Blaudruck Werkstatt Haase'. Inside was Herr Haase's 'Blueprint' textile workshop with beautiful, intricate patterns on blue cloth hanging over all the walls and more in the process of being printed on a large table in the middle of the room.

A calming and magical place, full of blue, I assumed the workshop and its techniques had been in the Haase family for many generations and that this friendly grey-beard in red and yellow was its latest warden, charged with taking care of all the blue. This is true of Herr Haase but in fact his family took over the workshop from its previous owners only one generation ago; today the 'Blueprint' workshop is one of only a handful of its kind still active.

Herr Haase produced an old hardback book with black and white photos and took me through the whole, highly involved printing process in great detail, which was impossible for me to follow. But I enjoyed the lesson nonetheless, as what's not to like in a world of blue? At one point I said, 'I'm sorry, my German isn't very good.' But Herr Haase ignored this, replied, 'Your German is good' (which it clearly isn't), and proceeded to pat his heart. I thought at the time he was reminding me that it's the goodness inside that counts, but thinking about it afterwards I think he might have meant, 'Your German is indeed hopeless but at least you're still alive.'

Later he would tell me – then tell me and my fiend Jan, who I took to the 'Blueprint' workshop the next day and who got the same detailed explanation of the printing process; and then tell me and my wife, who I also took to the blue house the day after that and who also got the same detailed explanation – that he speaks three languages, what I heard to be: German, Bad German, and gobbledegook. Never mind that the second of these was actually *Platt* German, a dialect of the Northern Low German language, it was the gobbledegook that was certainly true and what I came to love him for. Still, on this first visit Herr Haase and I shook hands, patted our hearts agreeing that they were in good working order, and I went on my way thanking him for showing me his wonderful blueprint.

Jan arrived a few hours later in good health and in time for the match, and before I'd even had a chance to tell him about meeting this joyful and eccentric man in his blue world, by chance he started telling me about another connotation of Blue Monday. Jan is a teacher and in the middle of his half-term so didn't need to avoid work to get to Rostock today. If he had done though, he explained, he'd have been having a *Blauen Montag* – a translation of the English 'pulling a sickie' or skive off, and a phrase which some say originates from Blaudruck workshops like Herr Haase's. The day the cloth was traditionally hung out to dry, and in the process turn blue, was a Monday. This might take all day and there was little else to do but put your feet up, have a cigarette on the bench outside your shop or go to the pub. Others cottoned on to this as a potential excuse for doing the same and when asked claimed it to be a Blue Monday.

Feeling the opposite of the Blues, something about Herr Haase's insistence on a healthy heart and the fact that he repeatedly exclaimed *Freude* (joy) having put a spring in my step, as if on an unexpected day off, I move on to think about the life of this place and its football club. It's what I'm here to do after all, day off or not. I think about the lifeline of Hansa Rostock. A quick glance at it suggests this one is different from all the others, its line unlike most of the clubs I've been to on my journey through the Oberliga. The shape of Hansa Rostock's history is as idiosyncratic as Herr Haase's hat.

Hansa Rostock are known as the *Kogge*, in reference to the sailing ships, called cogs, which moved between the ports of the Hanseatic League – a trading confederation of merchant guilds and towns along the Baltic and North Sea coasts in the late Middle Ages. So it's apt that the football club of this Baltic port city remembers its maritime past.

But this is peculiar too. The club's origins are actually a long, long way from the sea or from here, in fact as far away as a town called Lauter on the Czech border, just down the road from Aue. Midway through the 1953/54 season it was decided, in one of the more ridiculous of the dismantling and reshuffling of East German clubs, that while the area of Saxony around Aue had more than enough competitive clubs, Wismut Aue and Motor Zwickau among them, the area around Rostock in Mecklenburg-Vorpommern could do with one. With the season in full swing the team of Empor Lauter, then top of the Oberliga, was moved pretty much wholesale 300 miles away to the other end of the country to become Empor Rostock and take the Lauterers' place in the Oberliga.

They fared fairly well fairly quickly, and established themselves as the team that liked to come second: finishing runner-up in the league five times and losing the cup final on four occasions between 1955 and 1968. At the time of the establishment of the 11 football 'focus clubs' in 1965/66 they became FC Hansa Rostock, in a nod to the Hanseatic League, and remain so to this day, cogs and silver medals and all. The poor Lauterers were the real runners-up though, as the team has struggled on in a number of guises in the lower reaches of local football, not quite 20,000, but quite a few leagues under the Baltic Sea.

Meanwhile, throughout the 1970s and early '80s Hansa Rostock were a mid- or lower-table Oberliga side with four single seasons in the second division. But they were in no rush to the top, it seems, and the real history of the club was to be written late on, in the very dying days of the DDR itself. As pretty much out of the blue, and not having won anything before, Hansa Rostock won the last ever DDR-Oberliga (for that season called the NOFV-Oberliga), claiming the title with three games to spare after a home win against second-placed

Dynamo Dresden. They followed that up by beating Stahl Eisenhüttenstadt 1-0 in the cup final at the Jahn Sportpark in Berlin to take an unforeseen league and cup double. Due to the abundance of the hairdo of the day among the squad, what became known as the 'triumph of the mullets' saw the *Kogge* finally set sail.

Sailing proudly into the Bundesliga for its first season post-reunification, alongside Dynamo Dresden who'd finished second, Rostock promptly finished in the bottom four and were relegated to the second division. They did, however, put some icing on the cake by beating Barcelona 1-0 in the second leg of their European Cup first round match (despite the fact that Laudrup and Goikoetxea had already eyed up the cake in the first leg with three goals between them). But four years later Rostock were back up again, after winning the second division title, and then marched on to play ten consecutive seasons in the Bundesliga, seven of them as the only club in the league from the former DDR.

Hansa Rostock is by a considerable distance the most successful East German football club in reunified German history. Despite falling to the 2. Bundesliga in 2005 and then, after one final fling in the top division, down to the 3. Liga in 2010, where they play today, life for the Blues of Hansa since the *Wende*, and against most of the odds, has been a healthy one.

For most of the clubs of the DDR-Oberliga Wikipedia shows a handy graph of the divisions in which they've played since World War II, including before and after the changes of the *Wende*. For almost all the clubs the line of the graph, which I'd come to see as a sort of historic health check showing each club's heartbeat through the decades, is very similar: a fairly consistent line performing at the highest level, before a sudden dropping down to the mid to lower end of the chart from 1991 onwards, and in a number of cases a further fall to the lowest levels. While in the case of a club like Lokomotive Leipzig the fall and rise is most dramatic, still the majority of the graph lines have roughly the same shape, before 1989 and after '91. This is Erfurt's, for example:

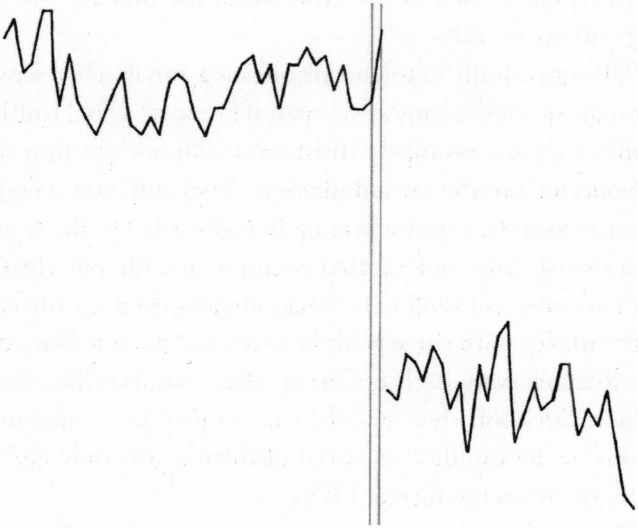

But Hansa Rostock is different:

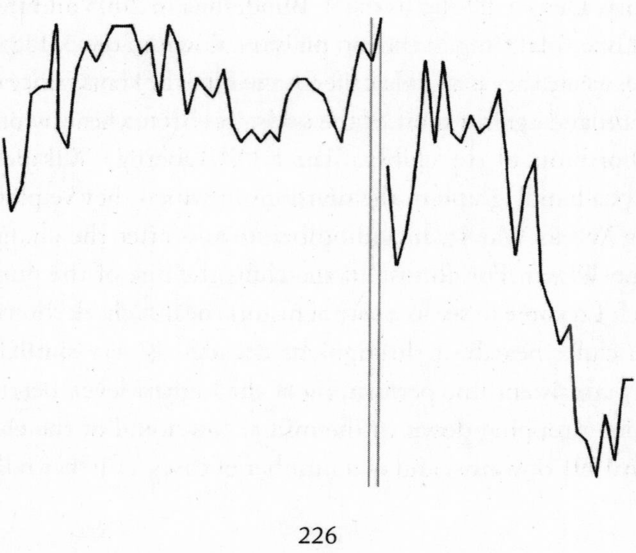

The health of a club is not measured by how high up the football pyramid it plays, of course. I nod again to Herr Haase who knows that a healthy heart means more than a medical; as I said I'll take the lower leagues over fizzy drinks football any day. And while Rostock's lifeline is different, its lifeblood is I'm sure the same.

The fans on the Monday night protests and the players who stick around to delight them are what hold a club together. Axel Schulz is one such player, a major part of this club's lifeblood for over 50 years and a loyal one-club man who has never forgotten how to be a fan too. Not to be confused with the heavyweight boxer Axel Schulz, our Axel is significantly smaller and I dare say gentler than the pugilist from Bad Saarow in Brandenburg; though checking now I can see that the boxer's known as 'The Gentle Giant', so maybe they're as gentle as each other.

Axel Schulz joined Hansa Rostock as a junior in 1967 and is still working for the club today. Slight-framed, he was a technical and intelligent midfielder who made 364 senior appearances between 1977 and 1993, scoring 61 goals. His time as a player crossed over the *Wende*; he appeared for Hansa briefly in the Bundesliga and played for East Germany three times as well as in a further six matches for the Olympic team.

Today he works as the club's sports coordinator, responsible for community and player liaison, and apart from a brief spell playing for a local amateur side at the end of his playing days, and a period managing the women's team of Polizei SV Rostock, he has been a lifelong and loyal fixture at the Baltic Sea Stadium. I chat to him there the day after the Monday night match in a room overlooking the pitch. 'I was born here. I've played for the club since I was eight years old,' he says. 'I like the idea that people stick to their club and don't look for a new one.'

Acknowledging that it's very difficult for anyone who didn't live in the DDR to understand the feelings of those that did, I ask Axel to think back to the time around the *Wende*, to what he remembers of 1989. 'It's quite a long time ago,' he says, 'so the memories aren't so clear. But I know the demonstrations were a big topic for a lot of people in those weeks. Of course, we were still relatively young and we were focused on football, our passion. But I was also interested in politics and I supported most of the demands of the first demonstrations, when it was still about reforming the DDR. In the end, I probably just didn't have the courage to join the demos. That doesn't flatter me much I know, but it's probably the closest thing to the truth.'

On 8 November, the night before the Wall fell, Hansa Rostock drew 3-3 with Lokomotive Leipzig in the pick of the week's results. Ten days into an uncertain future, after the events in Berlin and an international break, Hansa travelled to Bischofswerda (which must have existed then) and won 4-1. 'A lot of people demonstrated in Rostock too,' Axel continues. 'I was fine in the DDR. However, I saw a lot of things that were totally wrong in this state as well, but I was not a resistance fighter. And while as DDR citizens you couldn't go to France or even to West Germany, we as footballers had already been away on trips to capitalist countries. It wasn't so new for us.'

Axel had travelled with the national team but his club side had limited opportunity up until then. They'd qualified for the UEFA Cup in 1989/90 and in the first round tie against Banik Ostrava, from their own side of the Iron Curtain, were beaten 7-2 on aggregate. These would be the only competitive European club matches Axel would get to play in. He did still get to travel though, as he says, and remembers one trip to the west in particular from that time:

'It was summer 1989 and we went to play in Copenhagen. We had a player with us back then called Axel Kruse who played for Hertha Berlin later. But at that time he was with us. He was quite "lippy" and he'd actually had a travel ban for trips to the West previously. This was the first trip he was allowed to go on after the ban. We were room-mates, Axel Kruse and me. I think the match was on the Wednesday and on the Tuesday evening I wanted to go out for a smoke with my friend Juri Schlünz, and Axel Kruse asked if he could come with us. So we all went out and Axel Kruse said, "I'm just going to the shop to have a quick look, I'll catch you up." And we thought nothing of it. We carried on and then he was gone!

'We went back to the hotel and Axel Kruse hadn't turned up. Everyone was afraid the Stasi would come and question us. We didn't know what was going to happen, or if they thought we might have helped him escape or something. The chairman told me to prepare myself for a visit, and then someone from the Embassy did come. They spoke to me briefly and that was it. Nothing more came of it. We met Axel Kruse again about six months later, after the border was open. He came over and we laughed about it. He said he was sweating blood back then, and told us he'd had a liaison man there who had been waiting for him at the hotel, and that, yes, it was planned. It was funny afterwards, but at the time it was a bit edgy!'

The political turnaround matched the turn in fortunes of Hansa Rostock and thinking back to the next and final Oberliga season Axel can pinpoint the difference of the turn, 'The most significant thing perhaps, was that we got a manager from West Germany, Uwe Reinders, and he completely changed training.'

The relatively young Reinders, brought in from last night's opponents Eintracht Braunschweig in June 1990, introduced specialist football thinking, rather than the more usual imitation of the training plans for athletes and swimmers. But another significant reason related to the sale of the missing Axel Kruse. 'Once the Wall came down,' Axel Schulz explains, 'and he was able to play again [after the standard compromise period for players who'd defected] he transferred to Hertha Berlin and that deal was worth quite a lot of money to Hansa. Nearly all the other clubs in the Oberliga, and even in the leagues below, lost their best players to the west at that time, with players trying their best to earn some money there. But with the money they'd got from the Axel Kruse deal Hansa Rostock were able to keep the whole team from the season before together. There was a big advantage in this.'

Once the season started Rostock became unusually competitive, beating teams they'd never regularly fared well against, like Dynamo Berlin and Carl Zeiss Jena. After just three matches they were top of the league and they stayed there for the rest of the season. Axel stresses that Uwe Reinders remained a key factor in the success, 'He talked to the players well, as a friend, and we recognised that it was working and went from strength to strength.' So confident and smart was Reinders that he asked for a bonus to be put into his contract for winning the league and another for winning the cup. The board agreed, presumably thinking there was little to no chance of either. They were wrong. Already champions, by the time Rostock reached the cup final against Eisenhüttenstadt, Axel says, 'We were high fliers now and went into the match as favourites.' They won the cup 1-0.

There were Blue celebrations in Berlin that night but overall Axel remembers another feeling, 'People had others things to think about during that year – some had lost their jobs and had to deal with that, so there was less of a football atmosphere in society than there was in the years before and a lot less people in the stadiums.'

This had been starkly demonstrated when the Rostock players travelled to their own stadium to play the last league match of the season against Lokomotive Leipzig. Already champions, they hired a motorcade of eight cars and a motorbike for a victory parade through the city centre to the stadium. But no one turned up to cheer them home. Neither the manager nor the media knew what the players had planned, and nor did the fans. As Alan McDougall has noted, 'The only witness was an irate policeman.' Even if the fans had known about the parade it's clear they had other things on their minds at this time. 'The greatest season in Hansa's history was played in front of an indifferent public,' says McDougall (319).

Falling attendances – the average at the Ostseestadion in the double-winning year being half that of two seasons earlier, partly a result of rising ticket prices post-*Wende* – meant that football had to take a back seat, even in a motorcade.

As Hansa Rostock struck out into the Bundesliga, Axel's playing days were already approaching their end. His last full contribution had really been in the 1989/90 season and in the new world he was used infrequently and now as a wise *libero*, playing out from the back. He'd more than put in his shift though, rarely missing a match during the ten years up to that point. He played in eight matches in the Bundesliga and had to enjoy the 1-0 European Cup second-leg win against Barcelona from the stands like the fan he always was. 'I was injured,' he says, 'a cruciate injury which started in 1990. When I was able to play again the younger players were taking over! People ask me whether I was disappointed I didn't play for more years, because there was a lot more money involved by then. But I say no, we had fun. And perhaps more fun than nowadays, because with the pressures of social media the players are watched all the time now.'

It is telling and perhaps instructive for us today, that a player who spent most of his career as a citizen of a highly controlled and sophisticated surveillance state, says that modern players are watched all the time.

Axel doesn't need cheering up, but I point out anyway that he has an impressive record with the old national team. As well as cheerful, he's a modest man and doesn't seem to have realised that in his three caps – for matches against Greece, Mexico and Ecuador – the DDR were unbeaten. He was also part of the squad that qualified for the 1984 Olympics in Los Angeles but didn't go due to the Soviet-led boycotting of the Games. Axel has no regrets though and was happy to see that his club's best years were yet to come. For a full ten years from 1995 to 2005 Hansa Rostock held their place in the Bundesliga, perhaps the biggest achievement of all among any of the DDR-Oberliga clubs.

I ask Axel what he considers to be Hansa's greatest success: winning the double in 1991 or those ten years in the German top flight? 'For me,' he says, 'at the time the double was great, but bearing in mind that Hansa Rostock is now playing its eighth year in the third division, it's definitely the ten years in the Bundesliga that was the greatest achievement. We got a lot of things right over a long period of time,' as Hansa Rostock became the, self-proclaimed at least, 'club of the entire East'. (McDougall 326)

Axel Schulz was and still is a one-club man. Thinking back to the Axel Kruse story I ask him if he ever considered the same: fleeing from here, or leaving freely once he could? And it's clear from his answer that it's not only the club that he loves but the place it plays for. 'I never wanted to go away, because Mecklenburg-Vorpommern is my *Heimat* [homeland],' he says. 'It was never a discussion for me whether I would leave here and go to the west or anywhere else. This area is so wonderful

– the Baltic Sea coast, the islands, the lakes. Just a perfect place to live. Have you been to Warnemünde?'

He adds that family is far more important nowadays. A grandfather of three, his 60 years are hard to spot behind the youthful spirit. But this man has lived 30 years either side of the *Turn* and there is a wisdom to him, a sense of perspective carried from that. I also attribute the perspective, unashamedly romantically, to the blue Baltic Sea north of here – to the lighthouses of Warnemünde, where we did go as Axel said we should, and which is indeed lovely – and to the spirit of the city and its people. 'People here have a very strong connection to the club,' he says. 'It's an economically weak area, but the people are empowered through the football club. Hansa is important and a part of their lives.'

As we leave the Ostseestadion, through the gates placed here in 1954 after the long trip north from Lauter, I ask Axel if he has a favourite goal of his own. A *Tor* is a gate as well as a goal and despite mainly creating for others and later making things tick as a *libero*, he bagged a few too. 'It was two goals in the same game actually,' he says with a cheeky smile. 'The first one was a penalty against Stahl Riesa, a *Panenka*! And the other one was …'

He stops and points at the pitch behind us, and as he mimes curling the ball into the top corner from the edge of the box, his 60 years roll away in an instant.

He is as forever young as wise old Herr Haase sitting on his bench on Blue Monday.

*Postscript: The match between Hansa Rostock and Eintracht Braunschweig was one of three played that Monday night in the German higher leagues, the other two in Stuttgart and Offenbach. At the time of writing these were the last three matches played in any of the top four divisions in Germany, since social distancing measures were put in place as a result of the coronavirus pandemic. The same was soon true for most other countries. There were European club matches played later in that week but all behind closed doors, as* Geisterspiele *or ghost matches. The metaphorical cutting of the stadium lights I referred to at the start of the chapter has become a reality and football, among other things where people gather together, has paused – and been put into perspective by the awful effects of the virus worldwide. I was glad to have been able to see Rostock play, just in time, and to have completed my journey, but most glad to have met people like Axel and Herr Haase and so many others along the way. I headed home and I wish them well.*

# Crossing the line

THOMAS GOES to school in Wedding. Every day he crosses the bridge and later crosses back again. Unless he's going out to see Hertha play in the westend. Then he'll come back later via another bridge. His mother was born in West Germany. She moved to West Berlin in the mid-1980s and was on the other side of this bridge 30 years ago, welcoming the people when they crossed. His father is from this side, the east side, and 30 years ago he crossed over the bridge too. I don't know whether they're still together, after those first euphoric days and however many years. But every day Thomas, who's 17, walks across the same bridge, from east to west just like his dad did to meet his mum. 'It feels right to be here tonight,' I say to him on the Bösebrücke at Bornholmer Straße. 'I wanted to be on the bridge.' 'Me too,' he says. 'If it wasn't for this bridge I wouldn't exist.'

I'm here with Chris and Beke and about 500 other people of all ages at the Platz des 9 November 1989, on 9 November 2019. We're here to celebrate the anniversary of the *Mauerfall.* This is not one of numerous official events marking the anniversary: an outdoor video installation at seven sites across the city; a concert stage at the Brandenburg Gate; a ceremony on the Glienecke Bridge; an art installation of 30,000 messages floating above the city.

This is informal, a gathering, of the people. But at first it's as if the people don't really know what to do here without officialdom. But then that's maybe as it should be, as it was. We're happy to stand it out and wait until something happens, something to cheer. It doesn't take long. A car passes, honking its horn. Then another not honking, so a few people step into the road to slow it down, encouraging a press on the horn with smiles on their faces, only letting the car pass once the honk is agreed to. Then another car is waved by, then another. A bicycle passes, its rider with both hands in the air. There are big smiles and a big cheer for the cyclist, another cheer for a Trabi, a DDR car, then more cars honking their way across the bridge. Just like they did. I'm sure some drivers are crossing over, nipping down a side street and doubling back so they can cross over again. I imagine them taking off a hat or putting on a false beard to go again under cover, as someone else. As another of the thousands who crossed this bridge on this night 30 years ago.

Everyone's going the same way, every car and bike and Trabi. From east to west. Except the trams that is, they're going both ways. Some people on the trams aren't smiling and I don't know why not. The rain's stopped and more and more people step into the road to slow the cars and encourage a honk. A honk, then a cheer, then cross the bridge. I'm in the road now and have to jump out the way of a bike, which very nearly gets me squashed between a car and a tram coming the other way. It is wonderful. *Die Mauer muss weg!*

Earlier this afternoon Chris and I walked from Alexanderplatz towards the Brandenburg Gate to see what was going on. The evening's big gig was still a few hours away but already large crowds were heading westwards along Unter den Linden towards the gate. We'd already decided we wouldn't stay long. It wasn't the sort of celebration we were looking for: large scale, official and for broadcast. But soon the decision was made for us. Ironically, for an event marking the anniversary of the removal of a barrier, as we got very close to where the inner wall once stood on the east side, metal fences rose up in front of us.

Chris asked a policeman who said there was no way to get through and that going round would involve a very long walk. Better to head back east and take public transport all the way so that we could approach the gig from the front, he said, from the west. Right on the line of the old wall another had been built. Temporary, flimsy, but another barrier. For security, for the gig and the cameras. No thanks. *Die Mauer muss weg!* We leave as quickly as we can and have a beer on Torstraße. *Goal Street.* With a failing defence Egon Krenz, interim leader of the SED government in 1989, said, 'You know, in a game of football, when a free kick is awarded, a wall is formed in front of the goal. Free kicks are the results of fouls by the other team. Let us make sure together of fair play.'

* * *

Last night Dynamo Berlin played a Regionalliga Nordost fixture against Viktoria Berlin. The Lichterfelde Stadium near Tempelhof in the south-west is just ten miles from the Jahn Sportpark in the north-east where Dynamo plays. It's easy to draw a short line through the city from one ground to the other, but this is a Berlin city derby that couldn't have happened on that night 30 years ago. By the very next day though, it was already conceivable.

The tree-lined Lichterfelde Stadium on the banks of the Teltow Canal has a conspicuous police presence despite a crowd of 529, with the away support fenced in at one corner; while most of the home fans sit in the beautiful, curved art-deco main stand. 'This is real football,' says Daniel among the Viktoria supporters. An engineer from Neukölln, Daniel's parents fled East Berlin in the mid-'80s, he grew up this side of the divided city and was 11 when the Wall fell. He's here with his friend, a Viktoria fan, but Daniel likes to watch Dynamo whenever he can. 'We used to visit my grandparents in the East,' he says, 'and whenever I drive through Mitte now I can see myself as a little boy – but like in a black and white film. Nowadays we have colour.'

I ask if he'll be celebrating the colour tomorrow. 'I'm part of the history. I don't need a big party.' Daniel, who helps build the roads that connect the city, adds, 'Often, when I'm working somewhere like Potsdamer Platz, I think about that time, but in my own way.'

Back on the pitch Viktoria have the better of the first half, step up the pressure after the break, hit the post and have a shot cleared off the line. The atmosphere is cheerful. Before the final whistle the police are tucking in to bratwurst, and perhaps in homage to the spirit of 8 November 1989 the contest ends goalless. It doesn't lack bluster and blunder, including a booking for the Dynamo bench, has moments of flair in the drizzle, but it's all square in Berlin. Fittingly, in the dying minutes a Viktoria striker is brought down with a late tackle just outside the box. The Dynamo players gather to form a wall, the keeper screaming at them to move this way and that, to keep tight, not let anything through. I doubt very much if the players in the wall see any significance in their defensive job (I think it's just me!) but as the ball flies high over the crossbar the wall breaks up, dismantled by those that formed it.

On the evening of 8 November 1989 around 2,000 supporters gathered at the Friedrich-Ludwig-Jahn-Sportpark in East Berlin's Prenzlauer Berg district to watch Dynamo Berlin play out a goalless draw at home to Stahl Eisenhüttenstadt. The Berlin club's Oberliga dominance was already over and harder times were to come. On Dynamo Alan McDougall suggests, 'It is hard to imagine a more potent symbol of the decline of the game in the East after 1989.' (McDougall, 321)

The Jahn Sportpark holds about 20,000 so there was plenty of room for a wind of change that night. The stadium sits right up against what was the inner Berlin Wall in the east, the hinterland just behind it where the Mauerpark runs today, and is just a short walk from the bridge at Bornholmer Straße. Meanwhile, BFC Viktoria were struggling in the lowly Berlin Landesliga. In the old world before the *Wende*, in footballing terms at least, the two clubs were a world apart – Dynamo at the top level of East German football with those ten consecutive (albeit questionable) Oberliga titles to its name; while FC Viktoria's predecessors, BFC Viktoria and Lichterfelder FC (despite a successful pre-war history) were playing in the regional amateur leagues of the West German game. And they were in different countries. Sometimes something as simple as a game of football can shine a light on the absurdity of lines drawn. Thirty years on they are just two local teams, kicking a ball about not very well, in one city.

The world turned on 9 November 1989 but the turning season played on and six months later came to its own conclusion. 'Unruly and unpredictable, even when the destination of the league title was all too predictable, football was emblematic of the mixture of conformity and quiet rebellion that characterised society in the GDR's final decade.' (McDougall, 244)

The climax to the 1989/90 season was suitably wilful, in the balance until the very end, and ultimately finished a thriller. Going into the last day on 26 May 1990, Dynamo Dresden, FC Magdeburg and FC Karl-Marx-Stadt were all tied on 34 points at the top of the table, with Dresden edging into first place over Magdeburg by a single goal difference. Dresden would play an underperforming Lok Leipzig at home, while Karl-Marx-Stadt and Magdeburg would face each other in Karl-Marx-Stadt. Meanwhile, at the bottom of the table things were just as tight. Stahl Eisenhüttenstadt, Wismut Aue and Fortschritt Bischofswerda were tied on 16 points, with Bischofswerda (which I *think* exists) sitting bottom with a weaker goal difference. Two of the three would be relegated.

At half-time, with Dresden losing 1-0 and no goals in Karl-Marx-Stadt, Magdeburg are top of the league, as they have been for much of the season, and would be champions. Then for half an hour, between Karl-Marx-Stadt's goal on 52 minutes and Dresden's second to give them a 2-1 lead in their game, it is Karl-Marx-Stadt who would be champions. They cling on to the top spot until ten minutes before the end of the season, when the league's leading scorer Torsten Gütschow's strike on 81 minutes, followed by a third from Sven Ratke in the last minute of normal time, sees Dresden retain the title on goal difference. Karl-Marx-Stadt beat Magdeburg and finish second. A week later Dynamo Dresden make it a double with a cup final win against second division club PSV Schwerin.

It was equally gripping at the bottom. In a mirror of the other end of the table, relegation contenders Eisenhüttenstadt and Bischofswerda would face each other in the Iron Works Town; while Aue would travel to Berlin to play a sinking Dynamo. In only their second win of the whole season, Eisenhüttenstadt beat Bischofswerda 2-0 to survive and send Bischofswerda down. Meanwhile, despite winning 4-1 in the capital, and being safe for a tantalising five-minute period midway through the first half, Wismut Aue are relegated for the first time in 39 years. The Violets miss out on playing in the last Oberliga season and the unruly scrap for Bundesliga places.

A year later, 18 months after the fall of the Wall, the last ever goal was scored in the DDR-Oberliga: Heiko Weber, for

Carl Zeiss Jena against Energie Cottbus. On the last day of the previous season there had been 32,000 in the Dynamo-Stadion to watch Dresden clinch the title, but on 25 May 1991, in a new Germany, there were less than 3,000 there to see Weber net, fittingly in the 89th minute.

* * *

Back on the bridge, in 2019, we finally take the plunge. Chris, Beke and I start walking, crossing over the Bösebrücke past Bornholmer Straße station into west Berlin. We pause on the bridge for a photo. No one cheers us but we were cheered inside and ready for a drink. We continue on before turning the second left we come to down Jülicher Straße, heading for the Offside pub. 'This is where the people came 30 years ago, it must have been. The first pub you come to,' I insist to Chris and Beke. I don't think they believe me, but they're thirsty enough to humour me. They know that I've been seduced by the name. Offside. A pub with football ghosts, in a city full of them.

Chris says he thinks the Offside refers to the other meaning of *Abseits*, standing apart or out of the way. I think there's a sort of contrariness to lower league football fans everywhere, which is also worth celebrating, so either way it's perfect for a quiet pause on our gentle re-enactment of the peaceful revolution. But when we get there it's rammed. And the people don't look like they've just arrived after the revolution; they look like they've been here all evening avoiding the celebrations elsewhere. I need to plug in my vape, so I do. There's a loud bang and a flash of flame. Far from peaceful, I very nearly blow up Offside.

There's a game of darts going on. We call my wife and she says we're drunk. She's probably right, but we haven't noticed. We finish our drinks and Chris gets another from the corner shop opposite. Chris and Beke swear by the *Wegbier*. It feels doubly important now as it's a beer for the *way*, for the walk home, but also a beer for the 'going'. *Die Mauer muss weg!* The Wall has got to go! We go, continue down Jülicher Straße and turn left again on to Behmstraße. We're doubling back on ourselves, passing the site of *Die Plumpe* where Hertha Berlin played in front of thousands, and then across the Behmbrücke. I think about those fans from the east who couldn't get to the Plumpe ground after the border was strengthened so had to stand on this bridge and listen, taking their cues from the voices of the friends they could no longer stand beside. I wonder if some of them were there with us on the Bösebrücke tonight.

We're crossing back into the east now, heading towards the Jahn Sportpark and home to Prenzlauer Berg. After we cross the footbridge a small light catches our eyes, glistening just inside a playground at the north end of the Mauerpark. The playground is named after Bärbel Bohley, a brave dissident artist from Prenzlauer Berg who along with others in the newly formed New Forum movement 'found power lying on the street and picked it up'. The little light we've spotted is in the *Bärbel-Bohley Spielplatz*. 'I will get out of here,' she once snapped at an interrogator. 'You won't.'

We walk towards the little light. It's a tealight. A small candle left there by someone. But something about the way it's placed makes us look up and ahead. And there we can see another one – a small flame flickering a few metres ahead. This second candle directs our gaze in turn to the next one, a few metres ahead of that, and then to the next. We lift our heads to look further off and see a perfect line of lights, bending this way and turning that. They follow the course of the old wall, now gone after this night 30 years ago. In its place someone has placed a line of *Teelichter* here on the

Lichtburgring, for us to follow them all the way home. We are speechless.

# Appendices

## A) The DDR-Oberliga table (end of season) 1989/90

| | Goal difference | Points |
|---|---|---|
| Dynamo Dresden | +21 | 36 |
| FC Karl-Marx-Stadt | +15 | 36 |
| FC Magdeburg | +17 | 34 |
| Berliner FC Dynamo | +3 | 30 |
| Carl Zeiss Jena | +2 | 30 |
| Hansa Rostock | +5 | 27 |
| Energie Cottbus | -1 | 27 |
| Lokomotive Leipzig | +1 | 25 |
| Hallescher FC Chemie | 0 | 24 |
| Stahl Brandenburg | -2 | 24 |
| Rot-Weiß Erfurt | -11 | 19 |
| Stahl Eisenhüttenstadt | -9 | 18 |
| Wismut Aue | -11 | 18 |
| Fortschritt Bischofswerda | -30 | 16 |

## B) The 1989/90 DDR-Oberliga clubs at the start of the 2019/20 season

**2. Bundesliga** (second level)
Erzgebirge Aue
Dynamo Dresden

**3. Liga** (third level)
Chemnitzer FC
Hallescher FC
Carl Zeiss Jena
FC Magdeburg
Hansa Rostock

**Regionalliga Nordost** (fourth level)
Berliner FC Dynamo
Bischofswerdaer FV
Energie Cottbus
Rot-Weiß Erfurt
Lokomotive Leipzig

**Brandenburgliga** (sixth level)
FC Eisenhüttenstadt

**Landesliga Brandenburg-Nord** (seventh level)
Stahl Brandenburg

## C) The 'Eternal Table' of the DDR-Oberliga:

| | Points |
|---|---|
| **FC Carl Zeiss Jena** | **1,097** |
| **Berliner FC Dynamo** | **1,092** |
| **SG Dynamo Dresden** | **1,077** |
| **1. FC Lokomotive Leipzig** | **1,039** |
| **FC Wismut Aue** | **1,018** |
| FC Vorwärts Frankfurt/Oder | 1,012 |
| **FC Rot-Weiß Erfurt** | **972** |
| **1. FC Magdeburg** | **920** |
| BSG Sachsenring Zwickau | 888 |
| **Hallescher FC Chemie** | **874** |
| **FC Hansa Rostock** | **808** |
| **FC Karl-Marx-Stadt** | **769** |
| BSG Chemie Leipzig | 733 |
| 1. FC Union Berlin | 423 |
| SC Aktivist Brieske-Senftenberg | 395 |
| BSG Lokomotive Stendal | 356 |
| BSG Stahl Riesa | 326 |
| SC Einheit Dresden | 320 |
| BSG Rotation Babelsberg | 255 |
| **BSG Stahl Brandenburg** | **174** |
| BSG Waggonbau Dessau | 163 |
| BSG Stahl Thale | 121 |
| BSG Fortschritt Meerane | 117 |
| **BSG Energie Cottbus** | **117** |
| BSG Wismut Gera | 111 |
| SC Fortschritt Weißenfels | 102 |
| BSG Stahl Altenburg | 71 |
| BSG Chemie Böhlen | 65 |
| **BSG Stahl Eisenhüttenstadt** | **61** |
| BSG Empor Lauter | 60 |

| | |
|---|---|
| BSG Motor Steinach | 44 |
| BSG Chemie Zeitz | 44 |
| BSG Motor Wismar | 41 |
| SC Dresden-Friedrichstadt | 39 |
| **BSG Fortschritt Bischofswerda** | **33** |
| ASG Vorwärts Stralsund | 33 |
| BSG Turbine Weimar | 26 |
| BSG Einheit Pankow | 23 |
| FC Sachsen Leipzig | 22 |
| SC Neubrandenburg | 20 |
| SC Lichtenberg 47 | 20 |
| ASG Vorwärts Schwerin | 11 |
| BSG Chemie Buna Schkopau | 11 |
| BSG Motor Suhl | 5 |

Teams listed in bold competed in the 1989/90 Oberliga season.

(From *Zeitspiel* magazine, December 2019)

## D) *Das Rekordspiel*

On 8 May 2020 Lokomotive Leipzig played a significant match at their Bruno-Plache-Stadion. It was significant for a number of reasons. In the middle of the coronavirus outbreak, with football suspended it was a rare chance to cheer, at least from home, and to raise much-needed funds for the club. It was significant too for the number of tickets that were sold: 182,612. This smashed the record set at the Zentralstadion for their European Cup Winners' Cup semi-final against Bordeaux in 1987 (even bearing in mind that nobody really knows how many were there that night, and also bearing in mind that tickets for this latest match were €1 each).

Perhaps less significantly, but most delightfully, Leipzig's opponents at *das Bruno* were invisible. In line with and beyond social distancing guidelines there was only ever one Leipzig player on the pitch at any time, and 11 invisible opponents. There was much of the normal stuff of a matchday: exuberant goal celebrations, effing and jeffing from the touchline, pyrotechnics from the Fankurve, and a late appearance by the Leipzig mascot Lokki the lion. It was expansive football (there was a lot of space!) meets Poor Theatre.

As with Massimo Furlan's performances of football most of the players were imagined, in a ghost of a game. But unlike Furlan the Leipzigers did at least have a ball, and had scored five times by half-time. At which point the invisible opponents threw in a literal towel (which later appeared hanging over a microphone at the virtual press conference offering silence). So, a 5-0 home win, a record (virtual) attendance and a lot of fun in strange and uncertain times. In the English commentary for the game Matthias Löffler from Leipzig and Matt Ford mused on the nature of an imagined away leg. What does the invisible stadium of an invisible team in an invisible city, look like?

## E) A chat with Massimo Furlan

***What inspired you to make your football performances?***

'Growing up, I never played in a real football team but I started to play alone in my bedroom. I could transform my bedroom into a stadium and be the one scoring goals and winning every time! Imagination, creating something, is a kind of protection too. Then one day my uncle in Italy gave me a very small radio so that I could listen to live commentary of Italian matches. I would play five minutes with Juventus, five minutes with Roma, five minutes with Fiorentina. But sometimes I lost the frequency. So then I started to make up the commentary myself and I became a real hero and the best football player in the world (of my bedroom).'

***When did you decide to move from the bedroom to the stadium?***

'When I was 37 years old. I'd dreamt all that time that the coach of the Italian team would one day call me up to play in the real team. But you know by that age football players have retired, so as an artist I decided it was time to retire this dream of mine too. After that I started to build the concept of the performance: to recreate famous matches with one or two "players" and no ball, and with the original archive radio commentary for the spectators. The first match I did was in 2002 in the Olympic Stadium in Lausanne, recreating the World Cup Final between Italy and West Germany in 1982. I went on to perform that match in Germany, Portugal, Poland and South Korea.'

***How many different players have you played?***

'I don't remember exactly. The first one was myself. It was me in the World Cup Final in '82. But since then I've been Michel Platini in France, Zbigniew Boniek in Poland, Enzo Scifo in Belgium, Rabah Madjer, Jürgen Sparwasser and others. Whenever I'm asked to do the performance in a particular country I think of a famous match to recreate and decide which player I'll be. Depending on the country, the player I play changes. But when I do the performance in Italy I tend to play myself.'

***And it's always the full match?***
'Yes. Ninety minutes. Plus extra time, if it happened!'

***One of the games you've recreated is the World Cup group stage match between East Germany and West Germany.***
'Yes, I've done that one in Halle, at St Pauli's stadium in Hamburg, and in Munich. In Munich I played the goalkeeper Sepp Maier and another guy, Franz Beil (an actor of East German origin) played Sparwasser who scored the goal.'

***And was Franz Beil really injured that day?***
'Yes, after three minutes! It was crazy. Sparwasser ran very fast. I remember it was hard for me when I played him in Halle. And I saw Beil was running really fast down the wing. He was excited and nervous, I think. Then I saw him fall down, and he stayed down. I thought, "What's he doing? Is he being funny?" But no, he really was injured. So I played alone for the rest of the match as Sepp Maier.'

***Have Jürgen Sparwasser or Sepp Maier ever seen the performance?***
'Yes, Sparwasser saw it in Halle. And he cried that day. For him it was emotional to see it: to see himself and to remember that time.'

***How do you hope the performance will make the spectators feel?***
'When I first did it I had no real intentions regarding the audience. Because I was quite sure nobody would come to see it! But what happened was completely crazy. A lot of people came. In Lausanne, for that first performance, it was December and very, very cold but the people came. And I was really surprised when they started to *perform*. They started to sing and act just like a crowd. I wasn't expecting that. Then afterwards, when I'd finished and was Massimo again, they kept going and drove back into the city klaxoning, celebrating the victory like after the real match. Everywhere I do it now the spectators play their role really well.'

***I wonder if it has something to do with collective memory. The importance of getting together to watch the match in the first place, but then the possibility of remembering it collectively.***
'Absolutely. And a football match is like a story. Sometimes the stories are really beautiful. Remember when you're a child, you ask to be told a story again and again, because you think it's beautiful. This is the same thing I think.'

***You only tend to use one or two players/performers. Is that important?***
'Actually we do a new version now – we did it in Paris last year and have plans to perform it again in Rennes – where there are 11 players on the pitch. Trying to recreate the entire match still, but with 11 and a mix of men and women. I wanted to try to share the performance a bit more with others. Then it becomes something more like a big choreography, something in between Maurice Béjar [dancer and choreographer] and *Monty Python*.'

***It did make me think of the* Monty Python *Philosophers' Football match.***

'Ha, yes. In fact I'm touring a new project now which is a kind of Eurovision Song Contest of philosophy!'

***How hard is it to learn the moves?***

'I need three months to study the movements and to prepare myself physically. I watch the game up to 30 times and try to memorise the player's moves as much as I can. Then I make a recording with my own voice giving orders of what to do: run, go to the left, go to the right, back again etc. It's 90 minutes of that. I don't hear the same radio commentary as the spectators as I need really precise instructions, so that I can then be synchronised with the commentary.'

***When you're being these players, does it feel to you like the match is really happening?***

'Sometimes, yes. But it's more a childlike feeling: like a child playing and quite sure that they really are that hero. When I run I really feel like I'm Sparwasser, or whoever. And in those moments I forget who *I* am! At the same time it's a strange and physical challenge. You're alone and the pitch is so big, it never ends: you run, you run, you run, so it's a mixture of feelings.'

***What do you remember of that 1974 World Cup match? The* Bruderduell*?***

'I was young, nine years old, and I remember that World Cup through Panini stickers, really. I collected them. I had the Germany '74 album but I don't remember watching that game. I'm not sure if they even showed it live on TV where I was in Italy. Maybe it was on the radio.'

***Do the spectators hear the East or West German radio commentary?***
'We offer both. In Halle, for example, a lot of them chose the DDR commentary; and in Hamburg too. It's an interesting one. You know a lot of people say that game was a gift from West to East Germany!'

***Thanks Massimo. If you ever do the World Cup '74 match again, I'd like to offer myself for the role of Sparwasser!***
'Really? Okay. I'll call you! But you need to know: when I played Sparwasser in Hamburg and Halle I was quite sure that in a match like that, in 1974, they wouldn't run that much. I thought it would be quite easy. But my God, it was terrible for me physically. Sparwasser ran all the time! He ran as a forward but he was also following Paul Breitner everywhere he went.'

# Select bibliography

Alan McDougall, *The People's Game: Football, State and Society in East Germany* (Cambridge University Press, 2014, paperback edition 2016).

Ulrich Hesse-Lichtenberger, *Tor! The Story of German Football* (When Saturday Comes Books, 2002)

Mike Dennis, *Behind the Wall: East German football between state and society* (GFL-Journal no. 2, 2007)

Other sources:

Dave Wangerin, *The Fussball Book* (Dave Wangerin, 1993)

Barbara Happe, Martin S. Fischer, *Haus Auerbach von Walter Gropius mit Adolf Meyer* (Ernst Wasmuth Verlag, 2003)

*Zeitspiel: Magazin für Fußball-Zeitgeschichte*

*The Abseits Guide to German Soccer* (website)

weltfussball.de (website)

@FussballDdr (Twitter account)

# Notes

In 'Vorwort' the quotes describing the Public Art Munich festival 2018 are from www.pam2018.de.

The quote about Massimo Furlan's work is from www.massimofurlan.com.

In 'Halle: a tragedy' details about the fire in Eindhoven are from Craig McCracken, *Beyond The Last Man: Guardian Sport Network*, 28 September 2016.

In 'Hinterland, a fiction' the Klaus Taube quotes are from 'Border Control', Paul Joyce, *When Saturday Comes*, 299, January 2012.

References to the 'Bielefeld Conspiracy' are from Wikipedia.

In 'Crossing the line' the quotes relating to Bärbel Bohley are from *The Economist*, 23 September 2010.

Part of 'Crossing the line' was first published in theguardian.com (9 November 2019), Michael Wagg, *East v West: FC Viktoria and Berliner Dynamo meet in a united city.*

# Picture credits

*Front and back cover (players)*: Getty Images
*Back cover (floodlight)*: Duncan Palmer

*Page 14*: PAM 2018 (Public Art Munich)
*Pages 35*; *157; 226*: Jan Stöver
*Page 243*: Chris Baltes

Centre section:
*Pictures 1; 4; 5; 10; 13; 14; 15; 18; 20; 22; 23; 25; 26; 27; 28:* Getty Images
*7; 8*: Lok Leipzig
*11*: Walter Wagner
*16*: Martin Finkler
*17*: Duncan Palmer
*24*: Uwe Karte

*All other photos*: Michael Wagg